MONTH-BY-MONTH GARDENING

PACIFIC NORTHWEST

Brimming with creative inspiration, how-to projects, and useful information to enrich your everyday life, Quarto Knows is a favorite destination for those pursuing their interests and passions. Visit our site and dig deeper with our books into your area of interest: Quarto Creates, Quarto Cooks, Quarto Homes, Quarto Lives, Quarto Drives, Quarto Explores, Quarto Gifts, or Quarto Kids.

Inspiring | Educating | Creating | Entertaining

First published in 2019 by Cool Springs Press, an imprint of The Quarto Group, 100 Cummings Center, Suite 265D, Beverly, MA 01915 USA. T (978) 282-9590 F (978) 283-2742 www.QuartoKnows.com

Cool Springs Press titles are also available at discount for retail, wholesale, promotional, and bulk purchase. For details, contact the Special Sales Manager by email at specialsales@quarto.com or by mail at The Quarto Group, Attn: Special Sales Manager, 100 Cummings Center, Suite 265D, Beverly, MA 01915 USA.

ISBN: 978-1-59186-666-4

Library of Congress Cataloging-in-Publication Data

Names: Pfeiffer, Christina Ann, author. | Robson, Mary, author.
Title: Pacific Northwest month-by-month gardening : what to do each month to have a beautiful garden all year / Christina Pfeiffer with Mary Robson.
Description: Minneapolis, MN : Cool Springs Press, 2017. | Includes bibliographical references.
Identifiers: LCCN 2016030320 | ISBN 9781591866664 (sc)
Subjects: LCSH: Gardening--Northwest, Pacific.
Classification: LCC SB453.2.N83 P44 2017 | DDC 635.09795--dc23
LC record available at https://lccn.loc.gov/2016030320

Acquiring Editor: Bryan Trandem
Project Manager: Alyssa Bluhm
Art Director: Cindy Samargia Laun
Layout: Danielle Smith-Boldt

MONTH-BY-MONTH GARDENING

PACIFIC NORTHWEST

What to Do Each Month to Have
a Beautiful Garden All Year

CHRISTINA PFEIFFER WITH MARY ROBSON

COOL
SPRINGS
PRESS

Dedication

Pacific Northwest gardeners, may you experience the pleasures of gardening with its lifelong lessons on the beneficial connections between plants, people, and the environment. With thankful remembrance of horticulturist Liberty Hyde Bailey, who wrote, "Sensitiveness to all life is the highest product of education" (1898).

—Christina Pfeiffer and Mary Robson

Acknowledgments

I am ever appreciative of the innumerable horticultural friends, colleagues, and teachers who have enriched my life, personally and professionally. The influence of their shared knowledge and pleasure in the world of nature and gardening is reflected throughout my work on these pages.

Mary Robson, without whose encouragement I would never have made this journey, has been a generous mentor and collaborator in this and earlier garden books. Throughout her years in Cooperative Extension and as a horticultural educator, Mary's grounded sensibilities about gardening and being in tune with nature's rhythms have greatly enriched the experience of gardening for many in our region.

—Christina Pfeiffer

Contents

Welcome to gardening in the Pacific Northwest!

This is a region of vast proportions and wide variations in the natural landscape. It has a long ocean coast and the north–south run of the Cascade Mountains from British Columbia into California, with deserts east of those mountains and rainforests west of them. Rivers and lakes great and small weave through the terrain. The grand scale of these features creates a variety of climate and vegetation patterns, and they influence the character of the gardens and plant communities that thrive throughout. Garden tasks might occupy part of every day in milder western reaches or be concentrated into the few months of a hotter and shorter growing season east of the Cascades. Dry summer months are the norm throughout, with the majority of rainfall occurring outside of the growing season. The cultivation of drought-resistant gardens and the care of soil to optimize the capture of precious rainfall are becoming ever more important here.

A garden's beauty and benefits carry throughout the year. The rhythm of the seasons reminds us that plants don't live by the traditional written calendar, but according to the cues of light intensity and day length, of temperature and moisture patterns. Seasonal climate factors influence the cycles of growth and dormancy through the year. Monthly garden calendars serve as valuable reminders of what kinds of attention the garden and individual plants may need. But also stay attuned to the weather, as the patterns of temperature and precipitation will affect how plants grow and develop. Using sustainable gardening techniques helps us work in step with nature's seasonal processes to good effect. Most of us seek to spend more time enjoying the garden than tending it, so by using the timely tips and practical techniques described for each month in this book, you can reap greater pleasure from your garden and the process of gardening. As you become better acquainted with your own patch of earth and its seasonal benchmarks, you will be able to develop your own personal monthly guideposts.

KNOW WHERE YOU ARE

To garden successfully, you must first understand the local geography and its effect on climate. The Cascade Mountains divide the region north to south, creating different weather conditions on either side. West of the Cascades, ocean air keeps winter temperatures moderate, seldom dipping below the 20s, though locations along the mountains and in the Willamette Valley regularly turn colder. The high Cascade peaks retain much of the winter precipitation. Mild, rainy winters and cool, dry summers prevail. Most of this maritime climate area is in zone 8, a cooler zone 7 along the Cascade foothills, and a warmer zone 9 along the southern Oregon coast into northern California.

The inland Northwest, east of the Cascades and west of the Rocky Mountains, copes with frigid winters and sunny, hot, arid summers. It is sunnier and drier than west of the mountains. Most of this territory falls into zones 5 or 6, but the deep winter cold of zone 4 touches eastern Oregon's high desert country. The Okanogan spans an area from south-central British Columbia through Okanogan County of north-central Washington State. It has abundant summer sunshine and low precipitation.

The moderate maritime climate of western British Columbia, Washington, and Oregon—including the coastal areas of the Olympic Peninsula—welcomes a broad palette of plants. Conifers, ferns, and broadleaf evergreens dominate native forests. Summer temperatures are moderate, with a typical growing season of May through September, or April to November in the mildest locations. The occasional hot spell can intensify the already-droughty summer conditions. First frosts come around mid-November, earlier in the month to the north and in the foothills, later farther south. In lower British Columbia, the influence of the Pacific Ocean and steep mountain ranges causes wider variations in climate within relatively short distances.

Elevations below 1,000 feet, especially near water, often remain above freezing in average winters. Unexpected freezes can occur in spring or fall. November and December are typically the darkest and wettest months. Non-irrigated soils are usually at their wettest by March and at their driest in September. Northeast winds blowing out of the Fraser River Valley in British Columbia can rapidly draw temperatures down by 20 degrees in a few hours, killing plants from Bellingham and further south, on Whidbey Island, and in parts of the Olympic Peninsula.

The Tri-Cities (Richland, Kennewick, and Pasco) area boasts a greater number of frost-free days than other parts of eastern Washington. Even though it's east of the Cascade Mountains, a belt of warm, eastward-flowing air comes in from the coast and through the Columbia River Gorge stretching along the Yakima River through this part of the state. Winter temperatures here hover above freezing, at USDA zone 7.

Redmond and Bend in the Oregon central plateau are high, flat country with strong winds and temperature extremes. Frost can come any time of year. Pine, juniper, and sage dominate the native plant communities here. Farther east to Baker, a high basin between two mountain ranges, the area is occupied largely by juniper forests and savannahs. Summers are dry and hot, reaching 100°F highs. Temperatures in the long winters can plunge down to -20°F with scant snow cover. Annual precipitation is 11 inches.

Toward southern Oregon, the Medford area sits at a high elevation, with cooler temperatures and less than 20 inches of precipitation per year. Chaparral conditions with scrubby, dry-land plants are found here. Toward the coast, the vegetation becomes lush with the higher precipitation. Average January temperatures are around 38°F, though cold air draining off the mountains brings cooler night temperatures.

The coastal area of Northern California is home to some of the tallest trees on the planet, sustained by the mild temperatures and moist fog rolling in from the sea. There is little rain between March and November, with the annual 40 to 60 inches concentrated in winter months. In zones 8 and 9, there is a fairly long growing season lasting from mid-February to late November. Coastal mountain valleys can see freezing temperatures in winter and heat up to 100°F in summer. Farther

USDA PLANT HARDINESS ZONES

AVERAGE MINIMUM TEMPERATURE RANGES

ZONES	°F	°C
4	-30 to -20	-34.5 to -28.9
5	-20 to -10	-28.9 to -23.3
6	-10 to 0	-23.3 to 17.8
7	0 to 10	-17.8 to -12.3
8	10 to 20	-12.3 to -6.6
9	20 to 30	-6.6 to -1.1

This winter-rain/summer-drought pattern is the prevailing pattern of the coastal areas. The inland Northwest is dry country, with an average 12 inches (304 millimeters) precipitation per year.

In all parts of the Pacific Northwest, careful attention to water conservation and the use of garden practices that support drought-resistant gardens are a must. Our lack of reliable summer rainfall is probably the most limiting factor to garden cultivation here. Despite our national reputation, the weather doesn't actually deliver much moisture for the growing season.

inland from the coast, conditions are drier (only 10 to 20 inches annual precipitation) with hotter summers and cooler winters.

Recent weather trends point to higher seasonal temperatures with drier summers and wetter winters. Weather events may also arrive in stronger doses or for longer durations, stretching the limits of previous typical patterns. Gardeners need to stay attuned to each season's prevailing weather for its effects on plant growth in the following seasons. The stress of a drier or colder winter can leave some plants vulnerable to drought stress the following summer. Plants that have endured extremes of heat and drought without a reprieve by summer's end will be less resistant to cold damage in the coming winter.

IT WILL BE DRY HERE

The common impression that the Coastal Pacific Northwest has soggy rain year-round is more myth than reality. Though the region boasts genuine temperate rainforests with 100 to 200 inches (2,540 to 5,080 millimeters) of rain per year in parts of the Olympic Peninsula and Vancouver Island's west coast, these are small, isolated corners of the region. Indeed, in the rain shadow not too far to the east of these wet pockets, annual precipitation is a mere 13 to 24 inches (330 to 610 millimeters). Certainly, the 38-inch (965-millimeter) average in Seattle would be ample for gardening, but most of that rain falls during winter months.

MICROCLIMATES

In addition to the prevailing regional and local climate conditions, different microclimates can be found within a neighborhood or single property. The growing conditions within these small areas are modified by, and are slightly different from, the surrounding conditions, such as the shady side of a house or the reflected heat off large paved areas. These spots have slightly different light, wind, temperature, or moisture levels. You can see the microclimate effect on a neighborhood walk: you might pass a lilac bush bursting with color in full sun on the west side of the street, then half a block later see another lilac with no sign of color, in the shade of a pine, facing east with no morning sun. Paying attention to microclimate conditions can help you choose the right kind of plants, or explain why you can't grow a certain plant that thrives in the yard next door.

USING MICROCLIMATES TO YOUR ADVANTAGE

Altitude affects temperature, and as any hiker knows, higher elevation means cooler temperatures. Fall frosts come earlier, and spring frosts stay later as elevations rise. A large body of water will moderate temperature extremes. Gardens near Puget Sound, for example, are less likely to freeze late in the season. But surprisingly, these spots will remain cooler during summer months. Low valleys experience lower temperatures as cold air flows downhill like water. Fruit growers planting hillside orchards know that temperatures halfway down the slope will be more moderate than at the bottom. In urban gardens, be aware of heat radiated from pavement and buildings. A balcony garden facing west above Pike Place Market in Seattle will have modified temperatures: afternoon heat from a sunny day will radiate out of a concrete building after dark, adding to the moderating effect of nearby Puget Sound. A north-facing garden in North Bend that lacks these influences would stay colder as a result of the exposure and higher terrain.

Large trees can have a profound influence on a microclimate, changing it slowly as young trees grow and mature, and drastically when a large tree is removed. Tall trees provide shelter from sun and wind. Humidity is greater amid groups of trees. Deciduous trees make cool shade in summer but let in warmth and light in winter. Hedges can provide windbreaks as well as shade. Prevailing soil conditions—perpetually damp or freely draining, for example—also contribute to microclimate influences.

Understanding the microclimate details in your garden will improve the success of your overall gardening efforts. It can help you choose plants best adapted to each planting spot and to water appropriately. Microclimate conditions can be used to push the edges of temperature zone realities. A tender plant in the warmest garden spot with extra winter protection or placed against a south-facing stone wall can allow survival of a zone 9 plant in zone 8.

DON'T TREAT YOUR SOIL LIKE DIRT

Soil is the foundation for plant survival. It is the reservoir for moisture and nutrients where roots anchor. It is home to insects and microorganisms that decompose organic matter and improve soil condition.

How we treat the soil determines the success of the landscape. Many gardeners automatically assume their soil will need drastic help or that "better" soil needs to be brought in. In many cases, the resident soil may just need a little amendment and the right care to be a workable growing medium. Take the time to dig in and learn what kind of soil you really have.

■ *Ferns and woodland perennials are well adapted for a damp shade microclimate.*

REGIONAL NATIVE SOIL TYPES

Soil type will depend on the geological characteristics of the region. Deep loams in the Willamette and Puyallup River Valleys drastically contrast with nearby areas that have shallow, mixed gravel, rock, and clay soils left thousands of years ago by glaciers. One gardener described her western Washington soil as "clay except for the rocks." With low rainfall east of the Cascades, soils in high desert country tend to be higher in pH (more alkaline), contain soluble salts, and have lower organic content than coastal loam soils. Urban areas are always tricky to understand because so much ground has been heavily disturbed from its native condition.

Soil texture is determined by the percentage of sand, silt, and clay particles. Knowing the texture of your soil will help guide optimal plant selection as well as amendment and irrigation practices. Pick up a small handful of damp soil. Squeeze it into a ball, and then squeeze out a "ribbon" between your thumb and forefinger. Clay soil will hold together to form a ribbon inches long and will show the imprints of your fingers. Loam soil, a balance of clay and sand, will form a short but breakable ribbon. Sandy or gravelly soil won't hold together. Another method is to do a jar test (described on page 132).

Organic matter in soil comes from decomposed plant and animal residues, familiar to us as compost. It becomes dark-colored humus when completely decomposed. Organic matter contributes to soil porosity, fertility, and moisture-holding capacity. It supports an array of organisms that in turn contribute to overall plant health. Native soils west of the Cascades have about 5 percent by weight (10 percent by volume) of organic matter content; drier zones east of the Cascades have about half that amount. Gardeners should aim to match the "native" organic matter levels for their region and climate for best overall results.

CHARACTERISTICS OF SOIL TYPES

Fine-textured clay soils keep a tight grip on water. They drain slowly and are hard to dampen again when they get really dry. They hold mineral nutrients well and are generally more fertile than sandy soils. Course-textured sandy soils readily move water and oxygen to the root zone but can also drain and dry out quickly. They are difficult to keep moist in summer and aren't able to hold onto nutrients. Loamy soils strike a nice balance between the two, draining well and having good nutrient- and moisture-holding capacity.

Soil texture is not readily changed. Contrary to common belief, clay garden soil cannot be readily improved by adding sand! When you add sand, the tinier clay particles fill the spaces between the much larger sand particles, causing the resulting mix to be even denser. Gypsum, another material thought to be a cure-all, does not change soil texture either, but it can be used for correcting saline soils, a problem most common with arid soils and croplands and less common in average home gardens. Knowing your soil texture will help you choose the best types of plants and gardening practices to use.

Soil structure refers to how well soil particles stick together in clumps (called aggregates) and how much pore space is between them. Unlike texture, soil structure can be changed, for better or worse. Soil structure and porosity—the ability to drain well and also hold air—can be damaged by over tilling, over irrigation, and being handled when wet. Soil will become compacted and lose pore space—not so good for plant roots. The structure of both clay and sandy soils can be improved and maintained with modest annual applications of organic amendments and mulch. Organic matter and the associated organisms help soil particles stick together in aggregates. Organic matter helps sandy soils retain more moisture and helps increase porosity in clay soil. Soils with good porous structure will be more effective at capturing, storing, and filtering rainwater.

"Green manure" cover crops such as rye, buckwheat, or crimson clover can reduce weed invasions on bare ground and improve soil when they are later dug in to decompose in place. This practice is useful in vegetable and annual flower beds, which often lie empty between planting events.

HERE'S HOW

TO TEST FOR SOIL TEXTURE

1. Dampen about a tablespoon of soil with a few drops of water.

2. Roll it into a solid ball. It should be the consistency of putty.

3. Pinch the ball between your thumb and forefinger.

4. Gently push your thumb away from your forefinger to press the ball out into a ribbon.

   a. If it doesn't stay together in a ribbon, you have *loamy sand*.

   b. If the ribbon is less than an inch long before breaking, and when a pinch of soil is rubbed against the palm, it is:
   - gritty, you have *sandy loam*
   - smooth, you have *silty loam*
   - not very smooth and not very gritty, you have *loam*

   c. If the ribbon is 1 to 2 inches long before breaking, and when a pinch of soil is rubbed against the palm, it is:
   - gritty, you have *sandy clay loam*
   - smooth, you have *silty clay loam*
   - not very smooth and not very gritty, you have *clay loam*

   d. If the ribbon is more than 2 inches long before breaking, and when a pinch of soil is rubbed against the palm, it is:
   - gritty, you have *sandy clay*
   - smooth, you have *silty clay*
   - not very smooth and not very gritty, you have *clay*

UNRAVELING THE pH MYSTERY

Is your soil acid or alkaline? Most landscape plants grow well with a soil pH between 5.5 and 7.5 (7.0 is neutral). Native soils west of the Cascades tend to be acid, with pH between 5.0 and 6.0. Native conifers and plants such as salal and rhododendron are strongly adapted to grow well at these pH levels. Soils east of the mountains are mostly alkaline, up to 7.5 or 8.0. Grasslands tend to be more alkaline. Soil pH is also affected by the amount of annual rainfall, with alkaline soils more prevalent in arid regions. Forest areas, with high organic matter content, foster more acidic conditions. Urban soils, no matter the location of the city, also tend to have higher pH, due to disturbance and contamination from gypsum and lime outwash from construction activity.

Soil pH is important because it affects the availability and absorption of mineral nutrients. Some plant species have developed fairly specific pH adaptations: a rhododendron (adapted to acidic soil) will develop yellow, chlorotic leaves in very alkaline soil; its roots are unable to absorb nutrients when pH is too high. When the pH level causes rhododendron leaves to yellow, adding fertilizer will not help. A soil test is needed to measure the pH and determine what and how much amendment may be needed to adjust it. Sulfur will lower pH; lime increases it. Get the soil test before adding amendments.

GARDEN PREPARATION: TIPS FOR SOIL HANDLING & CARE

Start with a soil test before you install a large new landscape. This information will help you choose plants that are naturally adapted to your resident soil type and determine if amendments may be needed. Properly amended resident soil is often better than imported topsoil mixes. Some soil-test kits available in garden centers can help to check soil pH and certain nutrients. However, specialized soil tests will be needed if heavy metals or other contaminants are a concern. Master Gardeners and Extension offices can often help with referrals for soil testing (see Resources).

Check soil drainage well before planting time. Look at the surface grade and areas with persistent standing water. A simple percolation test will reveal if the soil is porous enough to drain well. Subsurface drain pipe, surface grading, or simply

■ *You can use a home soil test kit to check soil pH. A laboratory soil test will provide the most accurate measure.*

good cultivation to break up compacted ground are measures that can improve problems. Building a berm to create a mounded, raised planting bed is another option, especially if soil does not drain well.

Cultivate when soil is damp to dry. "Not too wet, not too dry" is the rule when handling soil. Cultivating soggy soil will cause compaction; clay soil that is too dry can be nearly impossible to dig.

Amend in moderation. Beware of mixing too much compost into your soil at once. This can lead to future problems with drainage, compaction, and plants settling below grade (with harmful results for trees and shrubs) as the compost decomposes and the soil settles.

Create a transition zone when adding new soil. Imported soil is likely to have a different texture than your native soil. If the two materials are stacked like a layer cake, drainage will be poor between them. To prevent this, lightly cultivate the existing grade and incorporate 1 to 2 inches of the new material before adding the full depth of imported soil. Water, air, and roots will be able to move through both soil types when this is done.

Keep bare ground covered. Left exposed to the elements and foot traffic, bare soil can quickly become compacted. Mulch freshly prepared soil 3 to 4 inches deep to protect it. It will also be easier to move the mulch out of the way at planting time than to apply mulch after planting.

Don't disturb the soil if you don't have to. An effective, no-till method to prepare a new landscape bed is to apply 6 to 8 inches of very coarse organic matter over the area weeks to months in advance of planting. It will need periodic irrigation or rainfall to stay moist. Coarse compost, shredded leaves, and wood-chip mulch are ideal materials. The soil will be softened and conditioned as these materials decompose. Just rake the excess material away to expose the nicely prepared ground when it is time to plant. If old turf or perennial weeds are present, cover them over with overlapping layers of newspaper and dampen before applying mulch. Apply mulch a little deeper if weeds start peeking through.

USING FERTILIZER: EVERYTHING IN MODERATION

While we casually call fertilizer "plant food," it is really more "soil food." Photosynthesis makes the food plants use. Nutrients from the soil are important to help plants produce carbohydrates and other compounds using energy from the sun. So we apply fertilizer to supply nutrients lacking in the soil.

Fertilizers come in different forms, from organic (derived from previously living sources) to synthetic (manufactured, generally from nonliving sources). Both types provide the same nutrient elements. However, organic fertilizers also support vital soil microorganisms. Some products contain both organic sources (such as cottonseed meal) and inorganic sources (ammonium nitrate).

Your garden may already be getting enough essential nutrients if you regularly use compost and organic mulch. Be sure fertilizer is really needed and to apply the right amount of the right nutrients. The way plants grow and their leaf color may be indicators of nutrient problems.

FERTILIZER IS NOT A CURE-ALL

Resist the urge to add fertilizer just because you suspect a plant problem. Fertilizer cannot fix poor soil or bad drainage that may be limiting plants. Nor can it help if plants are installed in the wrong light conditions—a shade-loving *Skimmia* turning yellow from too much sun won't green up with a fertilizer application. Nutrients cannot be absorbed when root rot or waterlogged soils are present. In fact, fertilizers should generally be avoided on severely declining or diseased plants. For best plant health, use fertilizers sparingly. Disease and insect difficulties can intensify on plants receiving too much nitrogen; aphids and powdery mildew are examples. Overfertilized plants will also require more water, difficult to supply in dry summer conditions. And in more arid regions, excess fertilization can lead to a harmful buildup of dissolved salts in the soil.

If plants have normal color and produce good bloom, leaves, and new shoots each year, then fertilizer is not needed. This is especially the case for most trees, shrubs, and other woody plants. Herbaceous perennials may need an annual boost with a moderate nitrogen formula such as a 4-2-2 broadcast on top of the soil and watered in when spring growth begins. Annuals and perennials grown in containers should receive a liquid form of complete fertilizer (with trace elements) twice per month until frost to keep them growing well. Hybrid tea roses and others grown for exhibition typically require monthly fertilization.

UNDERSTANDING NPK

Nitrogen, phosphorus, and potassium (NPK) are the nutrients found in complete fertilizers, with formula numbers indicating the percentage weight of each element per 100 pounds. Nitrogen is the most limiting element to plant growth, and its availability varies at different times of year. Nitrogen moves rapidly through the soil away from root zones during rainy weather, especially if soils are sandy or gravelly. Phosphorus and potassium are less likely to be lacking in landscape soils and don't need to be applied as often. Indeed, excess phosphorus applications add to runoff pollution and also suppress the beneficial mycorrhizal fungi, which aid roots in moisture and nitrogen uptake. Apply fertilizers only as needed, choose materials with lower P and K, and avoid times when heavy irrigation or rainfall can wash nitrogen away.

NPK is slowly released from organic products such as fish emulsion, cottonseed meal, manures, and compost through decomposition by soil fungi and bacteria when the soil is warm and moist. For synthetic slow-release products such as Nutricote or Osmocote, release rate depends on the coating type, temperature, and moisture levels. With all fertilizer applications, soil must be moist for nutrients to be available to roots. Don't apply granular fertilizer to dry soil; it will be ineffective and may burn roots. In drought conditions, use less fertilizer. The plant will grow more slowly and need less water.

APPLICATION RATES

Actively growing plants, such as trees and shrubs, can benefit from moderate late-spring applications during the first years of establishment. Once established for three to five years, trees and shrubs need little or no fertilizer if they are growing well.

TO CALCULATE FERTILIZER AMOUNTS

It pays to calculate the proper amount of material based on amount of the actual nutrient element needed per application area. To apply one pound of actual nitrogen per 1,000 square feet with a 21-0-0 NPK product, divide 1 pound by the percentage of nitrogen in the product:

1 pound nitrogen $\div$ 21 $\times$ 100 = 4.75 pounds of 21-0-0 fertilizer

This is also a helpful way to calculate the relative cost of different products. To apply 1 pound of nitrogen per 1,000 square feet with 10 percent N, you would need 10 pounds of fertilizer—about twice as much as the 21-percent N formulation.

Liquid fertilizers have label directions for mixing at different concentrations for different plant types. They are commonly used for containers, vegetables, and annual flowers. Start with the lower mixing rates and increase to the higher listed rates, if needed.

■ *This 12-0-0 feather meal is a nitrogen-only organic fertilizer.*

Plants with higher nutrient requirements, such as annuals, vegetables, turf, and containerized plants, will benefit from periodic fertilization during the growing season.

Both organic and synthetic fertilizer packages list NPK content on their labels. Some products include other trace nutrient elements such as sulfur and magnesium. Be sure to read the label directions and start with the lowest application rates. Too little nitrogen will result in poor growth. Too much will encourage leafy shoots and keep the plant from flowering.

COMPOSTING AT HOME

The garden trimmings and old leaves you may call "yard waste" may in fact be a gold mine for your garden. Composting—nutrient recycling through decomposition of plant debris created in the garden—is an age-old process. Properly done, it sustains native plant ecosystems and provides nutrients for the garden.

Composting doesn't need to be complicated. Small-sized plant debris can be left on the ground to compost in place. Allow leaves to fall naturally in autumn, raking them off lawns but letting a 2- to 3-inch layer build up under plants. "Mulch mowing" is a great way to allow lawn clippings and minced trees leaves to decompose in place.

Or make a pile and let nature to do its work. With time and moisture, all the leaves, twigs, and stems will break down into a crumbly compost material. Chopping up woody stems and shredding leaves will speed things up, as will periodic turning. Keep piles in a damp, shady location for best results. A variety of bins that hold more material within a smaller footprint can be made or purchased.

Keep your cleanest greens for composting. Heavily diseased plant parts, seedheads of weeds, and roots from persistent weeds such as morning glory or buttercup should go to a municipal composting facility (where these problems are destroyed in high-heat compost systems) or be separated out to a pile that will not go back into garden beds.

■ *There are a variety of good options for composting garden trimmings.*

Explore options for home composting to find a method that best suits your situation. More information is available from Master Gardeners and Cooperative Extension offices (see Resources).

MULCH MATTERS

Mulch matters—you will see this advice throughout this book. Most simply, mulch is a material used to cover and protect the soil. Mulch can be put down any time, except under very wet or saturated conditions. Apply mulch to cover bare ground after weeds are pulled, to reduce moisture stress around new plants, to protect plants from frost heaving in colder climates, and to suppress winter weeds and improve soil in regions with winter rain. As mulch decays, soil nutrients and organic matter are replenished. Over time, coarse mulch can even help improve compacted soil.

Mulch should be no more than a total of 3 to 4 inches deep for most landscape plantings. Never bury the trunks of trees or shrubs in mulch—it's

an invitation to basal rots and plant stress. It's best to let mulch break down far enough for the soil to start to show through before new mulch is added.

Maintaining organic matter for established plantings is best done with a surface application of amendments and/or organic mulch. Soil texture and nutrient content will be preserved, and the population of decomposers—insects, earthworms, fungi, and microbes—will thrive. Use a thin layer (about 1 inch) of fine, screened compost to top-dress lawns and groundcovers. Coarse, textured organic mulch can be applied 2 to 4 inches deep over open soil areas.

WHAT MAKES GOOD MULCH?
For maximum weed suppression and soil moisture benefits, mulch should be coarser in texture than the soil it sits on. When buying mulch in bags or bulk, look for products that contain a mixture of materials and plant parts. Composts with fine soil-like texture are best used as an amendment that is mixed into the soil or as topdressing that is less than 1 inch deep. Avoid fine bark, as its waxy fibers tend to crust into tight layers that exclude moisture and air from the soil. Very coarse bark is slow to decompose and may be most suitable for landscape beds with highly organic soil.

Wood chips from tree services have become a popular (and usually free) source of mulch. Find out how large the loads are before having a service deliver wood chips; you may want to share with

■ *Use a coarse organic mulch to suppress weeds, retain moisture, and maintain soil organic matter.*

HOW MUCH MULCH DO YOU NEED TO GET?

Begin by measuring the square feet of garden space to be covered. Remember some of the space is occupied by plant trunks and stems.

AMOUNT OF MULCH	SQUARE FEET COVERED (AT A 3- TO 4-INCH DEPTH)
1.5-cubic-foot bag	5 square feet or a 2.5-foot diameter circle
2-cubic-foot bag	8 square feet or a 3-foot diameter circle
3-cubic-foot bag	12 square feet or a 4-foot diameter circle
27 cubic feet	100 square foot area

0.25 foot depth (3 inches) × square foot area to cover = cubic feet of mulch required

a neighbor. Let fresh wood chips age for a couple weeks or more before use. The chips will have a darker, fairly uniform color when they are ready. Don't store mulch under or against large trees, especially if the pile will be stored for a while; the weight and heat of the pile can be damaging.

MAKING YOUR OWN MULCH

Leaf mold (partially composted leaves) is one of the best sources of coarse organic mulch for the garden. Garden compost with bits of leaves and twigs visible also works well. It can be screened, with the coarse pieces saved for mulch and the finer material used to top-dress lawns and groundcovers.

THRIFTY WATERING TECHNIQUES FOR HEALTHY PLANTS

The majority of our ground-penetrating rainfall occurs during the winter months, when plant growth is least active. Making the most of the garden while conserving water depends upon choosing the right plants, taking good care of the soil, and using the right irrigation equipment and techniques. Dry summer conditions don't always have to result in a desiccated landscape.

Remember that water is taken in through the roots, not the leaves. Speedy sprinkling over plants on a sunny day won't reach the roots. Quick rains from brief summer showers do not benefit roots either.

Plants lose water through their leaves during transpiration, a normal and necessary process. Plants wilt when soil is too dry or the weather gets too hot for roots to keep up with the demand. Overcast days with misty rain may not provide much measurable rainfall, but they do reduce plant water loss.

Keep track of how much rain is reaching your garden by using a rain gauge. What you may have thought was a big downpour could show up at a quarter inch or less in the gauge—not enough to replenish the soil. Another's day rain might add up to ½ inch or more and may be enough to replace an irrigation cycle. Keeping your own rainfall observations leads to better irrigation practices.

Use a rain gauge to help guide irrigation needs.

SOME IMPORTANT WATER-SAVING TACTICS

- When preparing soil for new landscapes, strive for a coarse, open texture 12 or more inches deep.

- Use coarse mulch to help retain soil moisture and improve water infiltration.

- Select plants adapted to manage dry times in your climate zone.

- Group and locate plants according to their water needs and cultural adaptations.

- Populate naturally damp garden zones with moisture-loving plants.

- Use a garden rain gauge. Probe the soil to check dampness and guide irrigation.

- Watch your water pressure: large, heavy drops are more effective than mist.

- Water for long, deep drinks, not sips.

Soil type and texture determine how much water a soil will hold and how quickly it can absorb that water. One inch of water applied to a sandy soil will readily penetrate to 12 inches deep. An inch of water will move anywhere from 6 to 10 inches into a good loam soil, but in clay soil the application may percolate down only 4 to 5 inches. Adjust the delivery rate to match how quickly the soil can take it in: if water is sheeting off the surface, it needs to be applied more slowly.

TARGET THE ROOT ZONE

To maintain a deeply rooted, drought-resistant garden, water deeply and infrequently. Use a trowel or shovel after watering to see how far down the water really went. Whether you use an irrigation system, a soaker hose, or hand water, the objective is the same: water deeply! The shallower the root zone, the more quickly it will dry out and the more often it will require water. New plants (even drought-tolerant species) require good, deep watering their first two to three summers while their roots are expanding into planting soil. Be sure to run drip systems

long enough to reach the depth of the rootballs. The worst thing you can do is to water a little bit every day; it leads to shallow roots with no buffer against hot dry spells.

Soaker hoses and solid irrigation tubing with pressure-compensating emitters are an easily installed, efficient means of supplying water. Soaker hoses perform best in short runs (less than 100 feet) on level ground, while pressure-compensating emitter tubing can deliver water evenly over slopes and longer runs. Both soaker hoses and irrigation tubing can be covered with mulch for better appearance and water conservation. Bubbler heads used for manual or automatic systems are another method of getting more water to the roots with less evaporative loss. Some irrigation companies have begun installing soaker hose below sod with great results in turf health and water savings. Zippered, slow-release watering bags, which are filled from a hose, are a great tool for watering new trees.

The overriding benefits of all these methods are avoiding water loss from evaporation or run-off across pavement, promotion of deeper rooting and drought resilience, and reducing some leaf blights by keeping leaves dry.

■ *Water deeply to promote a deep root zone.*

WEEDS

Pulling weeds can be the bane of leisure gardening. Or it can become a satisfying routine that immerses you into the life of your garden. Tips to keep weed control manageable include:

- Use well-adapted plants that compete and crowd weeds out.

- Use coarse organic mulch. There will be fewer weeds and those that do crop up will be easier to pull.

- Eliminate weeds before they have time to flower and go to seed.

A spading fork and the hori-hori soil knife are two of a gardener's best tools for getting weeds out, roots and all.

Fabric or plastic weed barriers are often seen as a quick fix for weed control, but they can cause more problems than they solve. Some weeds, such as horsetail, are known to punch through these landscape fabrics, while morning glory vines easily find their way under the fabric and emerge through small gaps and edges. Other weeds end up growing in mulch or organic debris on top of the fabric. One of the biggest disadvantages is that weed barrier fabrics prevent replenishment of organic matter into the soil and disrupt the life of beneficial soil organisms and insects.

A better option for reclaiming beds overrun by weeds or for establishing a new bed is sheet mulching with newspaper or cardboard (materials that will decompose once their work is done) covered with about 4 inches of mulch. Four-ply layers of newspaper are easier to work with around established plants. Make sure mulch completely buries the paper or cardboard and to wet it all down at installation.

HANDLING MONSTER WEEDS
Special tactics may be needed to subdue very dense weed growth or particularly persistent weed types. Information on identification and control methods for difficult weed species can be obtained through regional noxious weed boards as well as

Cooperative Extension offices (see Resources). Control of some noxious species that pose serious economic and/or environmental threat is required by law. Tansy ragwort on rangelands is one example. Purple loosestrife and Japanese knotweed are problem weeds that threaten wetland native plants and riparian areas.

PLANTING TECHNIQUES: TREES & SHRUBS

For larger installations, it's best to prepare the entire planting bed in advance. You may have heard old advice to add organic amendments only to the planting hole, but research has found roots tend to stay confined to that small, improved area, impairing good establishment. If the soil is not already soft and loose, prepare the entire plant bed to fracture existing soil at least 8 to 12 inches deep, remove larger rocks, and incorporate organic amendment (if needed). Cover the unplanted soil with coarse mulch and water in or allow rain to help settle it for a week or so before planting.

PREPARING & INSTALLING THE ROOTBALL
Proper planting means caring for the roots and planting at the proper height. Two common mistakes that lead to plant failure are leaving tight rootballs undisturbed and planting too deep. Score the rootball and loosen root ends before planting. Do not bury the crown or trunks with soil or mulch. Take great care to get trees and shrubs installed at or slightly above grade. Planting holes are best prepared shallow and wide.

All types of nursery stock need some gentle root disturbance with tools and hands to stimulate new growth and to put the roots in direct contact with garden soil. Left in the shape of their containers, rootballs can remain like a ball in a socket, with roots never getting a good grip into the surrounding ground.

Plants are sold in containers, balled and burlapped (B&B), or dormant bare root. Give new plants a good watering the day before planting. Keep exposed roots covered with damp burlap or mulch to keep them from drying out during the planting process.

■ *Gently loosen the rootball to spread roots out in the planting hole. Prune circling roots.*

Check container stock for matted or circling roots that follow the outline of the pot. Gently rinsing off of some of the container soil can help expose problem roots. Prune any circling or tightly matted roots, so new growth will extend horizontally from the cut ends. Remove any excess soil that may cover the base of the stems. Balled-and-burlapped plants come with fabric and twine wrapped around the rootball. Carefully remove all wrapping. There is a common misconception that these materials can be left buried in the planting hole—don't do it! Root growth can be hampered by buried materials that are slow to break down or don't decompose at all. Remove any excess soil covering the trunk or stems, down to the flare at the base where the top lateral roots start. Now you will have the actual height of the rootball and know how deep to dig the hole. Once the rootball is set in the hole, remove all wrapping and ties from the top and sides of the rootball. Before filling the hole, use a hand cultivator to loosen the sides of the soil ball (especially slick clay often found with B&B) so root ends will be in direct contact with the backfill.

Trees sometimes come in grow bags made of synthetic fabric that must be completely removed. Don't worry about any roots that may be poking through the fabric. The resulting root pruning will stimulate new growth.

Dormant bare-root plants are available in early spring. They come with their roots covered in damp sawdust. It is important to protect the roots from drying or frost before they are planted. Soak the roots for a few hours before planting. Prune any dry or broken root ends. Fill the hole gradually, holding the plant with one hand, keeping the roots spread and placing soil carefully around roots. Gently water as you add soil to eliminate air pockets. Make sure to plant at the correct height, with the soil covering the roots but not the flared base of the trunk. The root collar boundary is usually visible by a change in bark texture where root structure begins.

WHAT ABOUT STAKING?

Trees that are wobbly in the ground will need staking at planting, especially bare-root trees. The goal is to anchor the rootball (not the trunk). Drive stakes into undisturbed ground outside the planting hole and attach ties at the lowest position on the trunk that will hold the tree upright. Young trees need some trunk movement with the wind to stimulate strong wood and support roots. Use soft, pliable ties and avoid wires that can easily dig into the trunk. Healthy, well-planted trees should not normally need staking past the first season. Stakes and ties left in place too long can kill or severely deform the tree by girdling the growing trunk.

■ *Bare root*

■ *Balled and burlapped*

■ *Container*

1. Remove all twine, burlap, and other wrapping. Gently loosen the sides of the rootball so the exposed root ends extend into the backfill soil.
2. Place the root flare (where the first lateral roots start) slightly above grade. Do not bury the trunk in soil or mulch.
3. Provide staking if a newly planted tree is not stable in the ground at planting time.

PRUNING TREES & SHRUBS

Pruning is the garden task that can be most daunting or challenging for home gardeners. Here are some tips for how to prune so you won't have to prune so often.

- Put plants in positions where they can grow to their natural habit and dimensions. Don't fall for the idea that a plant will be easy to keep small with pruning. "Right plant, right place" means less pruning over the long run.

- Avoid heading and tipping branches, and resist the urge to trim and shape every plant. The more you do this, the more you'll have to keep pruning.

- Use selective pruning that follows the natural growth habit. Remove a branch that is broken all the way back to the place where it is attached to a larger branch or trunk, or even back to the soil in the case of multistem shrubs.

- Prune in moderation. The harder the pruning, the greater the growth response.

- Know why you are pruning, and prune only those plants that truly need it.

Don't overwater or overfertilize woody plants. This can push excess growth and pruning demands on plants that otherwise might not have needed any pruning. A lean but healthy culture makes less work for plants and gardeners.

MAKING SENSE OF PLANT NAMES

We know many of our favorite garden plants by their common names. Like nicknames, they are useful and easy to remember. Lilacs are unmistakable by their common name. Hydrangea

WHAT DO WE MEAN BY "ESTABLISHED PLANTS"?

"Establishment" means that plant roots have penetrated the surrounding soil and that new root growth has replaced roots lost from transplanting. Established plants will maintain healthy growth with less water. Count on two to three years of weekly attention to watering, mulching, and care. Once established, drought-tolerant plants may get along with relatively little or no extra summer irrigation, making a true water-wise garden. Plants such as azaleas, rhododendrons, and hydrangeas may always require supplemental water no matter how long they have been in the ground.

Well-established plants will settle into a pattern of seasonal growth with fewer requirements for water and fertilization. Their growth slows as summer progresses, settling down to ripen seeds and prepare for dormancy. Dry months of July and August may show leaves turning color early. This is predictable and generally not harmful for established plants, but early fall color and leaf loss are less tolerable during a plant's first three years in the ground.

Pruners and loppers with curved bypass blades provide the cleanest cuts when pruning woody plants.

Prune trees and shrubs to match their natural form for optimal plant health and less frequent pruning work.

is both the botanical and the common name. Some plants have so many common names it can be confusing as to what kind of plants they really are. The botanical name is the same the world over and can be most useful in helping you identify the correct plant in a nursery or garden reference book. Here is a brief summary of how plant names work.

In the case of the European highbush cranberry (its common name), the plant's botanical name is *Viburnum opulus*, a label that contains two parts: the genus and the species. The genus is the general group, which may include many species within it. It is usually depicted in italics and is capitalized. The species name identifies a single plant in the genus group. It, too, is italicized, but is not capitalized.

Many plant names will also have a third component, the cultivar and variety name; these are not italicized. These plants will differ from the basic species by some quality of leaf color, fruit color, size, height, or form. They may also have their own common name. Cultivar names are contained by single quotes: *Viburnum opulus* 'Nanum', for example, is dwarf European highbush cranberry. Variety names are an extension of the species name: *Viburnum opulus* var. *americanum* is American highbush cranberry.

Finally, some plants are hybrids. Hybrids are made by crosspollination of two related species, indicated by a name shown with an "×" in the middle. *Viburnum × burkwoodii*, for example, is Burkwood's viburnum—the result of *Viburnum carlesii* crossed with *Viburnum utile*. You will also see cultivars of hybrid plants, such as *Viburnum × burkwoodii* 'Mohawk'.

Some newer cultivars, varieties, and hybrids will have a legally protected trademark name as part of the common name, indicated by a ™ or ® symbol. It will be distinct from any part of the common name. For example, *Betula nigra* 'Cully' is Heritage™ river birch.

It's a good idea to save the name tags that come with new plants for future reference. It can be difficult, even for experts, to identify some types of plants, especially among cultivars and hybrids. Knowing the correct name can make all the difference when diagnosing plant problems, knowing how large a plant might grow, or finding out how to best prune and maintain certain plants.

WHAT IF SOMETHING GOES WRONG?

PLANT HEALTH CARE & INTEGRATED PEST MANAGEMENT

Plant Health Care (PHC) and the more complicated term IPM (Integrated Pest Management) mean looking carefully at possible plant problems and choosing the least toxic controls only when needed. These approaches are provided by many professional services and are

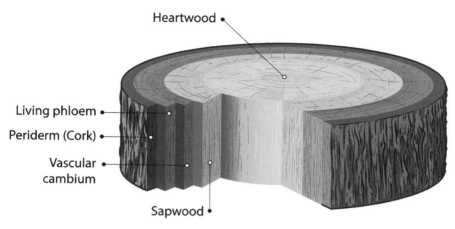

Heartwood

Living phloem
Periderm (Cork)
Vascular
cambium

Sapwood

■ *Trunk and stem anatomy of trees and shrubs:*
1. Bark (periderm): the protective outer covering.
2. Phloem and vascular cambium: the bright green layers just beneath the bark. Phloem conducts water and nutrients between roots and branches. Vascular cambium produces new phloem and xylem.
3. Sapwood: young xylem cells, which conduct water upward. As sapwood ages, it becomes part of the heartwood.
4. Heartwood: The growth rings seen in a cross-section are made up of old xylem. The inner wood is no longer actively growing, but is still a functioning part of the plant, providing support and energy storage.
When bark is cut or torn, water and nutrients will no longer move through that area. The wound does not heal. New layers of wood and vascular tissue will grow around it and may eventually cover the wound.

also useful to the home gardener. Both methods consider maintaining the health and function of the entire garden ecosystem.

1. **What's happening?** Problems almost never attack the garden as a whole, unless it is a large weather event, such as freezing, flooding, or drought.

Most plant difficulties happen to one type or group of plants: rose diseases, such as rose black spot, will not transfer to sunflowers and onions. Experience in observing and caring for your garden will help you notice plant changes and find symptoms of pest presence.

2. **Know the plant.** What is the normal appearance of leaf, flower, fruit, and bark? If you installed the plant, you may know its identification, but if you work in an older garden, their names may be mysteries. You may not recognize whether a change in leaf color is normal or a symptom of difficulty. Use university-based Internet resources for your region to help get acquainted with plant identification and problems (see Resources).

3. **Collect a sample.** Choose pieces that show a stage of the problem, as well as a piece that looks normal. University-trained volunteers at Master Gardener diagnostic clinics in some areas will be able to help, or you may take the samples to a nursery. Write your observations down: When did the problem begin? What parts of the plant are most affected? Is it a single plant or several? The more information you can gather, the more help that will be to anyone you consult.

4. **Evaluate the threat.** Once you have identified the plant and the problem, look at the landscape as a whole. Is this plant problem aesthetic or life threatening? How important is the plant specimen to the landscape? Don't be afraid to replace plants that aren't readily restored to good health or are not well suited to the growing conditions. And be prepared to accept some damage and imperfection as part of the normal life cycle of the garden.

Most gardeners are surprised to find that many common plant problems aren't caused by

■ Odd-looking insects on your plants can be a good thing. This lacewing and its larvae feast on aphids; it does not bother people. To avoid losing valuable beneficial insects, make sure you identify the problem before applying insecticides.

Routine, garden-wide application of insecticides, fungicides, and herbicides leads to the loss of beneficial organisms that would otherwise outnumber and keep most pest organisms in check. When routine chemical use is stopped, there may be a spike in some pest issues as a result. The good news is that such problems are usually short-lived, as beneficial insects, fungi, birds, and other organisms repopulate the garden ecosystem.

If you garden where a shed, garage, or basement contains old garden chemicals, gather them up carefully (wear gloves and goggles), box them, and get them to the next toxic waste residue pickup event in your county.

pests—poor soils, too little or too much water, overcrowding, the wrong amount of light and too much fertilizer all can lead to plant decline. As you read through this book, you will find references to "right plant, right place." Sun-loving conifers can dwindle if placed in too much shade or damp soil. Often, plants can benefit from being transplanted to a more agreeable spot in the garden. However, a severely infested plant that continues to decline may need removal and replacement with a more pest-resistant type. Check with garden advisors and nursery personnel about pest resistance. (A disease, by the way, is also considered a pest because its cause—fungal or bacterial or viral—is a live organism, just like an insect.)

5. **Choose and use pest controls carefully.** Be sure that you have considered steps 1 to 4 before selecting a pest control. This book does not specifically recommend any particular products, because it's necessary to have clear identification of the plant and the source of problem before selecting a product. Do not select a pesticide until you are clearly informed about what it does and how it may work on your specific problem. Do not use anything without proper personal protection to avoid being injured by spills or sprays. Read the label.

6. **Gardening for plant health care will lead to greater enjoyment.** As you become acquainted with the seasonal rhythms and life cycle of your garden and learn to work in sync with those cycles, you will come to see gardening more as a process and less as a battle with potential garden enemies. Landscapes are dynamic, and their growth and change through time present a great opportunity for interest and pleasure.

ENJOY YOUR GARDEN— MONTH BY MONTH

This introduction has presented up-to-date, basic techniques to help you care for and get the most out of your garden; come back to it as you go through the following chapters. As you spend time observing your garden, watching how your favorite plants respond to climate conditions and seasonal changes, you will find a flow of garden tasks and activities complementary to each season.

Learning from others adds to the pleasure. The resources offered in our reference will help you find great public gardens to visit and local experts who can inspire you.

Enjoy the journey. Whether you're a beginner or an experienced gardener who is new to the Pacific Northwest, you'll have a splendid time discovering how rewarding it is to garden here.

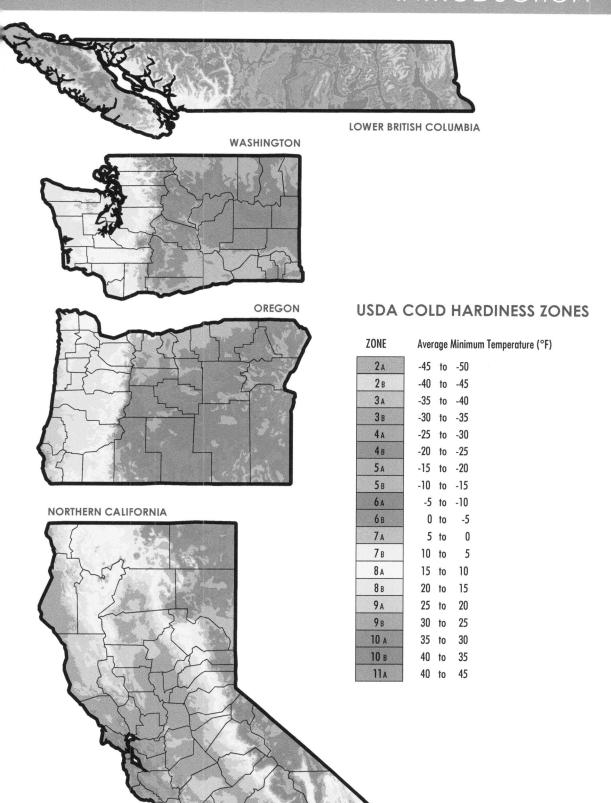

LOWER BRITISH COLUMBIA

WASHINGTON

OREGON

NORTHERN CALIFORNIA

USDA COLD HARDINESS ZONES

ZONE	Average Minimum Temperature (°F)		
2 A	-45	to	-50
2 B	-40	to	-45
3 A	-35	to	-40
3 B	-30	to	-35
4 A	-25	to	-30
4 B	-20	to	-25
5 A	-15	to	-20
5 B	-10	to	-15
6 A	-5	to	-10
6 B	0	to	-5
7 A	5	to	0
7 B	10	to	5
8 A	15	to	10
8 B	20	to	15
9 A	25	to	20
9 B	30	to	25
10 A	35	to	30
10 B	40	to	35
11 A	40	to	45

January

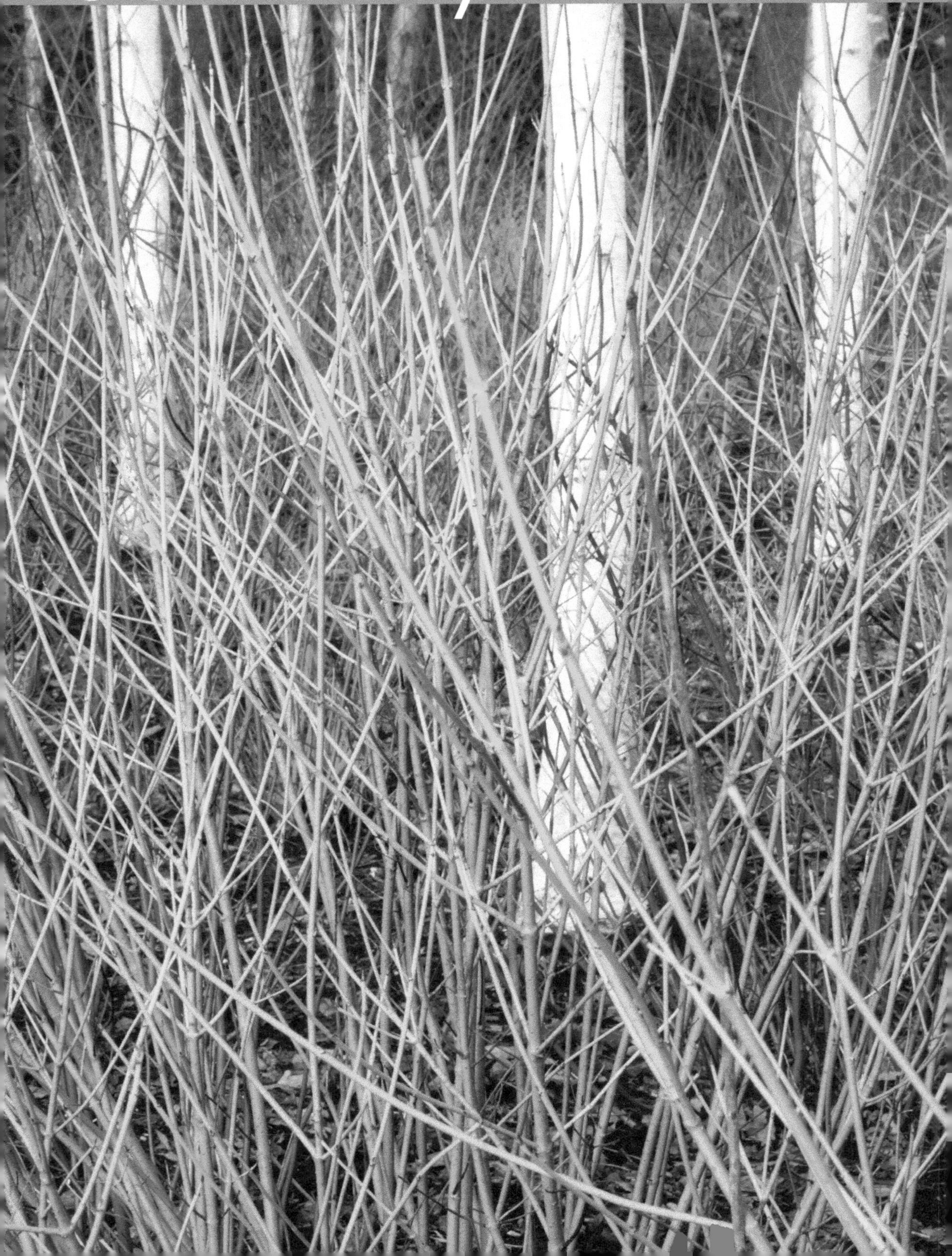

Short days and winter weather keep the pace slow this month. It is a time of repose for gardens and gardeners. Plants will be completely dormant, or nearly so, depending on the depth and persistence of the cold where you live. In colder zones, evergreen shrubs may sport burlap coats held in place with twine to ward off drying winds. Lichen and moss create a plush and iridescent blanket almost glowing in damp, low-light corners throughout the warmer coastal northwest.

Plant hardiness develops in early autumn, when leaves are falling and protective compounds accumulate in overwintering foliage, buds, and stems. Many of those protective compounds include the pigments responsible for the brilliant winter colors seen on young stems of red or yellow osier dogwoods and other deciduous plants, or the bronze-to-purple blush some conifer foliage takes on in cold temperatures. These winter hues are a function of survival that is beautiful to behold.

In colder zones, the combination of bright berries and colored stems with a backdrop of conifers provides bold color. Beautifully pruned deciduous trees strike a sculptural silhouette, dusted in new snow and in contrast with a snowy backdrop. The bark of ponderosa pine and birch add vivid patterns to the scenery.

Warmer zones host a variety of plants that bloom during this otherwise "off season," the surprise of their color and scent adding a lift to our winter days. In these places, while the rest of the plant is dormant, the flower buds on witch hazel (*Hamamelis*), sweet box (*Sarcococca*), winterblooming mahonia and camellias, and *Viburnum × bodnantense* burst through the subdued hues of winter with their bright and fragrant blooms.

When January weather keeps us indoors, the view to the outside can sustain our connection to nature and the garden. From an easy chair, with a supply of garden books and catalogs, we can contemplate the plants and details we want to add for an even more pleasing window on the winter landscape.

PLAN

ANNUALS

January is prime time to review seed catalogs and plan for which annuals you will grow this year. Think of annuals as the garden's accessories, as strong as a colored scarf on a neutral dress or like bold accent pillows on a sofa. They offer a big return for a small investment, and yearly changes add punch to the garden.

Annuals are plants that germinate from seed, mature, bloom, set seed, and die each growing season. Some, such as sweet alyssum, can be counted on to seed themselves nicely each year, but special cultivars require new seed packets each year to get their true colors and qualities. Biennials, less common than strict annuals, take two growing seasons to complete the seed-to-seed cycle. They are often sold as annuals in their bloom (second) year. Tender perennials are grown like annuals in climates where they cannot overwinter outdoors; geranium (*Pelargonium* spp.), coleus (*Plectranthus scutellarioides*), and banana (*Musa* spp.) fit this category throughout the Pacific Northwest.

Hybrid biennials with cultivar names—such as the wallflower *Erysimum cheiri* 'Ruby Gem'—will not produce seedlings that look the same. Seedlings from hybrid plants do not necessarily come true to type from seed, though they may still be beautiful. You will need to plant named seed again to get the same plant display.

BULBS

Summer-blooming alliums, begonias, cannas, and crocosmias are among the bulbs to include in your garden for seasonal color. Order summer bulbs now for spring delivery. Coordinate summer-blooming pink Asiatic lilies with shrubs such as lilacs: The lilies will bring fresh color as the lilac blooms fade. Alliums and lilies can be planted at the same time as spring-bloomers even though they bloom several months later.

INDOOR PLANTS

In this season, we may appreciate indoor plants the most. Quiet greens and intermittent blooming delight us. This month will join December in having the lowest light levels of the year. Where

HERE'S HOW

TO USE BIENNIALS IN THE GARDEN

Biennials produce a leafy rosette close to the ground their first year from seed. They are evergreen or dormant (depending on zone) over winter. During the second summer, they develop a flowering stem. Foxglove is a familiar biennial in the Pacific Northwest.

If you buy biennials with buds or blooms, they have completed their first year's rosette stage. They will bloom buoyantly when planted in your garden, set seed, and then die (much like this year's annuals). Their seeds will germinate to return as small, leafy rosettes their first summer. It is common to have biennial plants in both rosette and bloom stages in the garden at the same time.

■ *Foxglove is a familiar biennial in the Pacific Northwest.*

A light stand can give houseplants a boost during the darkest days in winter before it's needed for growing annuals from seed later in February and March.

light levels are too low, rotate plants between their display areas and positions in bright light. A light stand can be used to provide extra light for houseplants in winter and be switched over to start annuals indoors in mid-February and March.

LAWNS

Review the lawn's performance from last season to determine possible improvements. Function counts for a lot. Does the lawn get a lot of traffic? It is mostly a spot of color against a larger design? Is it a dog run? Do you fancy a croquet court? Be sure to plant the right seed blend for the intended use and existing light levels. Dark shade, tree roots, poor drainage, or hard-to-mow slopes make life tough for turf. When grass dies, weeds move in. Make changes to lawn areas for maximum effect and easier maintenance. For functions such as entertaining, a deck or patio may be more rewarding than turf.

Look for areas that hold water or freeze with puddles. If you have depressions in an older lawn, map these for renovation. Irregular surfaces will be harder to mow, and puddles can lead to poor grass growth. Plan now to prepare for lawn changes and renovation in March or April.

PERENNIALS, GRASSES & FERNS

A series of photographs on the first of January, first of April, first of July, and first of October will be helpful in seeing where sun-loving or shade-requiring plants can go. Or you may choose to photograph at the solstice and equinox dates. Learning the movement of light across the garden will be as important as studying the soil. Photographs offer an accurate record of how a garden grows and evolves over time. Perennials that are no longer in prime locations can be transplanted in early spring.

Consider stepping stones where there is too much shade or foot traffic on the lawn.

ROSES

Choose roses suited to your garden conditions, and plant as you would a shrub. Then weed, fertilize, and water as needed seasonally.

Consider the space available for new roses, selecting sunny spots with ample branch room for growth. Roses can be found in sizes from less than 1 foot among the miniature forms to 40 feet tall for scrambling climbers, such as the yellow 'Lady Banks', *Rosa banksiae* 'Lutea'. Groundcover roses need a lot of room to spread; use them on slopes or for season-long massed color in large beds.

SHRUBS

Garden shrubs can make for striking interest in the winter landscape. What do you see from your favorite windows? Is the view interesting or not? Does it lack a winter focal point? Begin a collection of photos to track the progression of seasonal change as viewed from inside, to use as a reference for choosing plants later.

Evergreen shrubs provide a dramatic backdrop when combined with deciduous shrubs, highlighting branch structure, colorful stems, and bright berries. Dramatic patterns and details emerge when plants are dusted in snow, outlined with frost, or even shining with rain.

Zones 4 to 6: Conifers and brightly colored stems of shrub dogwoods are a mainstay for winter season interest. Look for forms of multistemmed dogwood sporting a rainbow of bright colors, from reds to orange to brilliant yellow. You may need deer protection for these if that four-footer visits your garden.

Zones 7 to 9: Mahonia hybrids sport bright yellow floral spikes that attract hummingbirds, witch hazel (*Hamamelis* cvs.) casts a gentle sweet scent, and the intense perfume of sweet box (*Sarcococca* spp.) adds a tropical hint to the air. Visit your local nurseries now to see winter colors in prime display.

TREES

Conifers are nearly synonymous with Pacific Northwest trees. Long periods of moist weather, moderate temperatures, and overcast skies west of the Cascades provide ideal growing conditions for the native Douglas fir (*Pseudotsuga menziesii*), western red cedar (*Thuja plicata*), and shore pine (*Pinus contorta* var. *contorta*). These trees define the character of our forests and cultivated landscapes alike. East of the Cascades, ponderosa pine (*Pinus ponderosa*), lodgepole pine (*Pinus contorta* var. *latifolia*), western larch (*Larix occidentalis*), and western juniper (*Juniperus occidentalis*) are the predominant species. Native conifers are rapidly diminishing in many populated areas. Consider planting new native conifers and their cultivars where space permits.

Look to the native species that thrive in your area as indicators of which types of native and cultivated conifers to use in your garden. Existing and newly planted conifers can be easily incorporated into the landscape design as a dramatic backdrop or interspersed among deciduous trees. Many shades of greens, blues, and golds can be found among garden conifer cultivars.

VINES & GROUNDCOVERS

Focus on large areas of open ground with bare soil or chronic weed problems to add plants for year-round soil protection and weed suppression. Make note of the predominant weed species, as well as light and soil conditions. Browse garden books and catalogs to help choose plants that will thrive and compete. In addition to "standard" groundcovers, consider low-growing shrubs, such as Russian cypress (*Microbiota decussata*), dwarf Japanese spirea (*Spiraea japonica* 'Nana'), or *Rhododendron impeditum*. Shrubs that spread by underground stems are useful as a soil-anchoring cover for slopes. *Stephanandra incisa* 'Crispa' and *Sarcococca hookeriana* var. *humilis* (zones 7 to 9) are two examples. Prostrate junipers and low-spreading conifer cultivars provide hardy evergreen cover throughout the region.

■ *Prostrate junipers and low-spreading conifer cultivars provide hardy evergreen cover throughout the region.*

PLANT

ANNUALS

Zones 7 to 9: Pansies and primroses manage cool temperatures well and can be used to brighten up containers. Be sure to harden them off before setting them outside (see March).

BULBS

Pick up bargains on amaryllis bulbs this month. Choose firm, solid bulbs, and they'll thrive and bloom as vigorously as those potted two months ago.

Zones 4 to 6: Pot up any leftover daffodils or tulips that didn't make it into the ground last fall, using damp potting soil. Place them in an unheated garage or fruit cellar where temperatures stay between 32°F and 45°F/0° to 7°C. Don't allow them to freeze or go dry. When shoots emerge in

HERE'S HOW

TO TEST SEED GERMINATION

Sort out those old paper seed packets you have stashed away and find out what's still good. With dry storage, some seeds will stay viable for many years.

1. Lay about 10 seeds on a damp paper towel. Roll it up and lay it inside a plastic bag.

2. Unroll the towel in four to six days and count how many seeds have sprouted. Most gardeners choose to discard seeds that have less than 30 percent germination. For seeds gathered from a precious heirloom plant, any degree of germination will be good news.

Pansy (Viola × wittrockiana).

March, sink the pots in the ground outdoors where they will receive necessary light.

Zones 7 to 9: Can you plant bulbs now? Yes, you can, as long as the ground is neither squishy nor frozen. Tulips, daffodils, and hyacinths will be better off in the ground than languishing indoors. Discard any that seem dried or are soft and diseased. Set them at the same depth as for fall planting, and cover the soil with mulch. Spring bloomers planted now may not bloom the first season, but most will recover by the next year.

INDOOR PLANTS

A visit to the houseplant section of your favorite local nursery can serve as a great winter gardening excursion and an opportunity to add some new greenery to your surroundings.

LAWNS

Zones 7 to 9: West of the Cascades, it is possible to lay sod this month and nearly every month over winter when conditions aren't too cold or soggy. Though sod is less available this time of year, it can be found or ordered through garden centers. If sod cannot be planted, cover exposed soil with straw to protect and prepare the soil for later planting or seeding.

PERENNIALS, GRASSES & FERNS

Weather generally makes planting of herbaceous material this month impossible, especially in the coldest areas. Avoid walking or digging on frozen ground or on ground that's sodden from winter rains.

Zones 7 to 9: If it's a dry and pleasant day, planting or transplanting may be done.

ROSES

Zones 7 to 9: Late in the month in the mildest areas, bare-root roses can be planted and all rose types may be transplanted. Prepare bare-root roses for planting by soaking roots for six to eight hours in lukewarm water. Dig a hole with a conical center so you can spread the roots over the mound of soil. Install with the graft union above ground. Mulch deeply after planting to insulate the graft union against sudden February freezes. Dormant roses may be moved from one spot to another when temperatures are above freezing and the ground isn't waterlogged.

SHRUBS, TREES, VINES & GROUNDCOVERS

Zones 7 to 9: Evergreen and deciduous woody plants can be planted and transplanted during warmer periods when low temperatures are well above freezing and when soil is not sopping wet. Roots suffer freeze damage at higher temperatures than stems. Be sure to keep stored nursery plants insulated from the cold by surrounding the pots in mulch or compost.

■ *Trim dead foliage from warm season grasses when their appearance fades and any wildlife value is past. Cut grass clumps back before new growth emerges.*

CARE

Zones 7 to 9: Winter weeds may be appearing if weather has been mild. Look for rosettes of dandelion, plantain, and buttercup. Seedlings of dead nettle, shotweed, and herb-Robert (*Geranium robertianum*) that germinated in fall may be present. Nip these weeds now while they are small; distribute mulch over any soil left exposed. Remember to stay off saturated soil. If the day is dry and comfortable for a gardener to be outside, conditions are likely to be okay for plants and soil as well.

ANNUALS

Check the condition of any geraniums (*Pelargonium*) or fuchsias being overwintered inside. Prune out any blackened foliage and stems on the geraniums.

Zones 7 to 9: Protect pots containing winter pansies and primroses from sudden, heavy freezes. Tuck small pots into a sheltered, above freezing location such as a garage until the weather moderates. Protect larger pots by draping a cloth over the top, using some short stakes to hold it over plants without crushing them.

Remove any fall kale (*Brassica oleracea* cvs.) that has passed its period of good display. Remove dead leaves to tidy up ornamental kale that still look good.

BULBS

After amaryllis drops its petals, trim the stem down to the bulb.

Zones 4 to 6: Keep bulb plantings covered with 2 to 3 inches of mulch to insulate the ground and help protect them from freeze damage. Bulbs outdoors in containers are likely to be damaged if left unprotected. Bulbs in large containers, such as half barrels, can survive winter surrounded in the large volume of soil. Mulch and protect these containers from direct winter sun; thawing during a warm spell can shock bulbs into harmful premature growth.

Zones 7 to 9: Check any pots of bulbs during extended dry or frigid weather. If bulbs dry out now, after root formation has started, they will be damaged or killed. Keep them moist and covered in mulch. Group small pots together and fill spaces between with lightweight mulch. If temperatures drop below 25°F/-4°C, use a plastic bag filled with dry fallen leaves as an insulating "pillow" over the pots.

West of the Cascades, hardy bulbs die more from drowning than freezing over winter. Check gutter flows and divert heavy water flow away from bulbs. Otherwise, they'll rot rather than root.

INDOOR PLANTS

Wrap tropical plants when moving them from warm nursery conditions to the cold, possibly freezing, winter car. Prewarm the car interior. Many tropical plants, including ferns, can be damaged by exposure to temperatures lower than 50°F/10°C.

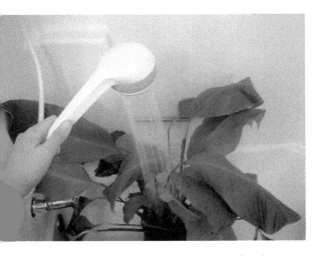

■ *Rinse dusty houseplants with a gentle spray of tepid water.*

Mid-winter often finds indoor plants coated with dust. Rinse in a tepid, low-pressure shower in a sink or bathtub. Don't soak or spray African violets or succulent plants; use a gentle brush instead.

Plants don't need "leaf polish." Waxy or oily products reduce air flow through stomates (natural openings) in the leaves.

Poinsettias: after their colorful leaf bracts drop, grow them as a tender house plant, in normal light, in a warm spot (65° to 75°F/18° to 24°C) without drafts.

LAWNS

Stay off frozen grass; walking on it will cause damage. Maintain barriers to protect new lawns from foot traffic.

Zones 7 to 9: In a mild season, lawns may grow enough to need mowing. If it's dry enough, go ahead and mow. But if rain is keeping things soggy, wait for drier conditions. Lawns that entered winter under stress will not be as thick and green as those with good fall care. Rake up any late deposits of leaves and fallen twigs. Moss flourishes with the cool, damp winter months. Often a seasonal feature, it does not always require management and can even help keep soil covered.

PERENNIALS, GRASSES, FERNS & GROUNDCOVERS

Zones 4 to 6: Plants may frost heave—literally pushed out of the ground by alternate freezing and thawing. New and small plants are most vulnerable. If you haven't covered them with mulch or evergreen boughs, do it now, walking on the ground as little as possible. Hope for snow, which is an excellent insulator.

Zones 7 to 9: Bishop's hat (*Epimedium* spp.) should be trimmed late this month or early February, before new basal growth is visible. Trim off old, tattered leaves. Large beds may be trimmed with a rotary lawnmower set to the tallest cutting height. Keep minced leaves in place as mulch. In March, plants will look renewed with fresh new leaves setting off their small spring flowers.

ROSES

Roses require little care while dormant. Check for sufficient water when planted under eaves; pull mulch over the graft union in coldest areas.

■ *Trim back old foliage of bishop's hat (*Epimedium*) in late January or early February in zones 7 to 9.*

SHRUBS

Evergreen and deciduous shrubs can be pruned when it's warm and dry enough to be comfortable working outdoors. Focus on removing dead and broken branches. Lightly thin multistem shrubs by cutting selected stems down to soil level.

Snowfall can occur in all regions. Gently shake snow loose with a soft broom to lighten loads on bent-over stems. Touching bent branches laden with ice risks breaking them; wait for a thaw unless broken branches need to be pruned for safety.

Zones 4 to 6: Check on winter protection installed for evergreens and tender shrubs.

Zones 7 to 9: Bring cut branches of flowering quince (*Chaenomeles* spp.), forsythia, and witch hazel inside to force them into bloom. Soak the branches in tepid water for a few hours to accelerate bloom.

HERE'S HOW

TO GROOM PERENNIALS

Grooming or pruning herbaceous perennials, ornamental grasses, and ferns will be easier when you understand the way different types grow.

1. Fully herbaceous perennials die to the ground and come back from a crown just above the roots. Remove brittle old stems that don't show a green inner core when broken, being careful not to catch any new green shoots.

2. In warmer areas, some herbaceous perennials become nearly evergreen. In late spring, pull out dead leaves on coast iris (*Iris douglasiana*). Trim evergreen daylilies (*Hemerocallis* spp.) just above the pointed green shoots.

3. Warm-season ornamental grasses whose leaves die over winter should be cut within 1 foot of the ground before new shoots emerge.

4. Cool-weather grasses that retain live foliage over winter often just need the unsightly dead foliage tugged out.

5. Sedges (*Carex*), mondo grass (*Ophiopogon*), sweet flag (*Acorus*), lily turf (*Liriope*), and blue oat grass do not require annual trimming. Trim off two-thirds of the height in years when foliage is tattered. Cutting any lower can damage growing tips and may open the crowns up to moisture and rot.

6. Hardy ferns don't need to be pruned every year. When dead fronds accumulate or old fronds look bad, clip them off just above the crown before the curled crosiers (coiled new fronds) begin to unfurl.

TREES

Zones 4 to 6: Winter desiccation can occur when needles on evergreens dry out from sun and wind exposure when soils are frozen. Needles may be protected with a spray-on antidesiccant when temperatures are above freezing. Smaller trees may be wrapped in burlap. Make sure newly planted evergreens go into winter well watered. Damaged needles will be shed and replaced the next growing season.

VINES & GROUNDCOVERS

Winter protection is most critical east of the Cascades. Check and adjust the attachments of mature vines to their supports. Secure any loose branches being whipped about by the wind. If heavy snows occur, gently shake the snow loose with a soft broom to lighten the load on permanent vine stems.

Zones 7 to 9: Mulch exposed soil showing through groundcover plantings to protect the soil surface from the destructive effects of hard winter rains. Prune out rampant branches that jut out of place or crowd neighboring plants on woody groundcovers, such as prostrate cotoneaster, Point Reyes ceanothus, or prostrate junipers.

WATER

Rain and snowfall provide moisture this month, no matter which zone you're in. Soils should be moist, and watering should not be a concern for landscape plantings that were well hydrated before winter. Check plants under protected eaves and overhangs, which may be suffering from lack of water.

BULBS

Indoors, keep amaryllis watered weekly after bloom is done to promote new leaf growth. Remove any decorative foil wrappers that impede water drainage.

Zones 4 to 6: Outdoors in high desert, check new bulb plantings to make sure none are dry. Bulbs under shrubs or overhangs may need water.

INDOOR PLANTS

Water sparingly this month; allow the top inch of soil to dry before watering. Take special winter care with succulent and cactus plants. Let jade plants dry out from mid-November through December, water once, and then wait until mid-February to resume normal watering. For cactus, pretend it's in a desert and keep them dry for now.

LAWNS

Zones 7 to 9: If an unusual dry spell sets in west of the mountains, check new turf installed in fall and water if needed. Pay special attention to the edges and seams on newly laid sod.

SHRUBS & TREES

Zones 4 to 6: If the weather has been milder than usual and snowfall sparse, garden evergreens may need supplemental water, particularly if they entered winter with dry soil. Check the soil and water needy plants when temperatures are above freezing.

FERTILIZE

No fertilizer for landscape plants or lawns.

INDOOR PLANTS

Don't fertilize indoor plants in winter. When a potted plant isn't growing, fertilizer may actually burn the roots. The exception is plants grown under lights and those that are actively flowering. They may benefit from one application this month.

PROBLEM-SOLVE

Zones 7 to 9: Woody weeds—tree seedlings, holly, Scotch broom, ivy, blackberry, and others—are easier to spot and pull from the moist ground this time of year. Search through garden beds and native plant borders for these invasive plants, and remove them before they are hidden in the flush of new spring growth. A specialized "weed wrench" is very effective at uprooting plants up to 2 inches in diameter with minimal soil disturbance. You may find them on the web or as a garden tool rental.

ANNUALS

Aphids may appear on plants brought into shelter. You will see little, green, translucent blobs the size of a comma. Rinse them off with warm water or treat with insecticidal soap. Just a few aphids can launch an indoor epidemic among your houseplants.

BULBS

Snow? No problem. Snow cover protects bulb shoots and other plants from drying cold. Ice storms bring the real peril. Fallen branches can crush tender shoots. Resilient bulbs will often bloom even if early leaf shoots were damaged in winter.

INDOOR PLANTS

Blooming plants may show symptoms of insufficient light. They may stop blooming, turn a paler green, drop yellow leaves, or lean and stretch toward light. This may be their winter condition, but they'll rally in spring.

Plants may slow down in January, but insect infestations don't. Keep a close watch for early signs. Isolate any plants with severe infestations to avoid infesting the entire indoor garden.

If you see sticky, cottony wads where leaves meet stems, the likely problem is aptly named: mealybugs. Regularly remove mealybugs with a cotton swab soaked in rubbing alcohol. A handheld vacuum can be used for whiteflies; dispose of them in sealed bags in outdoor trash cans. Disrupt fungus gnats by letting the soil dry out between watering and removing standing water from saucers. Insecticidal soap and light horticultural oil labeled for houseplants can be kept on hand. If you're not sure what's eating your plants, get an accurate diagnosis from a local nursery or Master Gardener clinic.

LAWNS

Zones 7 to 9: The sight of moss may compel you to do something now, but you should wait. The resulting bare spots would leave soil exposed to rain, weeds, and more moss. Address moss during March or April.

ROSES

Choose new roses that are known for ease of care and disease resistance in your growing area. Resistance isn't total immunity, but performance will be so much better. *Rosa rugosa* is a multistem shrub that is not only disease resistant, but is intolerant to pesticide sprays. The Knock Out® rose hybrids and "Carefree" series come in many colors and give gardeners great choices in disease-resistant roses. They thrive east of the mountains in hot summers as well as on the coasts. You'll find many more disease-resistant roses available each year, as growers respond to demand and more public gardens cultivate and test roses for disease resistance. This is a real revolution in rose growing.

PERENNIALS, GRASSES & FERNS

Zones 7 to 9: Slugs invade crowns of delphinium, iris, pulmonaria, and brunnera now if short leaf stalks are up. Some gardeners rake mulch away from plant crowns during late winter to remove cozy spots where slugs hide.

SHRUBS

Check the base of shrubs to be sure no leaves or mulch are piled up against the stems, as it can provide a warm haven for rodents that chew on the bark. Use fencing to surround young plants vulnerable to damage from deer browsing.

Be prepared to protect newly planted shrubs against severe cold snaps. Use light blankets, bushel baskets, or evergreen boughs for quick cover. In milder areas, remove covering when temperatures remain above freezing.

TREES

Winter storms can take a toll on trees; snow, ice, and wind can break limbs. Trees in water-logged soils may begin to lean or fall over. Check on your trees after any severe storm or wind events. Call an ISA Certified Arborist® for assistance with repair and cleanup of severely damaged trees, or those with large hanging broken limbs that could pose a safety threat (see "How to Hire an Arborist," page 80). Stay away from power lines when surveying tree damage after a storm, and contact your local utility if trees have come in contact with the power lines.

February

Snowdrops, early crocus, and petite narcissus push up through cool ground and offer pleasing hints that spring is near. Buds on the tips of tree branches may begin to show color. Days are noticeably longer. February is a mixed month; it can bring balmy weather that draws us outdoors or chilly reminders that winter is not quite over. Mild days offer gardeners the chance to get outdoors and be in touch with the earth. These early, short garden visits can provide a head start on tasks needed later in the growing season.

Garden soil can be at its wettest condition of the year. Tread carefully, as trampling and cultivating soggy, saturated soil leads to damage and compaction. It is too early for lawn care, but not for getting tools and equipment in order. Plant roots are easily pulled intact from damp soil, a boon to transplanting and to extracting stubborn roots of perennial weeds.

Branches cut from flowering quince, forsythia, cherry, witch hazel, and other flowering shrubs can brighten rooms as their flowers are forced open with indoor heat. Branches from red and yellow stem dogwoods add color used on their own or in mixed arrangements.

February can be a time of dramatic changes in seasonal cycles within the garden. In preparation for spring, flora and fauna are shifting and stirring from the depths of the soil to the tips of dormant stems. Keep watch for subtle moments of beauty and passing details. Taking note of where standing water persists during wet weather can let you know where plant or garden changes may be needed. Capture the unfolding of new growth with photographs. They will be an important part of this year's garden journal and future reference.

February can keep a long hold on winter's grip or rush ahead into early spring. Take advantage when the weather is nice enough to enjoy being outside; it can also mean the conditions are right for tending plants and soil with good results. Indoors and out, there is much to do in preparation for the gardening year.

PLAN

Consumer garden shows bloom this month through April. The displays, vendor shows, and seminars offer inspiration, education, and the welcome company of other gardeners. Check local news listings to find dates of upcoming events in your area.

This is a good time to sort out gardening goals and head off any problems from last year before they come up again. Are there bare areas requiring groundcover, shrubs, or perennial flowers? Do you want a cutting garden where you can gather flowers and colorful stems for arrangements? Thinking about growing edible plants? Start a list of plants to suit the growing conditions and design functions of those spaces.

Lay out some small, interior paths for easy access within large garden beds. Otherwise, working among fully developed herbaceous perennials might be difficult. A few flat stones, a mulched path, or small bricks placed over the ground are simple solutions.

BULBS

Order summer-blooming bulbs from catalogs, or shop at nurseries. Store bulbs in a cool, dry environment until April or May when soils are warm enough for planting.

INDOOR PLANTS

Colorful flowers abound this month at florists and nurseries. You may find primroses and florist cyclamen in deep raspberry, pink, and white. Early spring bulbs, crocus, daffodils, and tulips forced into bloom will be available. Plan to add a few to perk up the indoor scene.

February often brings gift plants, a celebratory rainbow of potted floral offerings. Some of these may become permanent house dwellers; others, such as miniature roses, will decline after several weeks indoors. That's fine; they can be considered long-lasting bouquets.

Late winter can find houseplants looking their worst, and the best-adapted ones will be obvious now. Don't hesitate to discard unsatisfactory indoor plants. You'll have the pleasure of adding new plants and keeping a collection that looks great.

LAWNS

What size is your lawn? Having an accurate measure is helpful because seed, fertilizer, and other granular treatments are calibrated in terms of pounds per 1,000 square feet.

Review your lawn needs and plan changes for easier care and improved appearance. Make mowing and edging easier by rounding out odd-shaped corners and widening adjacent beds for broadly curved edges. Draping a garden hose along the ground is an easy way to shape and visualize a new bed edge before digging out the excess grass.

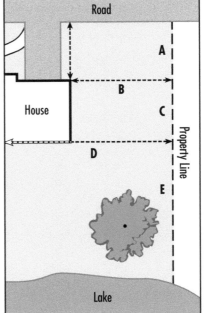

$$A \times B = X$$
$$B \times C = Y$$
$$D \times E = Z$$
$$X + Y + Z = \text{Total Square Feet}$$

■ *If you don't know your lawn area, measure it. Getting the approximate square footage will help calculate your seed and fertilizer needs.*

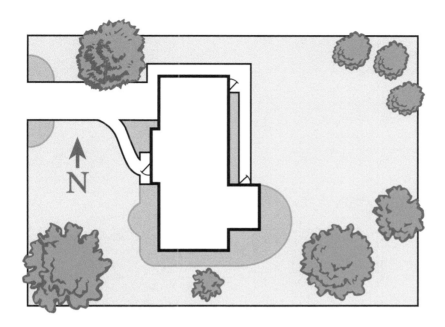

When planting new trees, but sure to place them where they will provide the best long-term benefits. Larger species planted southeast and southwest of a house offer the best energy-saving shade. Be sure to allow trees enough room to grow without crowding too close to the house or into overhead power lines.

If you plan to install or renovate a lawn, organize supplies for action in March and April. Seed choices, soil amendments, and tool rentals for thatching, aerating, and planting should all be on your list.

Extremely damp turf areas that are hard to mow through the summer might be turned into a landscape bed populated with moisture-loving specimens. Winterberry holly (*Ilex verticillata* cvs.), blueberries (*Vaccinium* spp.), western ninebark (*Physocarpus capitatus*), Virginia sweetspire (*Itea virginica*), Japanese sweet flag (*Acorus gramineus*), hosta, and ferns are among the many choices for enhancing damp locations.

SHRUBS

Tired of mowing grass on a steep bank? Replace turf with a bed of dense-growing shrubs that spread by underground stems. Salal (*Gaultheria shallon*), privet honeysuckle (*Lonicera pileata*), *Rosa rugosa*, and cinquefoil (*Potentilla fruticosa*) are a few rugged examples. Need a low screen that won't need constant trimming? Plant naturally narrow cultivars, such as the English yew (*Taxus baccata* 'Standishii'), American arborvitae (*Thuja*

occidentalis 'Rheingold'), 'Graham Blandy' boxwood, or dwarf heavenly bamboo (*Nandina domestica* 'Compacta').

TREES

Dormant planting season wraps up between now and March. Look at the sun and wind patterns around your property to determine optimal placement. Strategically placed deciduous trees can provide cooling shade in summer, while letting the light and warmth of the sun through in winter. Direct shade from trees can save 20 to 50 percent in summer cooling costs. Planting a long row of evergreen trees perpendicular to prevailing winds will deflect the impact of winter winds, especially in rural open areas, saving up to one-third of the heat loss from the building.

VINES & GROUNDCOVERS

With the garden at its most skeletal stage, this is a good time to review the edges, those places where turf meets shrub bed, perennial border meets sidewalk, garden meets wild slope. The shape and content of these edges hold some of the greatest impact on maintenance requirements.

Are you forever trimming a sprawling groundcover back off the sidewalk? Replace it with something such as Japanese spurge (*Pachysandra terminalis*), which has a more compact habit that will stay more neatly behind the pavement edge. Eliminate tight corners and peninsulas that are tricky to mow by reshaping the edges into broad sweeping curves. Fill the vacant spots with groundcovers that offer seasonal color, such as carpet bugle (*Ajuga reptans*) or 'John Creech' sedum. A border of low-growing plants along the front edge provides a gentle transition between a lawn or pathway and taller plants.

PLANT

ANNUALS

Zones 7 to 9: Plant sweet peas (*Lathyrus* spp.) outdoors in compost-enriched soil mid- to late February. Install a trellis for climbing types. 'Cupani' is a deep purple descendant of the original sweet pea with exceptionally fragrant, though tiny, flowers.

Zones 4 to 6: Start sweet peas indoors in mid-February; they can use a good head start for your area because they need cool temperatures to flower.

If you stepped into your favorite nursery's greenhouses right now, you'd find hundreds of new annuals just starting up. You may be planning to buy seedlings, but you may find it fun to grow them yourself. Some flowers and heritage vegetables may only be available as seed.

BULBS

Zones 7 to 9: Move or divide snowdrops just as blooms fade. Doing this while foliage is still green gives the best chance for blooming next year. Do you have some spring bulbs that didn't get planted? Discard soft or hollow ones and plant the rest by the end of the month. Bloom may not be normal this year. Hardy true lilies (*Lilium* spp.) of all types can go into the ground by month's end. Set them 6 to 8 inches deep in well-drained, loose soil. Place markers to avoid accidentally disturbing them before they emerge in May.

HERE'S HOW

TO START SEEDS INDOORS

Start now if you want plants for May, when annuals may be set out in all parts of our region. Start faster-growing plants, such as cosmos, marigolds, and zinnias, in mid- to late March.

1 **Get set up:** *Analyze your layout. It's easy to have room indoors when the seedlings are babies, but more space is needed when it's time to transplant them to larger containers. Start with a quantity you can easily care for until it's time for outdoor planting.*

2 **Light:** *In all parts of our region, winter lacks the daylight strength seedlings need. Plus, tender plants next to windows may suffer from cold air. A simple setup of fluorescent lights will do the trick. A 48-inch shop light on chains allows easy raising and lowering to keep the lights 6 inches above growing plants. Use a lamp timer to operate lights 12 to 14 hours a day.*

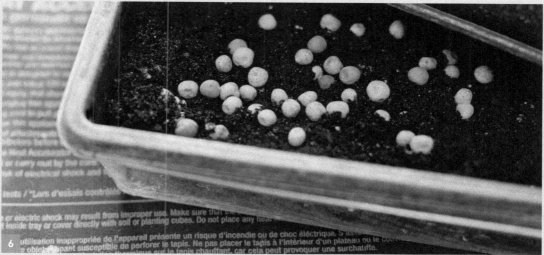

3   **When to plant:** *Check seed packet instructions and choose sowing time by working backward from the last frost date for your area. Ideally, the seedling you start will be just the right size when weather cooperates.*

4   **Material:** *Use bagged seeding soil mix and thoroughly dampen it before filling the containers. Wash and soak used containers for several minutes in a 9:1 ratio of water-to-bleach solution.*

5   **How to plant:** *Bury seeds about the same depth as their diameter, or as specified on the packet. Make sure seeds have good contact with moist soil. Cover containers with plastic to maintain consistent humidity until seedlings emerge. Starter trays with clear plastic lids are also a good option.*

6   **Heat:** *Seeds of annuals need warmth to germinate, 68 to 75°F/20 to 24°C. If your space is too cool, seedlings can be slow or fail to grow. Pots can be kept in a warmer location, and then moved to lights when seedlings emerge. Or use a seedling heat mat under the flat.*

INDOOR PLANTS

If you have a nice bright room with large window exposure, you can grow 'Meyer Improved' lemons indoors. They are typically available in early spring. Lemons offer fragrant flowers during winter months and often produce fruit once adapted to the location.

PERENNIALS, GRASSES & FERNS

Zones 7 to 9: Routine planting can be done toward the end of the month.

ROSES

Roses are sold in two growth forms: grafted or "own root." Grafted roses, like many fruit trees, combine two parts: the rootstock and a named variety branch stock. The graft location shows up as a knob or swelling just above the roots. In zones 4 to 6, plant the graft 3 to 4 inches below the surface. In warmer zones, keep the graft union above ground.

If the grafted rootstock produces its own canes, stems with different color or leaf shape from the variety will appear. Keep rootstock canes pruned off. This doesn't occur on "own root" roses grown from cuttings—all the shoots will be genetically identical.

Plant bare-root roses as soon as possible. Store them in their packaging in a cool place, such as an unheated garage, for up to three days to protect them from freezing if it's too cold to plant.

Zones 4 to 6: Plant bare-root roses when conditions are above freezing (see January).

Zones 7 to 9: Finish planting and transplanting roses by the end of the month, before they start full growth.

SHRUBS, TREES, VINES & GROUNDCOVERS

All zones: Nurseries will have bare-root stock of shade trees, shrubs, fruit trees, and small fruits over the next two months. They are sold packed in damp sawdust and plastic bags. The challenge is to keep roots from freezing or drying out: they should be planted within a day or so of purchase for best results. The advantages of bare-root plants are lower cost, lighter weight, and a head start on root growth. This is a good way to obtain a larger sized tree that you can handle planting yourself, since there is no heavy soil ball to lug around.

Zones 7 to 9: This is a good time of year to plant and transplant trees, shrubs, and woody vines. New plants will have better drought resilience their first season. Plant when the ground is workable and temperatures are above freezing—conditions that are also more comfortable for gardeners.

Bare-root and conservation stock of native plants are available from specialty nurseries and preordered from local natural resources and conservation districts.

CARE

Do you need a soil test? It's advisable if you plan a large landscape installation and are unfamiliar with the characteristics of the property, or if plants are not thriving. Testing for pH is helpful around new construction, where soils may have higher pH levels. Soil tests can confirm what kind, if any, fertilization or amendments are needed.

On the other hand, a soil test may not be crucial. Many people garden for decades without getting a formal soil test, relying on their experience and satisfaction with how plants grow. If you follow a regular program of replenishing organic matter to lawns and planting beds, and plants are growing well, soil testing may not be needed. See the Introduction for more information on soil testing.

Weeds can thrive at colder temperatures than we imagine. This is a good time to nip weeds in the bud, before they have the chance to put on more leaves, or worse, go to seed. Roots of persistent weedy plants are more easily pulled from moist soil.

ANNUALS

When bringing plants such as fuchsias, geraniums, and tuberous begonias out of winter storage, it's sometimes difficult to tell what parts are alive.

TO INSTALL BARE-ROOT PLANTS

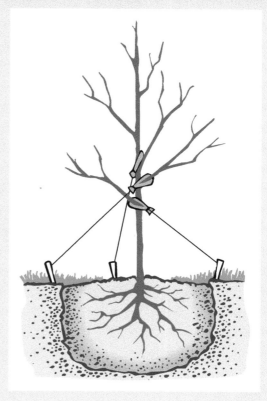

1. Keep roots covered in damp sawdust, compost, or soil until planting. Soak the roots in tepid water so plants are well hydrated before going into the ground. Prune broken, dead, shriveled, twisted, or kinked root ends back to healthy tissue. Nice new roots will grow from the cleanly cut ends.

2. Dig a shallow, wide hole no deeper than the actual root area so the root flare sits at or slightly above soil grade. Build a firmly packed mound of soil at the bottom of the hole to help hold the framework of roots in place.

3. Backfill with the same soil you dug out of the hole. Do not add any amendments or fertilizers to the planting hole; this can do more harm than good in the long run.

4. Gently water as the hole is backfilled to settle the soil in around roots. Gently tamp the ground with your hands so the plant holds firm without compacting the soil.

5. Trees will need staking until enough new roots grow for support. Drive stakes into firm soil outside the planting hole, and place ties at the lowest point needed to anchor the roots and hold the trunk straight. Remove stakes by the end of the first growing season.

6. Provide a generous ring of coarse organic mulch over the soil around the new plant. Never bury trunks or stems in soil or mulch. Coarse compost and wood chip mulch will improve establishment by retaining moisture, suppressing weeds, and slowly releasing nutrients as it decomposes.

Prune off obviously dead parts (such as blackened twigs on geranium). Otherwise wait until new leaves show before grooming. Fuchsia stems, for instance, can look completely dead but then sprout new leaves.

BULBS

Zones 7 to 9: Bring indoors any spring-blooming bulbs you potted up for forcing. They should have received 11 to 12 weeks of cooling outdoors or in a refrigerator at 35°F/2°C. You should see roots coming through the drain holes and new shoots popping up. Keep them in bright light and cool temperatures. A cool (50°F/10°C) location and fluorescent lights 6 inches above the plants for 12 hours per day is ideal for tulips, daffodils, and hyacinths. When buds show color, treat them as houseplants and move them to warmer areas and window light. Blooms last longer if plants are kept cooler at night.

Mow often enough to remove no more than one-third of the grass blade height. What if the lawn has gotten really long? Raise the mowing height to stay at the one-third rule, and then gradually bring it back down with the second and third mowings. Removing too much of the blade height weakens turf.

Check stored dahlias, gladiolus, and begonias. Remove rotted ones and dampen the withered ones with a spray bottle. The sawdust or coir fiber you've stored them in should be slightly damp.

Discard paperwhite narcissus with spent blooms. If you want to save them, remove faded blooms, fertilize, and then water until leaves fade. Store potted bulbs in a cool, dry place over summer. They may emerge again when watered in late fall.

INDOOR PLANTS

A small tarp, a watering can with a narrow spout, small clippers, a bucket for dumping excess water from saucers, and a trowel will make indoor plant care easier.

Use a soft brush such as a camera lens cleaning brush or cosmetic brush to clean dusty African violet leaves.

Gift plants of forced hyacinths, daffodils, and tulips bloom only once. After blooming, they can be fertilized, watered until the foliage fades, and then planted outdoors for possible bloom next season. Florist cyclamen (*Cyclamen persicum*) may bloom for a long period of time. Keep them in bright light. Do not overwater. Remove yellowing leaves.

Primroses do best in a well-lit, cool spot (below 60°F or 16°C). Baskets of primroses often grace mid-winter front doorsteps in zones 7 to 9. They cannot take freezing weather. They can be planted out in spring.

LAWNS

Sharpen mower blades and tune up mowers before the March and April rush.

Mowing frequency and height are extremely important to turf health. West of the Cascades, mow at 2 to 2.5 inches for fescue and perennial rye grass blends, and 1 to 1.5 inches for bentgrass. East of the Cascades, mow Kentucky blue grass 1.5 to 2.5 inches tall. As a general rule, mow shorter at the cool ends of the growing season and taller during summer.

PERENNIALS, GRASSES & FERNS

Maintain mulch and evergreen boughs over perennials this month.

Zones 4 to 6: Dead leaves of tall ornamental grasses may be getting tattered and messy. Cut back ornamental grasses and ferns now and next month, before new growth emerges (see January).

Zones 7 to 9: Perennial plant growth may start before the end of February. Gradually pull back protective mulch when shoots emerge, but be prepared to cover plants if a hard freeze is predicted.

Mulch is invaluable for weed management and moisture retention. When replenished now, soil will stay damp and cool longer into the spring. In cooler coastal areas, you may want to wait until May to allow the soil to warm up before replenishing mulch around heat-loving plants.

ROSES

Why prune? Roses produce flowers on new growth. Early spring pruning stimulates growth of new shoots carrying bloom. Left unpruned, many roses will gradually produce a tangle of old branches and fewer blooms. How to prune? That depends on the type of rose. Some require rigorous annual pruning, others only light shaping. Determine which roses you have before you begin cutting. Look for pruning demonstrations at public rose gardens to learn from local experts. Check with Master Gardeners or the American Rose Society website for reliable information.

Zones 4 to 6: Tie up climbers torn loose by wind. Keep protective winter coverings secure. It's too early to prune.

Zones 7 to 9: Unless February is unusually cold, gradually remove winter protection mid-month, taking a few days to completely uncover bushes.

Late February is a traditional time to prune roses west of the Cascades, with Presidents Day as the benchmark. A cold year pushes pruning into early March. Don't worry about removing stems that have already leafed out; rapid new growth will follow. Species and shrub roses, such as *Rosa rugosa*, are not cut back every spring. Use selective thinning as needed.

SHRUBS

Zones 4 to 6: Check that winter protection remains intact. When it is mild enough to work comfortably outdoors, begin pruning multistem shrubs. To enhance form and floral display, thin out a few of the largest stems on mock orange, forsythia, quince, lilac, spirea, and others. Remove individual stems as close to soil level as possible. Do not clip ends from the remaining stems (you'll be cutting away flower buds). Do remove broken

■ *On shrubs with multiple stems coming up from the ground, cut all the way back to the soil to thin out crowded stems.*

On trees and shrubs with a few main stems, thin out branches by cutting back to the point of attachment at a larger limb.

or dead branches. Bring quince and forsythia branches inside to force bloom.

Zones 7 to 9: Prune conifer shrubs and broad leaf evergreens. Repair winter damage, pruning back to a larger side branch. Begin pruning for summer-blooming shrubs that flower on new growth: glossy abelia, bush cinquefoil (*Potentilla* spp.), and hypericum. Remove about one-quarter or less of the oldest, unproductive stems. Make cuts near ground level.

Prune big leaf (mophead) hydrangeas every spring just as buds green up and swell. Thin out a few of the older, very crowded, and very spindly canes, cutting flush to the ground. Remove old flower heads, carefully cutting back to strong buds.

Oversized hedges can be renovated late in the dormant season. Yews, laurel, boxwood, privet, and other plants that produce new growth on old wood can be cut back to a bare framework. Buds and small shoots are often visible inside the plant on older stems or at the base of trunks, but this is not the case for arborvitae, juniper, or cypress: their old bare stems stay bare and plants may die if pruned too hard.

TREES

Winter storms may still occur. Inspect trees for damage after storms (see January).

Broadleaf evergreens and conifers can be pruned now.

Zones 7 to 9: Replenish mulch to a total of 2 to 4 inches deep when bare soil shows through. Keep the base of trees trunks clear of weeds and vegetation so the root flare area is clear and visible.

Continue dormant-season pruning. Maples and birches can "bleed" after pruning. The sap loss itself is not harmful, though continual wetness around larger wounds can sometimes damage stem tissue. Prune at the end of the dormant season (but before buds open) to reduce the amount of time sap flows onto the bark. These trees may also be pruned in summer.

VINES & GROUNDCOVERS

Winter weather can dislodge vines from supports. Prune any broken stems and re-tie loose stems.

Zones 7 to 9: Dormant season pruning of vines can begin. Prune Japanese wisteria (*Wisteria floribunda*), purple leaf grape (*Vitis vinifera* 'Purpurea'), and kiwi back to a main framework of older, thicker stems with side shoots cut into short spurs with three to five buds. Thin out alternate stems where several shoots are crowded together. Thin out overcrowded stems at the base of these types of vines.

Inspect new groundcover plantings for winter weeds, including small leafy rosettes of shotweed and herb Robert, grasses, chickweed, and dandelions. Smother large areas of tiny seedlings with coarse mulch. Herb Robert, also known as "Stinky Bob" for its characteristic foul odor, is notorious for its ability to germinate in shade and to shoot its sticky seeds broadly. Be sure to remove this weed before the pink blooms appear.

WATER

ANNUALS

Once seedlings are up, make sure they stay moist but not soggy. Mist them from the top or water from bottom trays.

BULBS

Monitor water needs for bulb plantings under eaves, in window wells, or under overhangs. Check moisture levels of bulbs stored in pots. In zones 7 to 9, they may be in active growth this month.

INDOOR PLANTS

Plants will begin to need more water when new growth starts. Resume watering kaffir lily (*Clivia miniata*) when flower buds appear. Remove foil wrappers or other decorative frills that prevent drainage from miniature indoor roses and other blooming gift plants.

Check all saucers under plants to be sure water has been absorbed by roots. Dump out any standing water. Logic might dictate the idea that water in the saucers is a good way to get extra moisture or humidity to plants. However, root rot is more likely.

PERENNIALS, SHRUBS & TREES

Moisture is normally ample this month. Check container plants in winter storage, as well as those in the dry shadows of eaves or evergreen canopies. Monitor newly installed plantings. The different texture of nursery soil can cause it to dry out even when the surrounding soil is still moist. Water as needed when temperatures are well above freezing.

HERE'S HOW

TO GROW AN EASY-CARE HEDGE WITH NATURALLY NARROW PLANTS

Rapidly growing shrubs that tolerate heavy shearing are often chosen for new hedges. But they can require frequent and difficult work to maintain. If you can have patience for slower growth those first years, shrubs that naturally form a narrow, easy-care hedge are best for the long term. Be sure to give plants enough room to grow to their mature width next to sidewalks and fences. Place shrubs that grow 4 to 5 feet in diameter at least 2 feet from edges and on 2- to 3-foot centers within the row. New selections of narrow shrubs and trees appear in nurseries every year. Here are a few examples that can be trained as an informal screen or sheared as a formal hedge:

- American arborvitae, *Thuja occidentalis* 'Degroot's Spire' (20 × 6 feet), or 'Smaragd', Emerald Green arborvitae (14 × 4 feet)

- Barberry, *Berberis thunbergii* 'Helmond Pillar' (6 × 3 feet)

- Boxwood, *Buxus sempervirens* 'Graham Blandy' (8 × 1.5 feet)

- Sky Pointer™ Japanese holly, *Ilex crenata* 'Farrowone' (6 × 3 feet)

- English yew, *Taxus baccata* 'Standishii' (4 × 1.5 feet) or 'Fastigiata' (20 × 5 feet)

HERE'S HOW

TO PRUNE CLEMATIS

Clematis vines are categorized into three main types, based on growth and bloom habits. Pruning is timed based on when they bloom.

Group I: These bloom in early spring on wood produced last summer. Prune lightly after it blooms only as needed to maintain shape and size. Overgrown specimens can be rejuvenated by cutting all stems to ground level right after flowering. All anemone clematis (*Clematis montana*), *C. macropetala* 'Markham's Pink', and evergreen *C. armandii* are in this group.

Group II: These include large-flowered hybrids that bloom in early summer on wood produced last summer and then again in late summer on new growth (such as *Clematis* 'Nelly Moser' and other hybrids).

Prune before new growth starts. Retain a framework of well-spaced old stems. All stems may be cut back hard to the ground periodically, resulting in larger blooms in late summer only.

Group III: These bloom in summer on the current season's growth and include *Clematis viticella*, *C. texensis*, *C.* 'Jackmanii'. Prune while dormant. Cut back to a set of well-spaced stems 6 to 12 inches tall. Stems can also be cut taller if needed for better display of new growth and flowers.

Zones 4 to 6: In high desert country, shade trees planted last fall benefit from occasional winter watering when the ground is not frozen.

FERTILIZE

Zones 7 to 9: Nitrogen leaches through soil during periods of heavy rain. Avoid fertilizing lawns and large landscape areas this month. Nitrogen can also leach from rich compost and mulch containing manure. Apply these materials later in spring.

ANNUALS

Repot stored tender fuchsias in fresh, compost-enriched soil and move to a well-lit location. Fertilize with half-strength liquid fertilizer when new leaves appear.

BULBS

Zones 7 to 9: To strengthen bulb health, use a water-soluble bulb fertilizer, kelp, or fish emulsion when new growth is 2 to 4 inches tall. Crocus, grape hyacinth, and the earliest daffodils appear this month. Fertilize snowdrops (*Galanthus nivalis*) after blooms fade.

INDOOR PLANTS

Fertilize amaryllis twice a month until September.

Use a liquid fertilizer with moderate nitrogen and trace elements for indoor plants starting new growth.

Newly planted roses will not be ready to take up fertilizer their first year in the ground.

PROBLEM-SOLVE

Zones 7 to 9: By the end of February, new weeds germinate. Winter weeds go to seed now through March. Keep bare soil covered with coarse mulch to deter new weeds.

ANNUALS

Watch seedlings started indoors for symptoms of etiolation (leaning and stretched out pale stems), caused by insufficient light. Move them to a brighter location or set them under a fluorescent light.

Sow seeds outdoors when soil is warm enough to prevent seeds from rotting in cold, wet ground. Most seed packets list optimal soil temperatures for germination. A soil thermometer gives the most accurate indication that soil is warm enough for your seeds.

BULBS

If you placed wire mesh to protect tulips and other bulbs from squirrels, voles, and birds last fall, remove it now (see October). Slugs will be active and continue feeding through spring, chewing holes in lilies, dahlias, and early bulbs. Tiny infant slugs can cause nearly as much havoc as their parents. Set out slug traps, handpick them, or use the least-toxic slug bait.

Not happy with the blooms? Your bulbs may have been planted too late or too deep. Daffodils in dense clumps that stop blooming may need to be divided. Carefully separate them when foliage yellows and flops over. Plant divided bulbs 2 inches apart. (You can also do this in September if you mark their location with small stakes).

INDOOR PLANTS

Check for aphids. Use a magnifying glass: the tiny green aphids hide and are exactly the color of leaves. Rinse leaves with water to wash off aphids. For serious, repeated infestations, insecticidal soap will work. Discard seriously invaded plants to avoid starting an aphid riot in your other indoor plants.

LAWNS

Red thread fungus (*Laetisaria fuciformis*) causes the tips of grass blades to turn a distinct reddish color, as if the leaf blade were touched with red ink. Often seen after mild, wet winters west of the Cascades, it can infect lawns in late fall, winter, and spring. East of the mountains, it's seen late summer through fall. It rarely kills grass and is common on lawns with low vigor. Hard fescue is resistant to the fungus, and healthy turf can outgrow it. The best treatment for home lawns is to fertilize and provide good cultural care (see April or September). While red thread is present, temporarily stop grass-cycling and bag clippings for disposal.

Monitor lawns now and in March for crane fly damage. Look for large bare or dying spots in the lawn with holes. The grayish-brown larvae are found in the upper 3 inches of sod. Dig out a square foot of sod and count the larvae. If there are 40 or fewer, healthy lawns can tolerate and outgrow their impact. Continue with cultural practices to maintain turf health.

ROSES

Using less water does not mean giving up roses. Many species roses survive with less water and are also disease resistant. Groundcover roses are worth trying for water thrift. The familiar hybrid tea roses are not currently classified as drought-tolerant plants. Further work could change this. Roses for drier gardens continue to be vital as gardeners plan for more water-wise landscapes.

SHRUBS & TREES

Zones 7 to 9: Webworm nests may be seen on junipers and cotoneaster (especially *Cotoneaster horizontalis*). Trim them out before caterpillars emerge. Horticultural oil can be sprayed on individual trees and shrubs where webworm, scale, aphids, leafhoppers, and mites were severe the previous year. Apply on dry days when temperatures are above 40°F/5°C. Dormant oil suffocates eggs and small insects on the plant. For large trees, spraying is best done by a professional service. Birds glean these tiny insects from branches over winter. Get help from a Master Gardener clinic or Cooperative Extension office for positive identification and recommendations.

March

With hints of spring, March is a mix of warm days and brisk chill. Will it be an early or late spring? The transition will be different each year. Tapping into stored energy reserves from the previous season, new growth emerges with the light and warmth of spring. While spring can appear practically overnight east of the mountains, the season trickles in over several weeks in the coastal Pacific Northwest. This is a time of growth and high energy and an abundance of flowers on all types of plants.

Many plants will still be dormant at the start of the month. Soon, the shining early risers will appear. Bright crocus and jonquil push up through moist earth. Forsythia, quince, and star magnolia blossoms line bare stems in clouds of color. Spring equinox arrives on March 20 or 21, when night and day have equal length. Sunlight lingers a little longer each day, and these longer, warmer days signal to dormant plants it's time to start growing.

Wrap up dormant-season tasks such as pruning, transplanting, and weeding before the growing season starts full tilt. These early efforts pay off with less work later in the year and help keep your garden looking tidy.

The garden is malleable at this time of year and receptive for change. Moist soil is easily worked for shaping garden beds, transplanting, dividing perennials and ornamental grasses, and for uprooting woody weeds and unwanted plants. Just be sure to keep off ground that is still really soggy so as not to damage it or your plants.

Each plant type has its signature cues and timing for breaking dormancy, with one plant in full force while its neighbor's buds stay snugly closed. Spring ephemerals—snowdrops, trillium, anemone, daffodils, tulips, and others—make an early appearance and fade away by the time the rest of the garden comes into season.

Be mindful of the last frost dates as you prepare to plant seeds and seasonal plants. The sap is running. The garden is calling—let's get growing!

PLAN

In February, it's "watch and wait." March defines itself—"march!"—when all gardening tasks leap into action at once, especially in zones 7 to 9.

No matter where you reside, local native species are a valuable part of cultivated gardens. Native plants honor regional character and enhance local habitats. It can be as simple as adding ferns and perennials or replacing lost ornamentals with native species that offer similar functions and qualities. Native plants in home gardens provide vital links with nearby habitat for native birds, bees, and butterflies.

Sometimes native plant seedlings show up on their own. Before yanking them out like weeds, stop to see if they might fit with the existing landscape. This is easiest with groundcovers and perennials, though a new tree or shrub might land in a good location. Contact your local Cooperative Extension office or native plant society for help with native plant identification (see Resources).

ANNUALS

Planning annuals for a special event? If the colors you need are only available from seed, plan to start at least eight weeks ahead. For a July 4 event, start seed indoors under lights in mid-March. Enticing nursery annuals often arrive earlier than you can plant them out. Be choosy about bringing home tender plants this month. They may have to be household residents until the weather warms. If you have a heated greenhouse or a plant light setup indoors, you'll be able to care for them appropriately.

BULBS

Photograph or diagram garden beds in early spring bloom as a reference for later changes and additions. Tag bulbs you would like to relocate after blooms and foliage fade.

INDOOR PLANTS

Finish reviewing the indoor garden. Check growth of each plant, and discard any that have disease or insect problems or have been unsatisfactory. Grow what fascinates you—be it orchids or cactus—and keep the indoor plants that thrive.

LAWNS

Specific timing for moving forward on lawn installation and renovation depends on both soil condition and air temperature. If soils remain soggy, wait for a drying trend before proceeding. In zones 4 to 6, April and May offer the best conditions for renewal. Mid-March through May is usually best for zones 7 to 9. Double check your calculations for square feet to cover in seed or sod, and review the shape of lawn edges for easy mowing.

■ *Native plants such as maidenhair fern add garden interest and enhance local wildlife habitat.*

PERENNIALS, GRASSES & FERNS

Review what's thriving and where there are gaps in the garden. Refer to photos from other seasons to remind you of plants that may not have emerged yet. Make a list to take when shopping. Impulsive discoveries can be wonderful, but finding a match for your "must have" list will be most satisfying.

Take time to research what types of mulch are available in your area. A medium-texture material, such as composted yard waste or shredded leaves or even pine needles, works well around herbaceous plants. "Fertile mulch," such as aged dairy manure mixed with compost, provides nutrients in place of added fertilizers. Fine-textured mulch gives a finished look when tucked around plants. Unfortunately, seeds dropping or blowing onto the surface can germinate rapidly—most bothersome when the newcomers are weeds.

The somewhat coarser texture of screened woodchip compost blends provides a uniform appearance while being less friendly to seed germination. Very coarse woodchip mulch (shredded tree trimmings and similar) can overwhelm herbaceous plants both visually and physically if placed too close around their crowns.

ROSES

Roses grow best where they receive at least six hours of sun daily (don't we all?). Combine roses with plants that need similar growing conditions. Sun-loving lavender, rosemary, sage, and other herb plants look handsome next to roses, but require much less water and nutrients. For a more compatible combination, miniature or small-stature roses in containers can enliven herb beds while being watered separately. Or place them in separate planting beds so that each can receive appropriate irrigation.

SHRUBS

This is a busy time of year for tending shrubs. Take a moment to review specific pruning requirements for your shrubs. Are they blooming well each year? How often do they need to be pruned? Have they become difficult to manage? If you have to rigorously prune a shrub more often than once every three to five years to "contain" its size, it is probably too large for the site. Don't

■ *There are many good options for mulch including (from top) grass clippings, leaf mulch, and wheat straw. Place mulch in perennial beds in March and April while plant growth is small for the best benefits and results.*

struggle trying to force it to stay small. Remove it or transplant in late winter or early spring to a roomier location and then replace it with a smaller-growing shrub. If growth has been especially long and lush, reduce water and fertilizer to moderate the growth. Heavy pruning on shrubs receiving ample fertilizer and water can push extra growth. Try scaling back on spring pruning, watering, and fertilizing before abandoning a favorite specimen.

Wait until summer to prune shrubs where less new growth is desired. Remove only the longest branches to reveal the smaller shrub within and to maintain natural form and flowering habit (see August).

TREES

Large trees respond poorly to dramatic changes to their root zone. Their fine feeder roots can be very close to the soil surface. Extra care is needed to preserve them during any construction. Advance planning to protect tree roots from trenching and compaction will make all the difference. Contact an ISA Certified Arborist® for help with tree assessment and a preservation plan (see Resources).

Spring-blooming trees seem to float like airy clouds, heralding the close of winter. Most are woodland species, adapted to grow where they are sheltered from the hot afternoon sun. Visit local nurseries now to choose among the different types and colors of early blooming trees.

Cornelian cherry dogwood (*Cornus mas*) is one of the earliest to bloom, bearing prolific tiny yellow flowers. Carolina silverbell (*Halesia carolina*) is a lovely woodland tree with pendulous white flowers that appear before the leaves. It's a fine companion with rhododendrons and is dramatic against an evergreen backdrop. Eastern redbud (*Cercis canadensis*), with deep pink blooms that line the graceful horizontal stems, and Eastern flowering dogwood (*Cornus florida*), with large, white leathery bracts circling its small green flowers ('Cherokee Chief' has red), both perform well east of the Cascades but have more difficulty on the west side. There are many forms of magnolias with magnificent early spring bloom. Magnolias establish better when planted in spring than fall.

■ *Inspect existing vine supports for maintenance needs or improvements. Doing the work this month coincides nicely with the timing for pruning and renovation of woody vines.*

VINES & GROUNDCOVERS

Take inventory of the existing and potential vine locations in your garden. Consider adding architectural details to your garden and entry areas with new arbors or trellises, followed by early spring planting of woody vines.

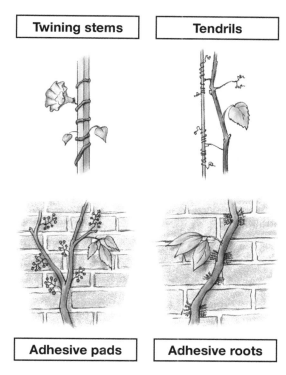

Twining stems

Tendrils

Adhesive pads

Adhesive roots

■ *Match the type of support with the way a vine clings: twining stems, tendrils, adhesive pads, or adhesive roots.*

PLANT

ANNUALS

Zones 4 to 6: It is still too early for planting outdoors. Toward the end of March, gather supplies to start warm-weather vegetables and tender flowers indoors. Sweet pea seedlings can be set outdoors around the last week of the month.

Zones 7 to 9: Cold-hardy annuals and annual seeds can land in the garden now as long as the soil is not soppy or frozen. Once sown, they can often withstand a light freeze before germinating. After emergence, they'll need frost protection. Keep a light cover handy to spread over tender seedlings if weather sends frost, hard rains, or hail.

BULBS

Tuberous begonias fill summer baskets with frilly flowers, perfect in lightly shaded spots. To get a head start, plant them indoors in early or mid-March (slightly later in zones 4 to 6). Place tubers with the concave side up, with only ½ inch of soil

cover. Water and store in a dark, warm location until shoots emerge. Then move them to bright light or under fluorescents for 12 hours per day. Wait until April to start them if you don't have enough light indoors this month.

INDOOR PLANTS

Spring's here: indoor plants will begin to grow again. Larger plants generally need new pots about every three years. Some may outgrow their pot in only a year. Roots sticking out through the drainage hole are a sign it's time to repot. Otherwise, tip the pot over and rap an upper edge lightly to loosen the soil ball and then slide it out to see if roots have filled the pot. If not, return it to the pot and top-dress lightly with fresh soil. Plants tightly stuck in the old pot may come out more easily if allowed to dry out for a few days. Plants do best "potted up" to a container about 2 inches larger than the old one. A kind of musical chairs can be done as larger plants are potted up and smaller plants are moved up to the empty pots.

When repotting, you may find some plants can be divided. *Clivia, Tradescantia, Tolmiea, Philodendron*, and many others may have rooted sections that can be pulled loose and tucked into smaller pots.

Terracotta pots should be cleaned to remove salt deposits before using. Cover the drainage hole with a broken piece of shard or a small square of window screen. Skip adding layers of rocks or gravel on the bottom—it'll make drainage worse by creating soggy soil above that bottom layer. Just fill the pot completely with a good, porous container-soil mix.

Shake the old soil loose and spread the roots out a bit. If the rootball is hard, soak it in tepid water first. Trim off circling roots. Place about 2 inches of soil in the bottom of the pot and set the rootball on it. Tuck soil in around roots. Tap the bottom of the pot lightly on your worktable to help settle out air pockets (don't compress the soil). Water thoroughly, and add more soil if needed. Keep the plant in low light for a week until the roots settle.

You can also wait to do this repotting outdoors in May or when weather is above 55°F/13°C.

Slide the plant out of its container to see if it's rootbound. Trim and loosen circling roots when potting up to a larger container.

LAWNS

Good lawns need deep, loose soil for deep roots. Shallow roots on compact soil lead to weak grass and constant summer drought stress. Cultivate soil 6 to 10 inches deep before planting. If soil tests show the need for lime, apply during cultivation.

Grass seed germinates best at 50° to 80°F/10° to 25°C. If your garden soil has warmed enough to grow lettuce seeds or spinach, grass seed will also germinate. Use grass seed blends developed for your region and follow seeding rates on the label. Rainfall should keep seeds moist, but be sure to water when there's no rain. Seedlings can die quickly if they get dry.

PERENNIALS, GRASSES & FERNS

Group plants according to their individual water needs when planting. This will make summer irrigation more efficient and effective. If you are adding companion plants near trees and shrubs, choose ferns and herbaceous plants tolerant of lower moisture and fertility to match the needs of the woody plants. Otherwise, the higher moisture and fertility given to the herbaceous plants can result in too much growth on the woody plants with roots in the same area.

When your catalog orders arrive, open boxes immediately and inspect the order for accuracy, plant condition, and any special handling instructions. Plant them as soon as possible after they arrive. They will keep in their opened packages for a day or two. If bad weather delays immediate planting, pot them up, water, and store them in a sheltered place outdoors.

Zones 7 to 9: March is a great time to change the layout of perennials, grasses, and ferns. Move plants to more suitable spots while foliage is small. They will grow more strongly when moved at this time of year than they will if moved later in the season. Herbaceous plants will need more water when transplanted in full growth during summer.

ROSES

Plant bare-root, boxed, and container roses this month when weather is above freezing. All types of roses demand good drainage as well as sun and open space for growth. Check drainage by digging and filling a hole with water before planting (see "Soils" in the Introduction). Add compost to the entire planting area (not just individual holes), or use compost as a 2 to 3 inch mulch if the soil has already been amended.

SHRUBS & TREES

This is a good month for planting. Temperatures are getting warmer and soils are generally moist.

Shape a small cone of soil in the hole to support bare-root roses at planting.

HERE'S HOW

TO INSTALL A NEW LAWN

Here is a "quick recipe" from OSU turf specialist Dr. Tom Cook for planting a new lawn from seed:

1. Choose the optimum time of year: May 1 to mid-June east of the mountains, April 1 to May 30 west of the mountains, or August 15 to September 15 for all areas.

2. Till and roughly grade existing soil. Turn in compost amendment if needed (no more than 30 percent by volume) and turn in lime west of the mountains, if required.

3. Spread any imported soil as a layer and mix it into the existing soil so there are no distinct layers.

4. Prepare the finish grade by raking and rolling to a firm surface.

5. Apply nitrogen fertilizer at 1.5 to 2 pounds actual nitrogen per 1,000 square feet before or after seeding. This is vital to stimulate growth after germination. High phosphorus has no advantage.

6. Apply seed with a drop spreader and lightly rake it in.

7. Apply ¼-inch fine mulch with a wire basket mulch roller.

8. Water thoroughly and with light repeated applications as needed.

9. Keep the seedbed moist for one to two weeks.

10. Mow as soon as grass is tall enough to cut, about three weeks after planting.

11. Fertilize again with a nitrogen-based fertilizer, four to six weeks after planting.

When installing sod, follow steps 1 through 4 above, then:

5. Incorporate preplant nitrogen fertilizer (as for seeding) if the sod did not come pre-fertilized.

6. Moisten the prepared soil just prior to laying sod.

7. Place sod so the edges fit tightly together with no gaps.

8. Soak it well immediately after planting.

9. Water the first two weeks while new roots establish, and make sure edges don't dry out.

10. Mow when grass is tall enough to cut off one-third of blade height.

11. Apply a nitrogen-based fertilizer in four to six weeks, sooner if color pales.

New roots have some time to develop before top growth starts, and new plants will have less summer transplant stress as a result. Bare-root nursery stock can be planted this month, a great option for shade and fruit trees.

Zones 4 to 6: Many types of native plants are available as restoration and bare-root stock from specialty nurseries, as well as through state DNR and local conservation district programs. If you are restoring native plants to a large area, mulch the entire area 3 to 4 inches deep in advance. Rake the mulch away to expose the soil for each planting hole.

VINES & GROUNDCOVERS

Woody species of groundcovers and vines such as clematis, honeysuckle, or kinnikinnick can be transplanted now, provided temperatures are above freezing and soils are not waterlogged. Groundcovers and vines planted this month will have time for quick root establishment before spring growth starts. Apply 2 to 3 inches of coarse mulch at planting time to help conserve soil moisture and to save time and water during summer.

When positioning vines, place the planting hole far enough from the support to give it room to grow, but close enough for stems to reach.

Zones 4 to 6: Start annual vines such as thunbergia, moonflower, and cathedral bells indoors three to four weeks before the last frost.

Zones 7 to 9: Multiply herbaceous groundcover plants by digging up divisions of plants such as ajuga, saxifrage, *Epimedium*, and pachysandra. This is a quick way to get extra plants for filling voids left after weeding.

CARE

Harden off plants that have been in protective storage before sending them back outdoors full time. Nursery plants that were under greenhouse protection will also need gradual exposure to the outdoors. Set containers outside during the day and bring them back in overnight for up to a week. Be prepared to cover any newly planted specimens with a light fabric cover in case of late frost. Early season mulching helps retain moisture, suppresses weeds, and replenishes soil nutrients and organic matter.

ANNUALS

Pinch out the tips of annual starts that begin to stretch out and appear weak and lanky. This can be a symptom of insufficient light.

Zones 4 to 6: When seedlings have two to three sets of true leaves, they are ready to transplant. Don't allow them to grow too long and get tangled in their first growing flat.

Zones 7 to 9: Choose the strongest plants at the nursery. Select short, stocky, green plants with sturdy stems and buds. Resist choosing plants in flower; their life in the garden may be shorter.

■ *Adjust lights over seedlings to keep the light 6 inches above them as they grow.*

BULBS

When blooms finish, snap off the floral stem and allow foliage to grow for at least six weeks. Don't fold, braid, rubber-band or otherwise mutilate the leaves. This is the period when leaves deliver nutrients to the bulb to form next year's flowers. The bulb needs as much of the "green life" from the leaves as it can get. When gathering cut flowers, leave the leaves!

Containers with forced bulbs can be placed outdoors in a bright spot while foliage ripens. Daffodil, crocus, and hyacinth may be planted directly into the garden after bloom fades, though it may take them a season or two to bloom well again.

Colchicum autumn crocus sends up a dense stand of foliage now. When the leaves begin to yellow in a few weeks, crowded plantings can be divided. Plant separated corms about 3 inches apart. The oddly shaped corms of *Colchicum* are very hardy and drought tolerant. They perennialize well and are a good companion plant under large trees. They will bloom in early fall without leaves.

Zones 4 to 6: Gradually pull protective mulch away as bulbs start emerging.

Zones 7 to 9: If stored dahlias have begun to produce shoots, plant them in shallow flats and set under lights or by a bright window to allow roots to develop before setting out in May.

INDOOR PLANTS

Houseplants must stay indoors this month. Some indoor plants grow so happily that they will need regular pruning back. Plants pinched back now will make strong new growth. Trim yellowing fronds from indoor ferns. New fronds should be emerging soon.

LAWNS

Keep reciting the lawn-care mantra: "Good mowing makes good lawns." Regular mowing is easier than intermittent mowing and results in a denser, healthier turf. Sharpen blades every six weeks, or have extra sharpened blades on hand to switch out.

■ *Use a core aerator to correct soil compaction and improve lawn health. Plugs can be easily raked into the lawn after they have dried out a bit.*

Practice "grass-cycling," which is allowing confetti-fine grass clippings to fall into the turf. It is a great investment in turf health and saves the time and energy of bagging clippings. Specialized mulching mowers are most effective. You can use a standard mower, but may need to make extra passes to fully chop and distribute the clippings. The key is to mow before grass is too long—removing one-third or less of total blade height—and to make enough passes so the clippings disappear into the lawn. As clippings break down, nitrogen, nutrients, and organic content are returned to the soil.

Zones 7 to 9: Does your lawn feel spongy when walked on? Or was it hard to water last summer? Then it's time to aerate so oxygen and water can penetrate the soil. If walking on it produces a squish-squish, the turf is too wet for aeration. You want it damp, but not saturated. A specialized walk-behind machine that pulls out plugs of old turf and roots work best (they can be rented). Allow the plugs to remain on the lawn where they

■ *If the thatch layer is more than ½-inch thick, it's a good time to dethatch.*

■ *Use a power rake for early spring lawn renovation and to remove thatch buildup. Make multiple passes in perpendicular directions. Rake up all loosened material before spreading new grass seed.*

will disintegrate. Gardeners sometimes stomp around the grass in spiked shoes, but in spite of the useful exercise, spikes have little lasting effect.

Dethatching is another spring task that will help invigorate lawns. This "power raking" pulls out dead material and thatch from around the crowns, enhancing turf growth. Thatch develops more readily in some types of grass than others; bentgrasses are particularly prone. Contrary to common concern, mulch mowing does not contribute to thatch buildup. To determine if thatch is a problem, dig out a chunk of turf, including the roots and soil, and look at the brown layer between the roots and the base of the grass blades. If the thatch layer exceeds ½ inch, lawn health will be improved by dethatching. All the dead material that is pulled out must be raked up and not left on the lawn. You can compost it in a pile reserved for future lawn care (where remnant grass seed would be welcome).

You must sow grass seed right after aerating or dethatching so new grass will quickly fill the gaps. Look for a topdressing seed blend developed for your region.

PERENNIALS, GRASSES & FERNS

Divide crowded perennials to increase them and improve their performance. Although some perennials can be divided in fall in warmer zones, spring division of most perennials suits all zones. (See September for dividing peonies.)

Clear away last year's foliage from around plants, being careful not to step on or cut emerging shoots.

Some perennials with persistent woody branches are referred to as "sub-shrubs." Among these are herbs such as lavender, rosemary, sage, and santolina. These plants can be evergreen in zones 7 to 9 but are too tender to overwinter outdoors in zones 4 to 6. Trim or shear them in early spring to remove last year's spent flowers and about one-third to one-half of last year's growth. You can also cut back to strong buds and emerging growth that appears near the base. Crowded or lanky stems can be thinned out.

Zones 4 to 6: Remove winter protection. Keep some extra light fabric on hand to cover plants in event of a late freeze in colder zones.

ROSES
Gardeners sometimes say, "Prune when forsythia is in bloom," which generally occurs between March and early April. This is a reliable seasonal marker.

Zones 7 to 9: Complete pruning.

Zones 4 to 6: Begin pruning when temperatures are above freezing—and the forsythia bloom!

SHRUBS
Remove about one-quarter of the old canes on multistem flowering shrubs, such as lilac, viburnum, native wood rose, mock orange, and deciduous azaleas. Remove any broken or dead stems. Plants will bloom as usual on the remaining stems that have not been pruned. You can also prune flowering shrubs as blooms fade.

HERE'S HOW

TO DIVIDE PERENNIALS

■ *Trim back excess foliage. Then use a sharp shovel to dig around the rootball and lift it out of the ground.*

■ *Divide the root ball into smaller sections, using a soil knife or shovel. Two garden forks set back to back can be used to pry dense roots apart.*

■ *Trim off any damaged or dead roots from each new clump.*

■ *Plant new divisions immediately. Plant them so the root crown is at the same height as it was before. Pot up extras for later planting.*

TO PRUNE ROSES

BASIC ROSE-PRUNING TECHNIQUES:

1. Identify the type of rose you have. If you don't know, prune it lightly this year, removing only about one-third of each cane. When the rose blooms, take a sample to a nursery for identification.

2. Remove dead and diseased wood on all rose types (such wood will look brown and may break readily). Cut back to visible green cambium (it's almost the color of a Granny Smith apple just beneath the bark, with clean white pith to the inside).

3. Proceed according to the rose type. (Note: after the first spring pruning, paint the cut ends of the largest canes with white glue to deter cane borers on hybrid tea and climbing roses. Do not compost debris).

Hybrid teas: These need heavy pruning, with all canes cut down to 1 to 1½ feet above the ground. Remove all small, weak canes (pencil size or smaller) down to the ground, keeping four to six strong canes.

Shrub roses: These keep more wood than hybrid teas. Saw out any dead canes. Balance the shape by removing overcrowded canes and/or cutting some canes back low into the shrub at an outward-facing bud. The multiple canes of *Rosa rugosa* don't need to be cut back each spring: it will stay more compact with less pruning. To manage size and width, remove the tallest or perimeter canes down to soil level.

Climbers: Allow new canes to grow for two years, tying the strongest ones to a support to form a framework for side shoots. Remove weak canes. After the second year, canes develop blooming side shoots from the main framework. Shorten side shoots and remove dead canes.

Groundcover roses: Once they're established, shear off at least 6 inches now, before buds begin to form.

Prune big-leaf (mophead) hydrangeas to remove older canes when buds are green, before leaves open. (See "Zones 7 to 9" in February.)

Overgrown multistem shrubs may be renovated by cutting all the stems off close to the ground. Staged renovation is less drastic: remove one-third to one-half of the stems now and again in summer. As all the old stems are gradually removed, healthy new stems take their place.

Zones 4 to 6: As the weather warms up, remove any winter protection.

Zones 7 to 9: Bring containerized shrubs out of winter storage. Lightly top-dress with fresh potting soil or screened compost. Water thoroughly. Apply a slow-release fertilizer. Repot plants that have outgrown their pots.

Apply or refresh organic mulch to 2 to 4 inches deep around new plants and any that suffered drought stress last summer. Always keep mulch from direct contact with plant stems and trunks.

TREES

Maintain coarse-textured organic mulch under garden trees. It is like the natural duff layer in forests, which replenishes soil organic matter and nutrients.

The smell of spring in the air inspires many to get busy trimming plants. Stop before touching trees: they are vastly different from plants such as roses or hydrangeas, which benefit from vigorous annual spring pruning. Your trees may be just fine as they are, or might be better pruned at a different time of year with a different technique.

Every spring, many otherwise normal trees end up with their limbs lopped off in efforts to "control" their growth. But pruning trees back hard, as you would with a rose bush or hedge, will permanently damage their structure, appearance, and long-term health.

Never use hedge shears on trees. Lopping or shearing the crowns of small trees into tight shapes not only ruins their form, but will lead to

For best color and appearance, thin out dull, older stems on colorful twig dogwoods. Cut stems cleanly to their base. Don't make any cuts on the remaining stems.

more maintenance in the long run. The resulting production of vigorous shoots depletes stored energy. Insect and disease problems can increase on the crowded tender growth. Decay eventually invades stubbed-off branch ends.

Large or small, trees are best pruned to follow their natural structure. The best pruning is almost invisible to casual observation. For healthy trees, not more than a quarter of the live branch area should be cut at one time. Place pruning cuts at the edge of the branch collar, the enlarged area around the point of branch attachment to a larger branch or trunk. Overthinning is harmful. The foliage on interior branches is important to tree health. Many trees only need periodic removal of dead, broken, or damaged branches.

If your trees have a lot of suckers around the base or water sprouts (thin vertical shoots) along their limbs, don't touch them yet. Instead, remove them during the last half of summer to discourage repeat flushes of new sprouts (see August).

Do general pruning before growth starts. Avoid pruning trees when buds are swelling and new leaves are just emerging.

What if your trees were already topped? Some smaller trees may be restored with careful selective pruning over a course of years. Replacement may turn out to be the more effective option. Large trees that have been topped should be assessed by an ISA Certified Arborist® for condition and safety.

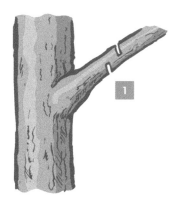  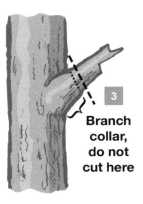

Branch collar, do not cut here

■ *When pruning branches from trees, always place the cut just outside the edge of the branch collar. The branch collar has protective compounds that help seal the wound and produce new callus growth to cover it. Don't cut flush, and don't leave a stub. To avoid tearing the bark, make an undercut several inches out (1) and then make a top cut to the outside of that cut (2) to remove the weight of the branch. Then make a clean finish cut at the branch collar (3).*

VINES & GROUNDCOVERS

Groom groundcovers, clearing out matted layers of leaves and debris. Carefully inspect for young weeds. The adage "a stitch in time saves nine" definitely holds true for this early-season effort. Eliminate early weeds before they go to seed. Add new plants and divisions to fill voids.

Reduce overgrowth of spreading woody ground-covers. Select the longest branches creeping over a walkway or lawn, and cut far back toward the center of the plant at a point of attachment or at ground level. The remaining shorter branches become the new edge. Remove "wild hairs" that stick out in vertical or odd positions.

Refresh herbaceous groundcovers with mowing or shearing, including bishop's hat (*Epimedium*), Japanese spurge (*Pachysandra terminalis*), *Vinca minor*, and creeping St. John's wort (*Hypericum calycinums*), before new growth or flower buds appear.

Zones 4 to 6: Begin early spring pruning of vines. (See "Zones 7 to 9" in February.)

Zone 7 to 9: Continue early season vine pruning.

WATER

Check watering equipment to see what repairs, replacements, or additions are needed. Adding quick-connect fittings to faucets, hoses, sprinklers, and water wands makes changing hoses a snap, prevents lost washers and leaky connections, and protects hose fittings from damage. Get rain barrels ready for the season and be sure screen-covered lids are in place to keep out debris and mosquitoes. Check sprinkler or bubbler head placement so that no plants are skipped: ensure function of irrigation equipment now before you need it.

Set up soaker hoses or emitter tubing in perennial beds and for all new plantings to make watering chores easier. Lay them out in broad curves and anchor them in place with U-shaped wire pins. These systems concentrate water near roots while keeping foliage dry and reducing water loss to evaporation or runoff. They can be covered with mulch. A simple faucet timer is helpful, but probe the soil after watering to make sure water goes deep enough. The slow delivery rate from soaker hoses and emitter tubing requires longer running times than sprinklers. Soaker hoses do not function well on slopes. With their pressure-compensating construction, emitter pipes are the better choice for drip-style irrigation on slopes.

ANNUALS

Keep indoor seedlings moist. Probe the soil to ensure roots are receiving enough water, and don't overwater. Spray gently with room-temperature water.

INDOOR PLANTS

Increase watering frequency as plants come into active growth. Keep forced bulbs watered while leaves are still green.

LAWNS

It is not yet time for routine irrigation, but make sure any newly seeded grass stays moist.

PERENNIALS, GRASSES & FERNS

Soaker hoses and emitter-tubing systems are very effective for perennial beds where large, lush leaves can interrupt delivery from standard sprinklers. Lay them out before plants get too large.

ROSES

Keep up mulch to help with water retention. Growing drought-tolerant roses? Roses with proven drought tolerance do best when watered regularly for their first two years. By their third year, watering may be reduced to deep soaking once or twice a month.

SHRUBS

Zones 4 to 6: Check for dry soil under evergreens and provide a deep soaking to support new spring growth. Keep container plants watered.

TREES

Zones 4 to 6: In high desert regions, new trees will benefit from a deep soaking as growth begins, especially if they have dried over winter.

FERTILIZE

ANNUALS

Fertilize any overwintering plants such as fuchsias or geranium (*Pelargonium*) as soon as new leaves appear. Use a liquid fertilizer with moderate nitrogen, such as a 9-6-6 or 6-8-8. Do not fertilize overwintered plants if no new growth is visible. For new seedlings, use half-strength fertilizer when the plants have two sets of leaves. Wait until you see new growth to fertilize repotted annuals.

BULBS

Fertilize bulbs once when shoots are 2 to 4 inches tall (see February). If rain is absent, water thoroughly when fertilizing. Dahlias and most summer bulbs prefer soil pH of about 6.5, about the same as for vegetable gardens. Hold off on planting dahlias until soil warms to 50°F/10°C.

INDOOR PLANTS

Increase the fertilizer routine when active growth begins. You may wish to sprinkle a timed-release fertilizer on the soil surface. Follow label rates according to the pot size.

LAWNS

No routine fertilization this month.

PERENNIALS, GRASSES & FERNS

Where "fertile mulch" containing composted animal manure is used, additional fertilizer may not be needed. Monitor plant performance before fertilizing.

Where needed, fertilize after all winter protection has been removed and the ground is damp. Immediately water in granular fertilizers.

ROSES

Fertilize or top-dress with fertile mulch after pruning. Avoid very high nitrogen applications, which push leaves instead of blooms. Slow-release organic fertilizers such as alfalfa pellets guarantee the presence of trace elements.

SHRUBS

Zones 7 to 9: Acidifying fertilizers, such as cottonseed meal and products containing ammonium sulfate, are helpful for camellias, azaleas, heath, heathers, rhododendrons, and other shrubs adapted to acid soils. Fertilize in moderation, and only as needed.

Provide slow-release fertilizer for ornamentals in containers.

TREES

No fertilizer this month.

VINES & GROUNDCOVERS

Top-dress groundcovers with fine compost, and wash residue off the leaves. Mulch around vines with coarse organic compost. For plants lacking good growth and vigor, a slow-release fertilizer can be helpful. It's important to get the cause for poor growth diagnosed and to test soil nutrient levels before applying extensive fertilizer. Visit a local Master Gardener clinic for assistance.

PROBLEM-SOLVE

Zones 7 to 9: Search through garden beds and native plant borders for invasive seedlings of evergreen woody weeds such as laurel, holly, and ivy. They are easy to pull when only a few inches tall. Damp soil makes the pulling even easier.

Maintaining organic matter for established plantings is best done with a surface application of amendments and/or organic mulch. Soil texture and nutrient content will be preserved, and the population of decomposers—insects, earthworms, fungi, and microbes—will thrive. These organisms help improve soil structure and promote root growth. Use a thin layer—about one inch—of fine, screened compost to top-dress lawns and groundcovers. Coarse-textured organic mulch can be applied 2 to 4 inches deep over open soil areas. Allow these materials to decompose before applying more, as it is possible to overwhelm the soil with too much compost and mulch.

Start monitoring for slugs as warmer, rainy weather returns. Check under rocks or larger debris for slugs and slug eggs. Eggs are about 1/16 to 1/8 inch big, pearly white or yellow, and often found in small clusters. Use a flashlight or headlamp to look for slugs just after dark. While they may not feed directly on all groundcover plants, they might take cover there during daylight hours. Eliminate slug eggs and slugs early in the season to reduce damage to tender new spring growth. As you poke about the mulch layer, be glad when you see ground beetles. These 1-inch-long shiny black beetles hang out under leafy debris and feast on slug eggs and several other insect pests.

ANNUALS

"Damping off" can cause indoor seedlings to suddenly keel over. This fungal infection occurs in crowded, damp conditions. Use sterile seedling mix and containers, and don't overwater or let plants sit in standing water. Thin seedlings out to reduce overcrowding.

Continue vigilance for aphid populations indoors.

BULBS

Tulip plantings can contract a nasty fungal disease called tulip botrytis (*Botrytis tulipae*), especially west of the Cascades. Flowers crumple into gray wads; leaves show brown splotches and roll inward. Confirm diagnosis at a local Master Gardener clinic or nursery professional. Entirely remove affected leaves, flowers, bulbs, and roots. Do not compost these. Fungal spores persist in the ground, so don't replant tulips in the same spot. Rotate plantings next year with other bulbs, such as daffodils, Dutch iris, or hyacinths, which don't get the blight. If the problem has been severe, plant tulips in pots with clean soil for next season.

Need deer-proof bulbs? Choose snowdrops, grape hyacinth, and daffodils. You'll need to protect tulips, hyacinth, and lilies. Containers on protected

■ *Clean leaves and trimmings run through a garden shredder are a perfect homemade source of coarse-textured organic mulch.*

decks are another option. The best defense is an 8-foot-tall fence or a motivated dog.

INDOOR PLANTS

Aphids, scale, whiteflies, and mealybugs can build up over winter. Gently wipe or wash aphids, scale, and mealybugs from plants. Small plants can be set in a sink or bucket and thoroughly washed off with room-temperature water. Clip off heavily damaged leaves or shoots. Use an insecticidal soap labeled for houseplants in a few weeks if pests reappear. Isolate or discard heavily infested plants.

LAWNS

Weeds move in where lawn grasses have moved out. The best defense against weeds is thick, well-maintained turf. Heavy weeds could be a symptom of other problems. Provide the early season cultural care listed on pages 61 and 62 as a first measure, removing problem weeds at the same time.

Manage weed problems in spring and fall. Pull or spot treat with an appropriate herbicide in spring. Accurate weed identification is needed to best manage chronic weed issues. Consult a Master Gardener clinic, nursery specialist, or weed information website (see Resources).

Dandelion is one weed everyone can identify. Scout out the rosettes before flowers open; they seem to go from flower to seed in moments at this time of year.

"Weed and feed"? Washington State University turf specialists don't recommend these products. It's better to separate weed control from fertilization. As with all pesticides, read the label. "Weed and feed" products contain herbicides that can damage plants other than grasses, including nearby trees and shrubs, especially if used too often or too carelessly.

PERENNIALS, GRASSES & FERNS

Young delphinium stalks are easy prey to slugs. When delphinium gets about 2 feet tall, they toughen up and slug damage diminishes.

Perennial weeds are among the worst invaders of perennial gardens. Dandelion, bindweed,

and quackgrass seriously interfere with garden success. Use a soil knife, narrow floral spade, or a spade fork to lift weeds out by the roots. For heavy weed infestations, lift perennials out and extract any weed roots from the rootball of desired plants. Pull any remaining weeds, then replant your perennials. The damp soil and cool weather that is ideal for transplanting at this time of year make it a good match for this kind of effort.

For extremely bad infestations, you may want to hold desired perennials in containers for a year while cleaning up the problem bed. Clear the soil of weeds, lay sheet mulch using several layers of newspaper or a single layer of cardboard, dampen them in place, and cover with 6 inches or more of mulch. Make sure the paper or cardboard layer stays thoroughly buried.

Be careful about "garden bullies"—plants that become unfriendly, space-grabbing hogs in the garden. Delicate plants can be overtaken by the spread of rugged, vigorous plants. A few notorious thugs include plume poppy (*Macleaya cordata*), Welsh poppy (*Papaver cambricum*), and *Euphorbia amygdaloides* var. *robbiae*. Yellow archangel (*Lamium galeobdolon*), once a garden favorite, is now on regional noxious weed lists. Check the local yearly noxious-weed list, because plants on those lists can change.

ROSES

Consider replacing struggling, disease-ridden roses with a disease-resistant selection. Transplant roses that are in too much shade to a brighter location to improve their health and performance.

SHRUBS & TREES

Zones 4 to 6: Dormant-season horticultural oil can be sprayed on evergreen and deciduous plants where insects such as webworm, scale, aphids, and mites were severe the previous year. Dormant-season fungicides can be applied to ornamental and fruit trees with threatening levels of leaf and twig fungus diseases. Contact a Master Gardener clinic or Cooperative Extension office for guidance.

April

April is awash in bloom and fresh green hues, though weather can be brisk or balmy. Frost is still a possibility, but the number of mild days is on the rise. Clouds of color spread across deciduous flowering trees and shrubs. Lawns become lush and long almost overnight, as do many weeds. Bees are about in their mission to gather pollen and nectar. Birds are singing and starting new nests. From earth to sky, change is about us. A new season has begun.

Gardening with the seasons means tapping into this month's high energy. For garden plants, it's about getting them off to a good start. For weeds, it's about early removal. "Nip it in the bud" is a good motto for April. Progress we make now with weeding, mulching, and planting will pay off with a great-looking garden and less work in summer.

Gardening can be a great form of exercise that offers many benefits to our well-being. With the return of nice weather and all that's going on in the garden now, it can be easy to overdo it with marathon gardening sessions. To keep it safe and fun, work in short sessions (maybe a couple hours or less at a time), stretch before and after, and use good form. You can find some great tips in "Gardening and Your Health: Protecting Your Knees and Back" (Virginia Extension Publication 426-065). Many gardeners have found certain yoga poses to be very useful.

In woody plants, there is a period when the bark is "slipping" as it practically floats atop the rapid flow of sap through the xylem vessels underneath it. Bark may readily peel off at the slightest touch, potentially damaging the tree. It's better not to prune or transplant when the bark is slipping.

The need to be careful around tender plants during early season gardening brings the opportunity to observe the beautiful details unfolding around us—sights, smells, and sounds we might otherwise miss.

Wherever you garden in the region and no matter how cool or warm a year it is, one thing is for sure: spring is arriving!

PLAN

Nature is celebrated in April. Earth Day is observed on April 22, with many communities sponsoring environmental stewardship projects. These events offer first-hand opportunities to learn more about the heritage of native vegetation unique to the place where you live.

Successful cultivation of native plants in urban areas comes not only through matching species with site conditions, but also through growing them in combinations as seen in the wild. This holds true for both naturalized and cultivated plantings. West of the Cascades we see Douglas fir (*Pseudotsuga menziesii*), Pacific madrone (*Arbutus menziesii*), salal (*Gaultheria shallon*), sword fern (*Polystichum munitum*) together. Where shore pine (*Pinus contorta* var. *contorta*) grows in coastal areas, it may be joined by kinnikinnick (*Arctostaphylos uva-ursi*), *Sedum spathulifolium*, coastal strawberry (*Fragaria chiloensis*), and Nootka rose (*Rosa nutkana*). Wetland areas on either side of the mountains host species of willow, hardhack spirea (*Spiraea douglasii*), red osier dogwood (*Cornus sericea*), and skunk cabbage (*Lysichiton americanus*). See Resources for more information on Pacific Northwest native plants.

Spring plant sales are prolific this month and next as community organizations and plant societies showcase garden starts, donated plants, and specialty nursery plants. Take your garden notes along and look for unusual treasures at these sales. Check newspaper calendars for dates and enjoy the "community fair" atmosphere of these sales.

ANNUALS

Thinking about growing food plants but not sure if you have enough room or time? Lovely, space-efficient plantings can be assembled by combining vegetables with annuals and other garden plants. Most garden vegetables are grown as annuals. Variegated 'Trout's Black' and other colorful varieties of lettuce function well as edging plants. Parsley combines with French marigolds and contrasts nicely with dark foliage plants such as burgundy New Zealand flax. Nasturtium bridges both worlds as annual color

■ *Nasturtium produces lovely edible flowers.*

■ *Edible swiss chard is a colorful companion in flower beds.*

and vegetable (the peppery flowers are a delicious addition to salads). Perennial chives make well-mannered ornamental vegetable companion plants; they can be sheared back when their purple blooms fade. Smaller annual vegetables without heavy root systems or tubers work best in mixed ornamental plantings.

BULBS

Choose and prepare garden areas for heat-loving dahlias, gladiolus, and cannas.

Once soil warms, small mignon dahlias can go in window boxes or containers with mixed annuals. If your favorite container still holds bloomed-out spring bulbs, you can lift those out and transplant them directly into the garden.

Review and photograph spring bulb plantings one more time, noting changes and additions for fall orders. On neighborhood walks, make note of bulb plantings you like. For more ideas, visit local public gardens. Excellent displays are found in British Columbia at Van Dusen Botanical Garden, UBC Botanical Garden, and Butchart Gardens. Bellevue Botanic Garden, Tacoma's Point Defiance Park, and Spokane's Manito Park are among Washington destinations. In Oregon, check out the Oregon Gardens in Silverton. San Francisco Botanical Gardens is a year-round northern-California showplace.

INDOOR PLANTS

Sort and clean pots to use for summer planting and for repotting. Many pots, especially plastic ones, lose their attractiveness after several years. They may be revived with paint (see May for details). Wash pots in soapy water. To sterilize pots that may have held diseased plants, soak them in a 1:10 solution of household bleach and water for about four hours. Rinse thoroughly and air dry. This also works on outdoor garden pots.

Orchids add elegance to the indoor garden. New methods of cultivation, including tissue culture, produce more variety and more economical orchids, giving us greater selection than ever. Orchids have become one of the most desired indoor plants.

Choose new orchid plants "in spike"—with buds forming—and you'll have six to eight weeks of display. Some orchid growers encourage keeping the plant only through its first bloom, then discarding it, but some types may be grown on fairly easily. Select an orchid suited to your growing conditions. *Dendrobium* and *Oncidium* hybrids need bright light; *Cattleya* and *Cymbidium* need the brightest conditions. In protected zone 9 gardens, many *Cymbidium* hybrids thrive outdoors nearly year-round.

Different orchids vary in their temperature preferences, water requirements, and light needs, and they require their own potting mixes. Hobby growers often invest in extra lighting, plastic enclosures, and misting systems. If orchids catch your interest, talk to suppliers and invest in a good basic book.

If you have a part-shade windowsill where ferns and African violets thrive, try moth orchids (*Phalaenopsis* hybrids).

■ *Many newer types of orchids are easily grown as houseplants.*

LAWNS

Plan to do renovation work now and in May. Spring gives lawn grasses their best chance for strong growth from either seed or sod. Lawn seeding does poorly between June 1 and late August, when warm, dry conditions make it difficult to maintain moist soil.

If you haven't been mulch mowing (grass-cycling), this is a good time to start. Specialized mowers have mulching blades and a closed mowing pan that minces clippings before dropping them back to the ground. Or, use a standard reel or rotary blade mower. The key is to mow frequently enough to remove no more than one-third the blade height at each mowing. If the grass has grown too long, rake or bag it for that mowing session. The benefits of mowing a little more often are better density and less need for fertilizer and water.

Zones 4 to 6: Even though lawns look tired and beat up in winter, they quickly green up as warmer weather arrives and may not be in need of renovation. (Think of the grasses in pastures; that's why they call this season "green up time.")

PERENNIALS, GRASSES & FERNS

Do summer winds disturb your perennial plantings? Try some cultivars with a lower

Keep a separate pile for excess grass clippings that can be composted for future lawn topdressing.

profile: Asiatic lilies, at 2 to 3 feet, manage wind better than the 6- to 7-foot Oriental hybrid lilies. Annual larkspur substitutes nicely for taller delphinium. Or select compact perennial *Delphinium grandiflorum* 'Summer Blues'. Many of these also suit smaller garden spaces.

Wind stress can reduce soil moisture in summer. Where winds and high temperatures prevail, choose herbaceous perennials best adapted to dry conditions.

ROSES

Nurseries will continue selling container roses this month. Miniature roses make nice specimens for containers and large hanging containers. Keep an eye out for disease-resistant and easy-care selections.

SHRUBS

Early flowering shrubs mark the beginning of warmer days, blooming alongside spring bulbs. In colder zones, dress up early spring color with shrubs such as *Forsythia × intermedia* 'Lynwood Variety', *Rhododendron mucronulatum* 'Cornell Pink', or *Fothergilla gardenii*. Place them in full sun with evergreens behind for brilliant contrast. Native Pacific ninebark (*Physocarpus capitatus*) has white flowers favored by native bees. Visit local gardens and nurseries to hunt out the most attractive early blooming shrubs in your area. Shrubs purchased this month can be planted right away for immediate results.

Sweet-scented lilacs grace May gardens. Choose among white, pink, and purple hues. Spokane became the City of Lilacs in the 1930s when local garden clubs launched an intensive lilac-planting campaign. Plan now for a May visit to the Spokane Lilac Festival. Lilac Days at the historic Hulda Klager Lilac Gardens in Woodland, Washington, runs from mid-April through Mother's Day.

TREES

Trees are long-lived, enduring inhabitants of our world. Fixed in place, trees must withstand a lot of changes in their environment over their lifetimes, including cyclical pests and periodic weather extremes, not to mention the many

■ *Make a plan to look at your trees closely each season of the year as a first step to keeping them healthy and safe. Take pictures. Like the relatives in our family photos, it can be amazing how much even seemingly full-grown trees continue to grow and change.*

insults people can impose on them. And, like all living things, trees can fall to ill health, the vagaries of age, and physical decline. To survive well in our communities, trees need our care and attention and protection against undue damage. And large trees with physical defects require routine inspection and attention to reduce potential hazards.

April is Arbor Day month in many parts of the United States (March in California). This year, honor the spirit of Arbor Day by seeing to the care and stewardship of valued trees in your landscape and community. If you have very large trees on your property, meet with a professional arborist to review their condition.

VINES & GROUNDCOVERS

Vines and groundcovers are a big part of garden flowers in all areas in the region. Note bloom dates and colors in a garden log, paying attention to color compatibility with adjacent plants. Vines and groundcovers should complement the adjacent plantings with color and texture.

Some good pollinator plants to add to groundcover plantings include low forms of Oregon grape (*Mahonia nervosa*, *M. repens*), native woodland strawberry (*Fragaria vesca*) for shade, or coast strawberry (*Fragaria chiloensis*) for sun.

PLANT

Make a point to keep track of the names of plants you add to your garden for future reference. This is invaluable for providing the right care practices, diagnosing problems, or for adding new plants that will grow in similar conditions. It can be as simple as writing the year on plastic tags and storing them in a shoebox, copying names and dates into a notebook, or organizing them on a computer spreadsheet. Plastic plant labels left out in the garden will deteriorate over time, so purchase weatherproof plant labels to keep out in the garden.

ANNUALS

Toward the month's end, complete planting of cool-season containers. Get creative by combining

■ *Save plant names and information from nursery tags for future gardening reference.*

annuals with perennials, ferns, foliage plants such as hosta, and even summer bulbs, including small gladiolus.

Seed packets sometimes include the optimal soil temperatures for germination. Most warm season crops require a minimum soil temperature of 60°F/15°C. Seeds can quickly rot if planted into soil that is too damp and cold. You can get a soil thermometer from your local garden center to check temperatures before planting.

Zones 4 to 6: Hold off on planting until the last frost date, except for the hardiest of annuals such as pansies. Make sure they are hardened to night temperatures before setting them out.

Zones 7 to 9: Sow these hardy annual seeds outdoors: sweet alyssum, cosmos, cleome, marigolds, California poppy, and sunflowers. If the garden isn't prepared yet, you can sow them in flats for later transplanting. Poppies do not transplant well and need to be directly sown. If your garden is ready, sprinkle seeds and mark the edges of the planting with twigs or stones and a label to help you remember to keep them watered as they emerge.

BULBS

After last frost and about the time deciduous trees come into leaf, dahlia, gladiolus, crocosmia, and canna can go into the ground in sheltered areas.

Gladiolus planted every two weeks until late June will keep the color show going throughout the summer. Because each corm produces only one flower stalk, it will not bloom again after it is finished. Sequential planting solves this. Consider some of the smaller *Gladiolus nanus* varieties, which do not require staking and bloom gracefully.

INDOOR PLANTS

Easter lilies can become part of the outdoor garden. Remove faded flowers, leaving a long stem, and plant them outside after last frost.

LAWNS

If the lawn has gotten thin over winter, now's the time to overseed. However, if you plan to allow the lawn to go totally dormant in this summer, without regular watering, do not overseed until fall.

Aerate or dethatch first if your lawn needs this attention. (See "Care" in March.) Don't be surprised at how scuffed, even scalped, the lawn appears after dethatching. You've made the beginnings of a good seedbed for the renewed lawn.

For all parts of the Northwest, perennial ryegrass is a good choice for scattering seed over an existing lawn, spread at about half the rate for seeding a new lawn. Use about 3 pounds per 1,000 square feet.

Seed is best laid out with a rolling spreader, going evenly over the lawn in two directions. Mulch with about ¼ inch of screened compost. After seeding and mulching, roll the lawn to get seed in contact with soil. Water thoroughly. If the seed doesn't make firm contact with soil, it will not germinate properly.

Correct any drainage problems before laying sod, and prepare the soil the same as for seeding (see March). Also roll sod to firm it. Some growers note that raccoons can roll the sod up while looking for grubs; you may need to pin it down.

PERENNIALS, GRASSES & FERNS

Plant herbaceous perennials in moist soil while they are still small. Work carefully around older plants with tender new leaves.

If catalog orders arrive bare root, without soil over the roots, soak them briefly (one to two hours) in tepid water before planting, or follow any instructions sent with the plants. Plant directly in the garden, or pot up in containers and wait for appropriate planting time. (See March for directions on handling mail-order plants.)

Zones 4 to 6: It's not too late to divide overcrowded perennials.

ROSES
Container roses can be planted now through spring.

SHRUBS & TREES
Choose plants with healthy leaves, plump green buds, and no broken or dead stems. Stay away from very small plants in large pots and very large shrubs in very small pots. Avoid potted plants with roots growing out of the bottom or that have thick woody roots visibly circling at the top of the container. Review planting tips in the Introduction.

Zones 4 to 6: Plant all types of nursery stock this month—bare-root, balled-and-burlapped, and containers. Remember to mulch.

Zones 7 to 9: Woody plants installed before the end of April will suffer less drought stress than those planted later. Create a shallow basin with a 2- to 3-inch rim of soil to aid watering. Mulch bare soil around new plants and keep mulch off of stems and trunks.

VINES & GROUNDCOVERS
This is a good month to plant herbaceous groundcovers: they will take off quickly in periods of moderately warm and moist weather. Finish up your planting of woody species.

Zones 4 to 6: Sweet pea can be sown outdoors. Sow other annual vines indoors about three to four weeks before last frost date.

Zones 7 to 9: As weather warms, plant out annual vines started indoors. Harden off transplants first by bringing them outdoors for gradually longer periods over a few days, bringing them back in at night.

When soils have warmed above 55°F/13°C and all danger of frost has passed, sow the following outdoors, all of which are attractive to hummingbirds: scarlet runner bean (*Phaseolus coccineus*), black-eyed Susan vine (*Thunbergia alata*), canary creeper (*Tropaeolum peregrinum*), cardinal climber (*Ipomoea × multifida*).

CARE

Remember to keep a gentle hand to avoid damaging tender growth on shrubs, and watch your step where perennial plant stems are just emerging.

Weeds are growing and blooming right along with our garden plants. Focus early-season weeding on what's in bloom and going to seed, such as dandelion and mustards. Practice weed birth control: don't let them reproduce. Immediately cover exposed ground with mulch or plant groundcovers.

Mulch is one of the best care practices you can provide for all types of garden plantings. For native and naturalized plantings, look to the natural plant habitats near your home and mimic the natural conditions and types of material covering the ground. Woodland gardens thrive with leaf mold and wood chips. Desert and alpine species are more accustomed to stone or gravel than to composted organic material.

ANNUALS
Harden off all annuals before planting outdoors. They can't go directly from the warmth of a greenhouse or your home without a staged adjustment plan: days out and nights in for about 7 to 10 days before they stay outside. Most annuals won't tolerate being set out in temperatures below 45°F/7°C.

Keep lightweight polyester garden cloth on hand to spread over annuals if night temperatures drop below 40°F/4°C. Use short stakes to hold the cloth above the plants to allow for a layer of warm air over them.

Be mindful that any system that protects from nighttime cold may cause plants to cook when temperatures go up during the day. Here's one solution: cut the large end out of a gallon plastic jug and set it over the plant. Replace the jug lid at night and remove it during the day. Though a little more complex to install, a portable plastic hoop house can also be used as protective cover. By the end of May, such protection should no longer be needed. However, in zones 4 to 6, freezes can occur into June and return in early September.

Monitor your garden for "self-sown" annual seedlings. You may want to keep some where they are or transfer them to pots. Scoop the seedling up gently, getting the entire root, and put in a 2- or 4-inch pot where it can grow larger. If you need to touch seedlings, hold them by the leaves; the fragile stems that carry water and nutrients are easily bruised. The plant will replace leaves but cannot mend if the stem is damaged.

Pinch flowers or buds from newly purchased annuals. They'll catch up and set new buds once new roots establish in the garden.

BULBS
Remove spent flowers from spring bloomers.

Zones 7 to 9: After last frost date, remove protective mulch from dahlias and gladiolus overwintered outdoors. Check for slugs around emerging dahlias.

INDOOR PLANTS
Potting mix significantly affects root health and thus the entire plant's health. Good potting mixes hold water yet drain well so roots don't sit in soggy, airless conditions. They're porous but heavy enough to hold the plant in place.

Look for a mix containing organic components (often listed as "forest products"). Gritty bits— either pumice or perlite— are vital to maintain extra air space and good drainage. When you squeeze wet container mix, it should fall apart in

your hand. If it sits in a wad with the pattern of your palm lines, it probably won't drain well. Add gritty material to equal about one-third by volume.

It's not necessary to buy potting soil with added fertilizer, microorganisms, or even "water-holding" beads. You can later add fertilizer as needed. If necessary, you can also add screened compost (about one-quarter by volume) for added nutrients and moisture-holding capacity.

Garden soil, scooped up and dumped into containers, doesn't work as potting mix. It is too dense and poorly drained when put in pots.

LAWNS
Expect to mow as least once per week in early spring. Keep pace with how fast grass is growing so you will mow off just one-third of the blade height. Set mower blades at 2½ to 3 inches. Avoid mowing too high or too short—both will weaken lawns. Bag or rake up clippings if the grass is too long or wet to mulch mow without leaving big clumps.

Zones 4 to 6: Core aerate (see March). Does your lawn feel spongy when walked on? Or did it resist water penetration last summer? You can increase oxygen to grass roots and improve water retention by aerating.

PERENNIALS, GRASSES & FERNS
Set supports or stakes while plants are small for tall-growing plants such as the larger lilies, or for those with top-heavy blooms, such as herbaceous peonies. Stakes should be about three-quarters the height of the mature plant. Use flexible ties. Be careful not to drive the stake through the bulb on large lilies; it will kill them.

ROSES
Weed and mulch rose beds.

Zones 4 to 6: Complete all rose pruning.

SHRUBS
Flowering shrubs may be pruned as flowers fade. Remove dead branches first. Use selective cuts to remove entire stems, or cut back to a natural point of attachment to maintain the

■ *Bushy or floppy plants are best held up with a circle of three or four short stakes with crisscrossed string like a loose net between them. Commercial wire hoop supports also work.*

HERE'S HOW

TO SHAPE NEWLY PLANTED HEDGES

Shape new hedges the year after planting to promote dense branching. Keep the top narrower than the bottom so lower branches don't get shaded out. Round the top if you live where snowfall is routine to reduce load damage. String a level line to guide an even pruning height. Remove no more than one-half to one-third of the shoot length at each trimming.

Fast-growing plants, such as laurels and Leyland cypress, that mature at tree sizes will require a lot more pruning than smaller, slower-growing selections. Scissor-style hedge shears provide a cleaner cut than power trimmers and are a good bet for smaller hedges. Power trimmers are faster and more useful for larger hedges with small leaves. For the neatest job, keep tools sharp.

Plants with small leaves work well for informal or sheared hedges. These popular hedge species produce new shoots on older stems, an advantage when renovation pruning is needed:

Japanese holly (*Ilex crenata*)

Box honeysuckle (*Lonicera nitida*)

Osmanthus (*Osmanthus delavayi,*
O. × burkwoodii)

Privet (*Ligustrum*)

Barberries (*Berberis*)

Boxwood (*Buxus*)

Yew (*Taxus*)

■ *A correctly pruned hedge will be slightly narrower at the top, which allows for lower branches to receive sunlight.*

Prune multi-stem shrubs to remove a few individual canes back to ground level.

natural growth habit. Don't leave short stubs when removing branches; they will either die back or produce an unwieldy cluster of crowded new shoots. Don't shear or round ornamental flowering shrubs, and make sure that any services you may hire don't do it as their general cleanup practice. This type of pruning typically results in the growth of long shoots like so many "wild hairs" sprouting from cut branch ends that demand even more pruning. Flower development may also be lost from such severe pruning methods.

Bluebeard (*Caryopteris × clandonensis*) blooms in summer on new shoots, and has a habit somewhat like hybrid roses. Prune them back each spring to a framework of well-spaced, 6- to 8-inch-tall stems before new growth emerges.

Zones 4 to 6: Bring container shrubs out of winter storage, including shrubby fuchsias, marginally hardy rhododendrons or azaleas, rosemary, and others. Clean up dead leaves and stems. Lightly top-dress with fresh potting soil or screened compost and slow-release fertilizer. Repot those which have outgrown last year's containers. In the landscape, apply or refresh the organic mulch around new plants and any that were drought stressed last summer.

HERE'S HOW

TO HIRE AN ARBORIST

An arborist is a specialist trained in the art and science of tree care. Arborists certified by the International Society of Arboriculture (ISA) must have at least three years of field experience, pass a comprehensive exam, and regularly attend training sessions to keep their certification current. Arborists can help with diagnosis and care for smaller trees and are essential when it comes to large trees. Some firms provide consultation only, and some provide both consultation and tree care services. Among the specialized services arborists can provide are pruning, diagnosis, and treatment of health problems, risk assessment, preservation during construction, and tree selections and planting.

The Pacific Northwest Chapter of the International Society of Arboriculture (PNW-ISA) web page offers these tips for selecting an arborist:

- Hire someone who is bonded, licensed, and insured and ask for ISA Certified Arborist® credentials.

- Check for membership in professional organizations such as the ISA, Tree Care Industry Association (TCIA), and American Society of Consulting Arborists (ASCA).

- Ask for references and check them. Get more than one bid.

- Beware of door-knockers. Reputable firms are generally too occupied to solicit work in this manner.

- Never allow tree workers to use spikes or spurs to climb for pruning and tree care.

Hiring a reputable service for your tree care needs will help ensure your trees' future health and beauty. Improper tree care and pruning can cause permanent harm.

Zones 7 to 9: When buds on hardy fuchsia (*Fuchsia magellanica* and others) begin to show color, remove dead stems and thin overcrowded canes. Keep cuts close to the base to preserve the arching form and to avoid overcrowded stems.

TREES

If there is bare ground beneath trees, provide a 2- to 4-inch layer of coarse organic mulch (composted leaves from last fall are a great choice). This is one of the best care practices you can provide for young and old trees alike.

Always be sure mulch tapers to ground level around the trunk so it does not hold moisture against the bark.

As spring sap flows rush up from the roots to feed swelling buds and shoots, the bark can be very easily torn during pruning work. It is best not to prune if you find that the bark is "slipping." Wait until after the first leaves and shoots have fully expanded.

Large or small, trees should never be rounded or topped. Be wary of hiring services who recommend pruning trees in this manner.

Zones 4 to 6: Remove from young trees the tree wrap that was used for sunscald protection. (see November).

VINES & GROUNDCOVERS

Stay a step ahead by frequently removing smaller weeds before they bloom to diminish the workload later. To suppress new weeds, replenish areas where mulch is thin. Shear spring-blooming heath (*Erica carnea*) as soon as blooms fade. Don't cut more than one-third of the green growth. Annual grooming will help keep plants full and prevent them from becoming leggy in the center.

Zones 4 to 6: Prune woody groundcovers such as kinnikinnick and prostrate cotoneaster. (See "Zones 7 to 9" in March.) Mow or shear herbaceous groundcovers before new growth begins for bishop's hat (*Epimedium*), Japanese spurge (*Pachysandra terminalis*), creeping St. John's wort (*Hypericum calycinum*), and *Vinca minor*.

Zones 7 to 9: Prune early-flowering vines as blooms fade. Evergreen *Clematis armandii* can be pruned this month, needing little more than selective thinning to keep it trained to its support system. Don't prune groundcovers while they are in a rapid flush of growth.

Zones 4 to 6: Bring tender vines such as clematis out of winter storage into a sheltered position. Water, top-dress with new soil, and reset supports. Repot to a larger container if the vine is pot bound. Keep them outside once night temperatures remain above freezing.

WATER

Keep track of rainfall this month. The month's rainfall can arrive in a day's deluge, leaving the rest of month dry. New plantings will need water first. Test manual and automatic irrigation equipment for good performance and coverage. Keep track of rainfall and warm days, and be ready to water if soils begin to dry out. Remember to allow soil to dry out a bit between watering

■ *Set up rain barrels so they will be full and functioning for the start of the growing season.*

and to apply enough water to soak in deep. The resulting shrink and swell cycle helps maintain soil porosity.

ANNUALS

April starts the summer watering regiment. Water plants recently moved outdoors. If you're using soaker hoses, make sure they run long enough for water to reach down to the roots.

BULBS

Tulips, hyacinths, and daffodils need water during and just after bloom; water when rainfall is scarce.

Do not allow newly planted summer bulbs to get dry once they've begun growth. True lilies, calla lilies, dahlias, and others need steady moisture from leaf emergence through their bloom time.

INDOOR PLANTS

Indoor garden plants will be growing strongly and will need regular watering. To test for dryness, poke your finger into the soil: water if it's dry to 1 inch down. Dump water out of saucers after an hour.

"Water-holding" polymers, which resemble gelatin when wet, aren't necessary for container gardening. After a while, they tend to migrate to the surface as strange-looking gray blobs.

LAWNS

Established lawns don't generally need watering in April, but keep emerging grass seed moist until blades are at least 3 inches tall. New grass will die if it dries out just after germinating.

PERENNIALS, GRASSES & FERNS

All zones: Set soaker hoses and check the irrigation system. Irrigation is typically needed from mid-May through September—sometimes into October—throughout our region. Water according to plant needs—well-established, drought-tolerant plants may only need attention during heat spells.

SHRUBS

Nursery soil mixes often dry out sooner than the surrounding soil, causing drought stress. This is one reason to gently remove some of the nursery soil from the edges of the rootball at planting time. Set up soaker hoses or low-volume emitter pipes to supply water directly to new plants that need water the most.

TREES

In desert areas, as temperatures warm and precipitation decreases, begin monitoring new and established trees for watering.

Check automatic irrigation systems to make sure water spray does not directly wet the lower trunks of trees. For both automatic and manual sprinklers, position them so the water spray touches the ground several inches away from tree trunks. Repeated wetting of the lower trunk creates stress and invites decay. Apply enough water to wet the soil several inches deep, and allow the soil to dry out a bit between waterings. Maintaining mulch will reduce the amount of irrigation needed through the season. Use a trowel to probe several inches down into the soil to check moisture levels.

VINES & GROUNDCOVERS

As with all garden plants, inspect transplants and new plants for watering needs. Established vines and groundcovers should receive adequate water along with the other landscape plants around them.

FERTILIZE

Review plant requirements and conditions before using fertilizers. Most established landscape plants don't require annual fertilization. If your plants show yellowing leaves, get the problem diagnosed before applying fertilizer.

On most soils, native species don't need fertilization (especially where leaf litter and organic mulch is present). Both native and ornamental species that are adapted to low-fertility soils may perform poorly if they get excessive nutrients.

Young trees, shrubs, and vines planted last year can be fertilized this month to promote strong growth and size during their early establishment. Nitrogen is the most essential element for spring growth. Use fertilizers sparingly if your garden is near water or an aquifer. Rainstorms can quickly wash nutrients away into watersheds. Herbaceous perennials generally thrive on moderate- to low-nutrient levels. If you use fertile mulch, it should provide adequate nutrients for most plants.

ANNUALS

Fertilize annuals in containers once just after new growth starts from their initial planting and then again when roots establish and there is a new flush of leaves. Container plants require regular fertilization because of the limited soil area and because nutrients wash out after watering. Fertilize every three to four weeks during the summer.

BULBS

Spring-blooming bulbs can be fertilized if it was not done last month. As they die back, hardy spring bulbs replenish themselves and set flowers for next year. They need only one spring application of a 9-6-6 or similar bulb fertilizer. If your bulbs are planted in beds with perennial flowers, the spring fertilization of the perennials with a 5-10-10 will also provide for the bulbs; they won't need separate applications.

Emerging Siberian iris and German iris (*Iris germanica*) may benefit from a low nitrogen fertilizer.

Indoors, continue to fertilize amaryllis bulbs every two weeks.

INDOOR PLANTS

Apply liquid fertilizer twice a month for most plants. Cactus and succulents need less. See March for more detail.

LAWNS

Fertilize in either April or May. The general recommendation for our region is to apply up to 4 pounds of actual nitrogen per year. Oregon State University turf specialists note that applied fertilizers can be cut in half (or eliminated on clay soil) with mulch mowing. In addition, they recommend using only ½ pound of nitrogen per 1,000 square feet in spring to prevent extra-early growth that will require extra mowing.

Zones 7 to 9: A general schedule is May, June, September, and October. Adjust lawn fertilization based on the use of mulch mowing and the overall performance and density of your lawn. Avoid weed-and-feed combination fertilizers.

PERENNIALS, GRASSES & FERNS

If you did not do so in March and added nutrients are needed, use a low-nitrogen formula such as 5-1-1 (liquid fish emulsion is ideal). If you applied fertile mulch to the garden earlier, perennials should not need additional fertilizer.

"Waterwise" plants, such as herbs, artemisia, and yarrow, become floppy and unattractive if overfertilized. If they grow well and look strong, no fertilizer is needed.

Caution: Do not fertilize newly divided plants until they show new leaves, which is the sign that the roots have established and can take in nutrients.

ROSES

Fertilize after pruning with a low-nitrogen liquid formula such as fish fertilizer. Keeping nitrogen levels low will allow leaf growth but not retard bloom. If you use a granular type, water it in well. Remember that newly planted roses do not need fertilizer until their roots are established. Look for the first bud or bloom before fertilizing.

SHRUBS

A single application of a slow-release 5-1-1 or similar fertilizer for young plants can be done this month. Nitrogen is the most essential element utilized for spring growth. Established shrubs should not need annual fertilization.

TREES

Established trees do not need to be fertilized every year, especially where organic mulch and leaf litter are maintained. Do not fertilize newly planted trees.

VINES & GROUNDCOVERS

Zones 4 to 6: To maintain good soil fertility and structure, lightly top-dress groundcovers with fine compost. Use a coarse-texture mulch around vines. For plants lacking good growth and vigor, a slow-release nitrogen fertilizer can be helpful. However, it is important to find out the cause for poor growth before applying extensive fertilizer.

PROBLEM-SOLVE

Nursery soil mixes often dry out sooner than the surrounding soil, causing drought stress to new transplants. This is not a problem for bare-root stock. For container stock, gently shake or wash off some of the potting mix from the outer edge so root ends make direct contact with garden soil. Plan to check and water the original rootball every day or so the first month after planting.

If your garden is plagued by leaf blights, such as powdery mildew, botrytis, or anthracnose, take measures to improve air circulation around the plants and to keep irrigation spray off of leaves. Soaker hoses, emitter tubing, and bubbler heads keep water close to the ground and plants dry.

Slugs are often out after a light rain, as well as in the evening. You can make a slug trap from a lidded cottage cheese container with 1-inch holes cut in the side, with the container then buried to the bottom edge of the holes. Or, cut the top one-third off of a plastic beverage bottle, invert it like a funnel into the bottom half of the bottle, and place it on its side in the garden. Beer or a solution of yeast and sugar are good attractants to put in these traps. Slugs will congregate under squares of corrugated cardboard laid on the ground overnight, ready to be discarded in the morning. Iron phosphate (often sold as Sluggo®) is a less-toxic form among commercial slug baits.

BULBS

Slugs can remove new lily and dahlia shoots just as they emerge, almost before you realize anything has grown. Pull mulch away from bulb plantings to reduce the slug-friendly habitat early in the season.

INDOOR PLANTS

If a plant does nothing when others are in active growth, slide it gently out of the pot and check the roots. Healthy roots are generally a light color, firm and vigorous, not mushy or black. Mushy, rotten roots generally mean the plant will die. Shake the soil off to look for healthy roots farther in. Cut off dead roots and repot. Be sure the container and soil mix are well drained. If the plant doesn't resume growth within six weeks, it's not likely to recover.

LAWNS

Moles are more common where soils are neither very dry nor very wet (therefore easy to tunnel through) and where earthworms are plentiful. They aren't chewing on turf or roots. The easiest solution is to coexist with moles, raking out soil mounds as they appear. They can be troublesome as they start feeding in spring. Take heart. Moles are an indicator of good garden soil. Most home remedies don't work anyway. Contact your local Master Gardener clinic or Cooperative Extension office if you need help managing moles.

Zones 4 to 6: Use a hard rake to break up any areas with snow mold fungus (*Typhula*). Thoroughly rake and reseed large areas. Lawns with prolonged snow cover are prone to snow mold fungus. Overfertilized lawns are more likely to develop it. Treat affected lawns with routine spring lawn care of dethatching or core aerating, overseeding, and top-dressing with fine compost.

PERENNIALS, GRASSES & FERNS

Aphids hatch as plants begin growth. As leaves mature, plants will endure a certain amount of aphid activity, but aphids can damage tender,

young growth. Wash them off with a gentle stream of water, encourage beneficial insects, and use mild insecticidal soap for the worst infestations. Repeat soap treatment in a week to catch newly hatched aphids; soap does not affect aphid eggs. Avoid toxic chemical insecticides; they can readily wipe out ladybugs, lacewings, and other beneficial insects that feed on aphids. Aphids tend to be less damaging later in the season as new growth hardens.

Flowers can attract beneficial insects. To help increase the "good guys" that aid pollination and feed on other insects, grow a wide variety of flowering plants in your garden. Lavender, angelica, cosmos, dill, goldenrod, sweet alyssum, and yarrow, as well as catmint, rue, thyme, and alyssum are among the top choices.

Dense perennial groundcovers may offer hiding places for slugs. If this is a problem, delay adding fresh mulch until after the spring growth flush is over and the soil dries a bit. Peonies succumb to fungal botrytis, especially west of the mountains. Stems will show blackening. Clean up all dead and infected leaves and stems. Watch emerging foliage for signs of black patches. Keep foliage dry when irrigating.

ROSES

Three diseases bother roses, the worst being blackspot. Infected leaves will yellow and drop. Even leafless canes may show the problem. Prune to open the plant to good air circulation. Remove all fallen leaves and trimmings from pruning; do not compost them. Disease-resistant roses will be less affected by this leaf blight.

Warm temperatures (70°F/21°C or above) and wet leaves lead to infection. Rain can't be stopped, but do avoid wetting the leaves when watering in warm weather. Rose growers sometimes cover roses for exhibit with umbrellas to protect their leaves and blooms from rain, but this is extreme.

Powdery mildew and rust are also common on roses, though less troublesome.

■ *Blackspot is a common leaf blight on roses. Look for resistant varieties when planting new roses.*

been spotted in a couple of counties in Oregon and Washington (and eradicated in some spots). They hang out in clusters on the leaves they skeletonize. Do pay attention if you see this metallic-colored beetle—it has a copper-toned back and a dark green head area—and contact your state Department of Agriculture insect management programs (www.oregon.gov/ODA or agr.wa.gov). Take action if you see them feeding in your garden.

Aphids may congregate on rose shoots in spring when growth is soft. You can wash them off with a gentle spray of water. Aphids multiply quickly, so this will need to be repeated. Many garden allies, such as birds, ladybug beetles, and lacebugs, devour aphids. If you choose to use a low-toxicity insecticide such as insecticidal soap, aphids will be reduced. However, using no pesticide for aphids is a better strategy to protect beneficial garden helpers.

SHRUBS

Zones 7 to 9: Aphids show up on succulent spring shoots. They can increase and persist on the extra-tender growth on shrubs that receive too much moisture and nutrients. Control persistent aphid problems with insecticidal soap, a hard spray of water, or hand removal. Moderate or eliminate fertilizer applications. Aphid populations diminish in hot weather, and lower populations won't do much damage to most shrubs. To protect beneficial insects, avoid broad-spectrum insecticides.

Insects are generally less troublesome than diseases. If you've moved into our area from another part of the United States, you may be surprised to discover that the dreaded, destructive Japanese beetle (*Popillia japonica*) is not a constant threat here. As of this writing, it has

West of the Cascades, in a rainy spring, bacterial blight can increase on lilacs. Young shoots and flower clusters turn brown and die back. Grow lilacs in full sun, and thin dense growth to improve air circulation. Cut out blighted stems as soon as they appear. Disinfect your tools with rubbing alcohol and coat with light oil. Disease-resistant selections include 'Maud Notcutt', 'William Robinson', 'Rutilant', and 'Guinevere'. Colder zones can rejoice because lilacs grow well there and have fewer disease issues.

TREES

Zones 7 to 9: Native dogwoods (*Cornus nuttallii*) are commonly affected by anthracnose leaf blight, which can leave them partially defoliated in summer. Blight is more intense after wet springs, and stressed trees are most vulnerable. Use wood-chip mulch and water in summer if needed to prevent drought stress. Regularly clean up and dispose of fallen leaves (not in your compost). If you are planting a new dogwood, choose among the disease-resistant *Cornus nuttallii* hybrids or Chinese dogwood (*Cornus kousa*).

VINES & GROUNDCOVERS

Fungal diseases can develop in herbaceous groundcovers growing in damp areas. Patches of browned, then rotting leaves and stems of pachysandra, ajuga, and vinca can signal a disease problem. Stem cankers, black root rot, botrytis, and other disease fungi are favored by warm, humid weather and encouraged further by overhead irrigation and waterlogged soil.

Apply water and fertilizer sparingly. Periodically thin out overly dense planting. Mowing with a lawnmower and cleaning out the clippings before new growth starts in spring every few years is one way to do this. Clean off any fallen leaves and other debris that accumulate on top of the plants. If you suspect disease in your plants, take a sample to a local Master Gardener clinic for diagnosis.

Japanese beetle are not common in the Pacific Northwest. Take action if you see them feeding in your garden.

May

May is mild and sweet, a prime time for flowers. Rhododendrons, azaleas, lilacs, roses, spirea, wisteria, crabapples, magnolia, hyacinths, and an array of perennials barely start the list of what comes into bloom this month. Families are drawn to public gardens on Mother's Day excursions to take in the splendid vistas of color.

While we marvel at nature's show, the colors, fragrant nectar, and artistry of spring flowers were not designed just for us. Each lovely bloom beckons bees, butterflies, and other insects to get close and, in the process, spread their pollen. The outcome of good pollination, of course, is plentiful fruit and seeds.

The plight of declining honeybee populations and concern for the impact to crop yields may be familiar to many. Perhaps lesser known is that native bumblebees and other bee species that are also important pollinators for both native and cultivated food plants are also declining. The good news is that gardeners across the nation are planting "pollinator gardens"—insecticide-free plantings with a broad variety of plants to provide flowers and habitat for their protection and survival. Every home garden has the potential to be host to valuable native pollinator bees.

Attracting Native Pollinators: Protecting North America's Bees and Butterflies, by The Xerces Society, offers a great launching point for getting started. You can also find more information on local plants and native bees from Cooperative Extension offices and websites (see Resources). At the very least, eliminating the routine use of broad-spectrum insecticides will go a long way toward improving life for all pollinator insects. Increasing the number and diversity of flowering plants (including native species) in your garden and keeping some areas of undisturbed soil for ground-nesting bumblebees creates a real haven. Gardens planted this way also provide greater seasonal interest for our enjoyment and vital links with nearby habitat for bees, butterflies, and birds.

As you admire all the beautiful flowers this month, take a look at the precious pollinators at work there. And then add some of *their* favorite plants to your spring plant shopping list.

PLAN

Rock gardens are a great choice for arid sites. Well-drained soils with spring moisture and crushed rock mulch to emulate mountain scree conditions are key components. Choice plants can be found at nurseries that specialize in native rock garden plants, where you can also learn more about how to grow them. Never collect live plants from the wild.

Lovely blooms are found on native *Lewisia*, shooting star (*Dodecatheon conjugens*), penstemon, and *Douglasia laevigata*. Dress up shadier rockery crevices with rock brake fern (*Aspidotis densa*), spleenwort (*Asplenium trichomanes*), and parsley fern (*Cryptogramma crispa*). For extended bloom add pussytoes (*Antennaria*). Sandworts (*Arenaria*) are easy to establish and have a long bloom period. These plants are thrifty in their water needs and attract native bees and other pollinators.

ANNUALS

Nurseries are chock-full of choices and color this month and in June. Select what you want now, especially if you are aiming for a particular color scheme. Include selections that support bees and other beneficial insects: sweet alyssum, cosmos, wallflower, angelica, zinnias, marigolds, sunflowers, helianthus, cilantro, and other annuals.

■ *Nurseries often have special sections highlighting plants for birds and pollinators.*

■ *Colorful butterflies are like living flowers in the garden, and they play a valuable role as pollinators.*

Freezing temperatures that are still possible in colder zones mean some protection may still be needed for new annuals. By the end of May, night temperatures east of the Cascades begin to moderate, especially at lower elevations.

BULBS

Catalogs for fall-planted bulbs may arrive now and in June; mark your favorites. Or try something completely new! It's easiest to think about good locations for spring bulbs now. By fall purchasing time, thinking of spring conditions becomes challenging. Give yourself some guidance by making notes now and through the end of spring bulb bloom season.

Tiny dahlias that suit containers and window boxes may be available at nurseries.

INDOOR PLANTS

Use your indoor plants for extra summer interest on the patio. Best suited for shade are begonias and fuchsias. Plants adapted to indoor conditions will need protection from brightest sun. Even some geraniums—those in the Stellar series—will appreciate afternoon shade. Wait until warm nights before setting plants outside.

Locate bricks, overturned pots, or wood stands for risers. Find some new pots to enhance the display.

Paint plastic pots to revive them for summer cheer, to complement flower colors, or to coordinate with interior colors. You can use either latex house paint or a spray-on plastic paint, such as Krylon®. The latex paint wears off quite quickly—it can look scuffed in a few months. The durable plastic paints come mostly in bright primary colors. If you're a fan of collecting inexpensive pots on sale in stores or at yard sales, they don't have to remain drab.

LAWNS

Maintaining a dense, green, weed-free lawn requires significant water, fertilizer, and effort to stay a step ahead of nature's tendency to evolve toward a mix of species. Assess how you use your lawn, and consider changes to lessen the work. In the pre-herbicide years before the 1950s, a blend of clover and grass was the standard. Ecologically, this makes great sense: clover "fixes" nitrogen in the soil, is drought tolerant, and dark green in color. Seed blends of grass with 5 to 10 percent new dwarf "microclover" are commonly available again. The dwarf clovers have a finer texture and are less aggressive than white clover. Coated microclover seed can be spread over established lawns in May. Try it on a single area of lawn as a step toward reducing your lawn-care workload.

PERENNIALS, GRASSES & FERNS

Spring bulbs may need some dressing up with perennial plantings to serve as "shoes and socks" to disguise their bare ankles and fading foliage. Lady's mantle (*Alchemilla mollis*), perennial candytuft (*Iberis sempervirens*), and prostrate rosemary (*Rosmarinus officinalis* Prostratus Group) clothe garden margins nicely.

Be careful about choosing commercial wildflower or meadow seed mixes. Many come mixed for a very broad region and may include seed for plants that may be unsuitable or problematic in your location. Many wildflower mixes contain nonnative species, and noxious weed species have shown up in some. Avoid seed mixes that don't list all the species. Look for wildflower seed mixes blended for a specific zone, such as Puget Sound Prairie or eastern Oregon shrub-steppe. Or buy individual seed packets. Native plant societies, Cooperative Extension offices, and noxious weed boards all have information on native seed sources, as well as alerts on invasive species of concern (see Resources).

ROSES

Roses reach their full blooming glory in about three years. Keep notes about performance, but be cautious and forgiving in your judgments of a newly planted rose. They often don't reach their full potential until their second or third year.

SHRUBS

Spring-flowering shrubs come into their glory with a variety of color and scents. Browse nurseries for interesting new selections, and rediscover reliable old-fashioned shrubs such as spirea, deutzia, and weigela. Also pay attention to leaf qualities that will be in full view as blossoms fade. Cultivars with variegated, purple, or lime foliage provide beautiful summer color and contrast: *Weigela* 'Florida Variegata', *Berberis thunbergii* 'Crimson Pygmy', *Fothergilla gardenii* 'Blue Mist', Black Beauty™ elderberry, and *Spiraea japonica* 'Firelight'. Shrubs with deep green leaves and bold texture offer dramatic backdrops to summer perennials.

Native shrubs attractive to butterflies, hummingbirds, and pollinators include wild lilac (*Ceanothus* spp.), evergreen huckleberry (*Vaccinium ovatum*), mock orange (*Philadelphus lewisii*), ninebark (*Physocarpus capitatus*), Oregon grape (*Mahonia* spp.), red-flowering currant (*Ribes sanguineum*), and western azalea (*Rhododendron occidentale*).

TREES

Spring-blooming trees are a great compliment to the garden. Flowering crabapples are an old-time favorite, but many of the older cultivars quickly dissolve into a mess of brown leaves as apple scab and powdery mildew take their toll, particularly west of the Cascades. Replace an existing poor performer with disease-resistant selections for better bloom and summer performance. These small (20 feet or fewer) trees are a great accent for smaller gardens. All are hardy to zone 4. *Malus domestica* 'Winter Gem' has a broad upright form. 'Prairifire' blooms deep pink, with maroon leaves for great summer color. 'Louisa' has a broad, weeping form. 'Royal Raindrops' has tiny red fruit and lobed leaves. Outstanding for small, narrow spaces is the late-blooming, columnar 'Adirondack', reaching about 12 to 15 feet tall.

HERE'S HOW

TO PLANT SEASONAL CONTAINERS

1 *The larger the container, the easier the maintenance. Aim for 3- to 4-gallon size, about 10 × 10 inches, or larger. Plastic and polymers are lighter weight than ceramic or wood. Disguise black plastic nursery pots inside woven baskets.*

2 *Drainage is important! Be sure water drains well through the soil mix and out the bottom of the container. Don't add a bottom layer of pebbles or marbles; these will not help drainage and only serve to decrease soil depth. Pots without holes are only useful for water plants such as small floating waterlilies. To prevent soil from pouring out the drainage holes, cover the holes with a piece of window screen, coffee filter, or a clay shard. Fill the pot about three-quarters full, and water well to check drainage.*

3 *Special soil is crucial. Soil scooped from the garden will be too heavy and soggy in the confines of a container. Make sure commercial potting soil drains well. Look for mixes that contain perlite or pumice. Added fertilizers, moisture polymers, and microorganisms are not necessary. If you find the potting soil you bought doesn't drain well enough, blend in more perlite before installing plants. To make a well-draining mix, blend one-quarter part garden soil, one-quarter part perlite for aeration, and one-half part bagged potting soil. Moisten thoroughly before filling containers.*

4 *Space plants from 1-gallon containers 6 inches apart, and from 4-inch pots 3 inches apart. Set tiny starter-pack plants in groups of three. Gently spread out tightly packed or tangled roots and water well to settle the planting.*

5 *Top-dress with 1 inch of screened compost or worm bin compost to contribute to plant health and soil condition.*

6 *Fertilize every two weeks with a low nitrogen-complete fertilizer with trace minerals. If using 20-20-20, dilute it to half strength. Do not overfertilize because that will reduce or eliminate flower performance.*

Few tree species tolerate cultivation in patio containers, but the dwarf *Malus* Lancelot® and 'Camelot' crabapples are good choices. They will need regular water and fertilization and should be taken out of their pots every few years for root pruning and repotting with fresh soil. Containers too large to move into winter protection will need insulation for protection in colder zones.

VINES & GROUNDCOVERS

Use low-growing plants along the front edges of perennial beds to provide a transition between beds and adjacent lawns or paths. Options for dense groundcovers under 8 inches tall include prostrate sedum 'John Creech', black mondo grass, Japanese spurge, and sandworts. Look for groundcovers that will complement the adjacent bloom and leaf colors, and are adapted to the existing light exposure.

PLANT

ANNUALS

Warm season annual flowers and vegetables germinate best when soil temperatures reach 70°F/21°C.

Zones 4 to 6: Plant hardy annuals, such as alyssum, cosmos, and lobelia. Hold off on installing tender annuals, such as cleome, nicotiana, and heliotrope, until night temperatures are steadily above 45°F/7°C.

Zones 7 to 9: Mother's Day marks a traditional date for planting patio containers. Combine all types of summer annuals with perennials. Helichrysum is a reliable addition for foliage interest. Be prepared to cover tender geraniums and other half-hardy annuals if temperatures dip below 45°F/7°C at night.

BULBS

Spring-flowering bulbs in containers can be planted in the ground after they bloom. Choose a sunny spot and plant them a little deeper than they were in the pot. Keep them watered until foliage fades.

New and stored dahlias can be set out early in the month. Place markers identifying them. If the dahlia is a dinner-plate size on a stalk soaring 6 or 7 feet tall, plant at 8 inches deep. Set a sturdy stake next to the tuber. Smaller dahlias can be planted 3 to 4 inches deep. In coldest zones, plant dahlias a week after the last frost date and keep covers handy to protect emerging shoots in case of a sudden freeze.

Zones 4 to 6: May is the last month to plant true lilies (*Lilium* spp.). The stress of later planting leads to late blooming and stunted growth. Lilies require well-drained soil and don't compete well with heavy tree and shrub roots; plant them far enough away for sufficient soil space and light.

INDOOR PLANTS

The Easter lilies (usually *Lilium longiflorum*) you've been keeping since April can be planted outdoors. Plant them in a part shade, part sun area. Keep them watered until the leaves die back in late summer. It may take two years for them to bloom again. They are hardy in zones 8 to 9 and warmer parts of zone 7.

LAWNS

If you are seeding a new lawn in an area full of perennial weeds, you will want to clear them out first. This might be done by hand with a spade fork, soil knife (hori-hori), or other hand tool. Multiple passes with a power-rake (thatching machine, vertical mower) to loosen weeds for easier removal is another option. This mechanical preparation works well and helps loosen the soil at the same time.

If glyphosate herbicide is used to manage severe weeds, it must be applied on a warm, dry day while weeds are actively growing. You will need to wait the two weeks or more it takes for weeds to die before continuing seed bed preparation.

Pick up big rocks, sticks, and other debris and correct any drainage problems. Loosen the soil about 8 inches deep with a power rake or rototiller. Work when the soil is damp but still dry enough to crumble in the hand.

Slope the surface grade away from buildings, and fill in any holes or dips for a smooth, level seed bed. Leveling will be easier with a lightweight, 3-foot-wide grading rake you can find at most tool rental outlets. If you need to bring in topsoil, it must be mixed into the existing grade (not layered like icing on a cake) to maintain good drainage. Use a lawn roller to firm up the soil before planting seed.

Soil temperatures around 50°F/10°C are ideal for germinating grass seed. (See "Here's How to Install a New Lawn" in March.)

PERENNIALS, GRASSES & FERNS

Some plants, such as hosta and lilies, emerge from the ground later than other perennials. Be sure to mark their locations so that you don't accidentally plant another treasure on top of them.

Zones 4 to 6: This is an ideal time for planting new perennials from pots and divisions. Perennials are best planted when they are about 3 to 5 inches tall, though they can also be planted at other heights.

Zones 7 to 9: As the garden fills with foliage, add plants for late summer and fall color: yarrow, black-eyed Susan (*Rudbeckia* spp.), Japanese anemone (*Anemone japonica*), and white boltonia (*Boltonia asteroides*).

ROSES

Container roses can be planted. Water them thoroughly the day before planting. (See "Planting Instructions" in the Introduction.)

SHRUBS

Woody plants installed this month will need extra care and irrigation to reduce transplant stress. Make sure to mulch. Transplanting is less feasible for larger shrubs now, though anything small enough to be lifted and moved on a shovel may move well if you attend well to watering over the following weeks.

Softwood cuttings of many shrubs can be taken just before succulent new shoots begin to harden in, starting in May through the summer.

HERE'S HOW

TO TAKE SOFTWOOD CUTTINGS

It can be fun to grow new shrubs from softwood cuttings. Try this with azaleas, barberries, boxwood, forsythia, fuchsia, spirea, weigela, and others. Some may take better earlier or later in the season, so don't be afraid to try again if the first set doesn't take. Roots should appear in two to four weeks.

Cuttings are best taken during the coolest part of the day. Collect them in a plastic bag to keep them from wilting. Look for long, healthy shoot tips from side branches with green bark that will break with a clean snap when bent. Prepare your cuttings in the shade. Make sure to use clean tools, containers, and soil mix. Use a light, well-drained seeding mix containing extra perlite or pumice. You can also use a mix of equal parts coir fiber and coarse sand, or equal parts perlite, coir fiber, and coarse sand.

1. Trim cuttings at 4 to 6 inches long with at least three nodes (points where buds and leaves are attached).

2. Remove leaves from the lower 2 to 3 inches of stem, plus any flower buds.

3. Dip the stem ends in a powdered rooting compound.

4. Moisten the soil mix and use an old pencil as a dibble stick to make a hole for each cutting.

5. Gently insert the cutting so leaves are well above the mix, then press the medium around it.

6. Cover securely with a plastic bag and set outdoors in a sheltered location out of direct sun.

A super simple method is to place a couple inches of moist rooting mix and the cuttings directly into a zip-top plastic bag, which can be easily opened and resealed to vent excess moisture. Pot cuttings up when roots are visible through the bag.

Check cuttings every few days to make sure they don't get too soggy or too dry. Once they have rooted, transplant them to individual containers in standard potting soil. Keep transplants in light shade. Some plants may grow large enough to plant out in the fall; others may need another season to grow before they are ready.

TREES

Complete tree planting before summer heat arrives. The best transplant treatments are to use good planting techniques, water well during the first growing season, and use mulch to help retain soil moisture and suppress weeds.

Special transplant products cannot make up for poor planting methods or lack of water. Repeated research has found no added benefits with Vitamin B-1. Many transplant products, including bone meal, are high in phosphorus. This element is rarely deficient in landscape soil and adding more can lead to problems: high phosphorus suppresses beneficial mycorrhizal fungi that enhance root growth and nutrient uptake, and the runoff of phosphates contributes to water pollution. Mycorrhizae inoculums have begun to show up in some transplant products, but consistent benefits have yet to be proven. Maintaining good organic matter is the best action to promote and maintain beneficial fungi already present in the soil.

VINES & GROUNDCOVERS

Choose cooler, overcast days for planting. Small new plants can dry out quickly on warm sunny days. Water regularly and watch for early signs of wilt.

Zones 4 to 6: After the last frost, seeds and transplants for many annual vines can be planted outdoors.

Zones 7 to 9: Take divisions early in the month from very dense groundcover plantings to use in other areas of your garden. Pachysandra, carpet bugle, ornamental strawberry, sedum, and saxifrage are among those that can be divided now. Softwood cuttings can be taken of climbing hydrangea.

CARE

Make sure all new plants from this year and last year are mulched to help conserve soil moisture. Consider leaving some "rough edges" in less visible corners of the garden with no mulch and a little less grooming. Undisturbed bare soil is critical habitat for ground-nesting bumblebees.

ANNUALS

If your annual plant starts came from a heated greenhouse, they'll need to be hardened off before staying outdoors. Follow directions for hardening off in April.

Pinch off spent flowers to promote continued blooming on many types of annuals.

BULBS

Dig and transplant spring-flowering bulbs after the foliage turns yellow. You can also mark the bulb locations with labeled stakes now to make transplanting easier in fall. Photos and sketches are also helpful references. Foliage from late-blooming daffodils may still be ripening; they can be cut about seven weeks after bloom. Remove faded flower stalks of early blooming bearded German iris; allow foliage to multiply through summer.

Allium foliage often disappears before the bloom opens, which is normal. Allium leaves can appear as early as February in the warmest zones. Allium bulbs burst into purple, cream, pink, or yellow this month. Taller types with prominent golfball- or

■ *Allium produce eye-catching globes.*

baseball-sized blooms ('Purple Sensation' and others) look lovely as flowers fade from green to tan. Many gardeners keep them as accents for most of the summer.

INDOOR PLANTS

Indoor plants may shoot into active growth when both light and warmth return. Check shade-lovers to be certain they aren't being scorched from more intense window light.

Check drainage holes to look for emerging roots; this is a good time to repot to a larger container.

■ *Wipe leaves to remove dust, because anything impeding the plant's ability to receive light will reduce health.*

Remove yellowing leaves and spent flowers. Houseplants require regular grooming to look their best. Don't let fallen leaves stay on the soil. Older lower leaves on rubber plants, philodendron, and prayer plants (*Maranta leuconeura* vars.) may turn yellow. If new, emerging leaves turn yellow, that's a serious symptom of root problems, potentially of root rot.

LAWNS

Rope off any new lawn areas to prevent foot traffic; leave the barrier up until after the first mowing.

Alternate direction each time you mow, ideally at right angles to the previous mowing. Grass can mat down if only mowed in one direction.

Mow often enough to remove only one-third of the leaf blade; if the mower height is set at 2.5 inches, mow when grass reaches 3.5 inches. Dull mowers tear the grass blades, resulting in dead, uneven ends that can turn yellow. Practice mulch mowing whenever possible—it cycles nutrients and organic matter back into the soil and can help improve lawn condition if done properly. It does not work if grass is too long or too wet.

PERENNIALS, GRASSES & FERNS

After you've tidied, divided, planted, and watered, mulch is the last touch. Keep it 2 to 3 inches

deep around, but not over, emerging crowns. Don't mulch over dry soil. Placed over moist soil, mulch helps retain moisture and lessen irrigation demands.

As spring bulbs finish blooming, allow leaves to die back amid perennial plantings without interference. Snowdrop, crocus, hyacinth, and tulip leaves need to be thoroughly brown, indicating that the bulb has ripened, before removing the old foliage; all daffodils (*Narcissus* spp.) may be cut back six to seven weeks after bloom finishes.

Trim back foliage of low-growing spring-blooming perennials. Candytuft (*Iberis* spp.), rock cress (*Arabis* and *Aubrieta* spp.), and groundcover phlox will put on a flush of fresh foliage after dead flowers are clipped off. This can be done with hedge shears.

Remove the top 3 inches of growth from fall-blooming asters and chrysanthemums to make the plants bushier. ("Pinch your mum on Mother's Day and the Fourth of July.") Two pinches will produce bushy plants for fall bloom. Bee balm (*Monarda* spp.) and tall phlox (*Phlox* spp.) benefit from one pinch.

Zones 4 to 6: Set support stakes of bamboo or metal next to emerging delphinium, peonies, asters, lilies, and other tall plants that tend to bend over when in bloom.

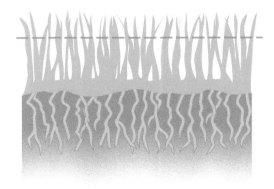

■ *Cut no more than one-third of the grass blade height at each mowing for a healthier lawn.*

■ *After you've tidied, divided, planted, and watered, finish with a covering of mulch.*

ROSES

Indoor roses: Miniature roses sold as gifts do not thrive in household conditions. You may wish to treat them as long-lasting bouquets and then discard them. To keep them outdoors, choose a sunny spot where they can grow without being swamped by larger plants. Pot them up into a larger container, water in, and fertilize after two or three weeks outside. Some of these roses are winter hardy in zones 5 to 9. You may have to experiment to see how hardy they will be outdoors.

Prune climbing roses, choosing healthy young canes to tie up and keep as the framework for flowering side shoots. Remove excess and crowded canes.

Don't prune newly planted roses now because canes need to grow and support root establishment. Many gardeners remove skinny "blind shoots" with no flower buds, which are sometimes considered a symptom of too much shade. Other growers suggest that keeping the blind shoots may contribute to vigor because they produce more leaves to photosynthesize. Use your judgment; blind shoots may be more helpful to young plants still getting established.

SHRUBS

If newly planted shrubs keep wilting and are difficult to keep watered, relieve the moisture stress with a temporary shade cover, because shaded leaves lose less water. Shade cloth is more effective than anti-desiccant sprays, which wear away as leaves expand. Use a light mesh fabric or shade cloth available in garden centers, or construct a simple teepee with long poles for smaller plants. In a pinch, an old patio or beach umbrella offers instant relief. The shade cover can be removed later in the summer or when it is no longer needed.

Natural form is best preserved when winter-damaged stems are pruned all the way back to the ground or to a larger main stem, rather than at the edge of the damaged section. Note where new growth is absent, and prune out entire weak or dead stems.

In very cold winters, less hardy shrubs may die back completely to the ground. Don't be too hasty to dig them up, as new growth may still emerge from the roots. Cut away dead stems, mark the spot with a stake, water, and watch for signs of new growth.

■ *When cutting roses for bouquets or pruning to remove spent blooms on repeat bloomers, cut down to a sturdy section of stem at an outward facing bud so the new stem won't grow toward the center of the shrub. "Old roses" bloom just once a year, usually in June.*

Zones 7 to 9: Prune evergreen rhododendrons, azaleas, and other broadleaf evergreen shrubs, if needed, just after they finish blooming. Spent blooms can be removed from lilacs and rhododendrons for neater appearance. Use hand pruners on lilacs; spent rhododendron trusses can be pinched off by hand, using care not to break off swelling buds. Most plants will bloom whether deadheaded or not. Many experts say the practice is mostly for appearance.

TREES

Provide a generous ring of mulch around trees growing in turf. Do not use fabric weed barriers—they prevent organic matter from reaching the soil and roots and are not a good choice around trees.

The lower trunk and root flare are like an Achilles heel for a tree. Bark injury in this area weakens growth and predisposes trees to other maladies. Common sources of damage are covering trunks in

HERE'S HOW

TO PRUNE YOUNG TREES FOR FUTURE STRUCTURE

1. Remove dead, damaged, and broken limbs. Make all cuts along the branch collar at the point of attachment to a larger limb or trunk.

2. Make sure there is one central leader. Remove one of the competing leaders if there are double leaders. If the cut is too large for hand pruners, you can also reduce the height of the competing leader by two-thirds, making the cut above a lateral branch. This should stunt that leader so it will develop as a smaller lateral branch.

3. Determine how high the canopy should be when the tree is bigger. Gradually remove the lowest limbs each year as the tree grows taller. This way, pruning wounds will be smaller and less injurious to the trunk. In the meantime, those lower branches will help the trunk develop good taper and strength. The canopy should remain at least two-thirds the total height of the young tree.

4. Thin out any tightly spaced scaffold limbs. The larger the mature tree size, the farther apart these larger main limbs should be spaced, both vertically and around the trunk.

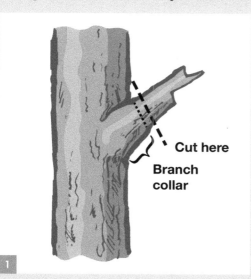

Cut here

Branch collar

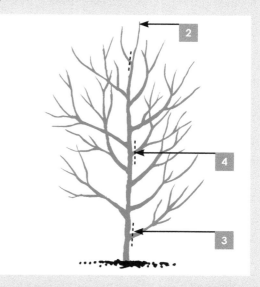

soil or mulch, mechanical injury from mowers or string trimmers, and repeatedly soaking the lower trunk with irrigation spray. Avoid these insults to preserve tree health.

Zones 4 to 6: Remove tree wrap used for winter protection on young trees. As their bark thickens with age, continued winter protection will not be needed.

VINES & GROUNDCOVERS

Tie in or prune out long, rambling shoots on vines. Check old ties, and remove any that have become tight against stems. Avoid using wire or nylon cord: they are the worst offenders for girdling woody stems. Sisal garden twine and adjustable rubber or plastic plant ties are better options. Position ties in a loose figure-eight loop. Prune spring-blooming vines after bloom. Five-leaf akebia can be kept in scale with selective thinning and then shortening the remaining shoots by one-third. Also thin and shorten stems of honeysuckle and similar vines. (See February for tips on pruning clematis.)

Begin a monthly schedule for pruning wisteria after it blooms, routinely cutting out the long, trailing whips. This will encourage more blooms, and keep the vine contained and attractive. As blooms fade out on spring heath (*Erica carnea*), lightly shear off about one-third of the green shoots to keep plants dense. Take care not to cut back into bare wood, which will not resprout.

Zones 4 to 6: Potted vines may be brought back outdoors toward the end of the month. Check supports and prune vines to prepare them for a new season's growth.

WATER

Routine water applications should start as the weather warms up and soaking rains diminish. Cover bare soil with coarse mulch. Remove weeds to reduce moisture competition. Check the soil with a trowel.

Don't overwater so soil is constantly moist, and don't let it get so powder-dry that it repels water. Both conditions damage soil structure and lead to compaction. Compacted soil cannot hold much water.

Soil that is well aerated and has good organic content will have a built-in moisture reservoir. Roots can grow deeper, giving plants better drought resistance. Coarse organic mulch serves to replenish organic matter and improves water infiltration and retention. For arid soils that take less organic matter, coarse materials such as small pinecones, bark chips, or lava rock will be ideal for moisture retention.

The greatest demand for water is in early summer when growth is most active. Identify the water needs of the different plants in your garden and water accordingly. Larger, established woody plants generally need less water than new plants, which should get regular deep soakings in the first few years of establishment. Most garden plants can tolerate dry spells better later in the season. When water is scarce, make watering trees and large shrubs a priority over lawns and perennials, which are more easily replaced should they be lost to drought. (See additional irrigation information in the Introduction.)

ANNUALS

Establish a planned watering schedule for annuals. Most cannot tolerate dry conditions.

■ *Squeeze a clump of soil in your palm. Is it too dry to make a ball, but still slightly damp? It's time to water. Is it like wringing out a wet sponge? Wait until soil has dried out more.*

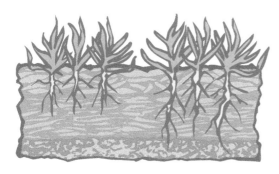

■ *Deeper but less frequent watering will promote deeper roots and better drought tolerance.*

A few exceptions are cosmos, portulaca, and sunflowers, which can endure drier conditions as summer progresses.

BULBS

Keep potted bulbs and newly planted summer bloomers watered. Once the foliage has disappeared on spring-blooming bulbs, they can manage without summer water.

INDOOR PLANTS

Take special care with plants that sulk when they dry out: Norfolk Island pines, ferns, grape ivy (*Cissus* species), and spider plant. All indoor plants require regular watering now; use the finger test, poking the soil about 1 inch, and watering when the soil feels dry.

Succulents such as jade plants (*Crassula* species) and cactus need moderate water, every three to four weeks. If the plant shows signs of root stress, stop watering and turn the plant out to check roots for dieback or to see if they are excessively potbound. If needed, repot in a soil mix with about one-third pumice.

LAWNS

Irrigate in the early morning or late afternoon; avoid the hottest parts of the day. Turn water off immediately if it begins to run off. If the soil is sloped or compacted, water will be easily wasted by runoff. In these conditions, irrigate just until runoff starts. Turn off the water, and turn it on again in about 20 minutes. Gradual slow watering

will allow water the time it needs to soak in to the needed 4- to 6-inch depth.

Deeper but less frequent watering will promote deeper roots and better drought tolerance. Plan to water a maximum of three times per week during the hottest parts of the summer. Once a week may be enough during cooler periods or when it rains. The general target is to provide about 1 inch of water per week to keep lawns green all summer. Eco-lawns and grass-clover blends remain green with less water.

PERENNIALS, GRASSES & FERNS

Newly planted or divided perennials will need careful watering through summer.

ROSES

Check the soil to maintain good moisture, especially east of the mountains, where rainfall can be low this month.

SHRUBS

Be prepared to keep new shrubs watered when there isn't enough rainfall to do the job. Remove weeds to reduce moisture competition.

TREES

Keep newly planted trees well watered and mulched. Zippered, slow-release watering bags filled from a hose are a great way to supply the extra water new trees need.

VINES & GROUNDCOVERS

Keep actively growing groundcovers and annual vines well watered this month. For woody vines and groundcovers, allow the soil to dry between applications. To decrease fungal problems on leaves, water groundcovers early in the day so foliage will be dry well before nightfall.

FERTILIZE

ANNUALS

Continue to fertilize annual plantings with a low-nitrogen liquid fertilizer, such as fish emulsion, when you see new growth starting.

■ *Fish emulsion fertilizer is suitable for annuals and seasonal containers.*

LAWNS

If you are mulch mowing regularly, your lawn may not need added fertilizer. Excess growth from over-fertilizing leads to higher demands for irrigation and mowing, and higher incidence of some diseases.

Zones 4 to 6: Use a slow-release fertilizer with a 3-1-2 NPK ratio. One way to remember the specific dates for the year in the inland Northwest is: Easter, Memorial Day, Labor Day, and Halloween. For lower-maintenance lawns, fertilize once in spring and once in fall.

Zones 7 to 9: Higher-use and formal lawns benefit from a nitrogen boost when growth slows toward the end of the month. Apply ½ to 1 pound of actual nitrogen per 1,000 square feet.

PERENNIALS, GRASSES & FERNS

Fertilize plants with higher nutrient needs in May only if you have not done it earlier in the year. One spring application is enough, particularly if composts and fertile mulch are used. If your perennials are grown among shrubs and trees, follow the lower fertility needs of the woody plants for best overall garden results.

Zones 7 to 9: Native soils west of the Cascades tend to be acidic. Compost and organic amendments help buffer this acidity; it's not always necessary to add lime. Some growers mulch

BULBS

Lightly fertilize emerging lily, dahlia, crocosmia, and canna shoots. If you are using compost and manure blend mulch, this may not be necessary.

INDOOR PLANTS

Plants will need more fertilization in May. Fertilize twice a month with a fertilizer that has trace elements, such as a fish or kelp fertilizer, and avoid very high levels of nitrogen.

The most common reasons for limited flower production are lack of light and overuse of nitrogen. Because indoor gardens contain so many different plant types, there's no "one fertilizer fits all" strategy, especially if you combine flowering and non-flowering plants, cactus, and ferns.

■ *Earthworms are part of a healthy soil system.*

sensitive plants with limestone chips. Consider testing your soil if plants aren't thriving.

ROSES

Fertilize about six weeks after pruning, and again six weeks later, up until the end of July, when the plants will slowly begin to approach fall dormancy and fertilizer should be stopped. Water thoroughly before and after fertilizing.

SHRUBS

Established shrubs should not need annual fertilization. A single slow-release application can be given to new shrubs planted within the last couple years and to any shrubs with poor growth over the past year. Use moderate rates: about 2 tablespoons of a 19-percent nitrogen product per 4-foot-diameter circle provides 1 to 2 pounds actual nitrogen per 1,000 square feet (see Introduction). Compost and organic mulch often provide enough nutrients without additional applications.

Hydrangea bloom color is affected by soil pH. Blues are maintained with aluminum sulfate or other acidifying fertilizers. Add lime, and the floral hues will shift to pink.

TREES

Young trees, except those planted this spring, will benefit from a slow-release fertilizer applied at 1 pound actual nitrogen per 1,000 square feet, or about 2 tablespoons of 15-percent nitrogen fertilizer per 3-foot circle. Rake granules into mulch and water well. Fertilize young trees during the first three years of establishment.

VINES & GROUNDCOVERS

Avoid applying too much nitrogen, which will push extra growth that will need more trimming and water. Fertilizing too often may worsen problems with aphids and some fungal diseases.

PROBLEM-SOLVE

ANNUALS

Odd leaf color? Red, maroon, or sometimes silvery color on annuals such as geraniums and tender fuchsias can signal overexposure to cold temperatures. As temperatures warm, this symptom will depart.

The tiresome twins, slugs and aphids, continue this month. Set up slug traps or iron phosphate slug bait. Lady beetles, hover flies, and tiny garden spiders may be seen moving in on aphids. Let these garden angels do their work before using controls.

BULBS

If any of your tulip plantings develop tulip fire (tulip botrytis), completely remove the bulbs and surrounding soil, and don't plant tulips back to the same location. Affected plants show distorted leaves and gray patches of spores. This tulip disease persists in the soil, so plant daffodils, hyacinths, Dutch iris, or other plant types there instead.

Tulip bulbs do best if kept dry during the summer. Bulbs mixed in well-watered flower beds don't repeat bloom as well. Crocus and hyacinths also prefer dry summer conditions.

INDOOR PLANTS

oor air circulation and damp conditions can bring on spotty leaves from fungus diseases; identifying the exact cause can be elusive. Isolate the plant and remove affected leaves. Keep the plant in drier conditions and monitor new growth. If it does not improve, discard it.

LAWNS

Little heaps of soil scattered on the lawn? This may be the work of nightcrawlers and earthworms, which burrow through the soil and shove little piles called castings up to the surface. It may seem annoying, but it's really an asset for a healthy lawn.

These worms draw their nutrition from organic matter in the soil, and their castings are extremely fertile. The tunneling of the worms will benefit compacted or poorly drained soils by opening up soil and enhancing drainage. Worms also aid decomposition of thatch and old grass clippings, thereby boosting soil fertility.

Lightly rake out castings as needed. Worms are most active in warm, moist soil. They stay deeper in the soil when surface conditions are warmer and dryer during summer, especially if deep, infrequent irrigation is used. All types of pesticides may harm worms as well as other beneficial soil organisms in the turf.

PERENNIALS, GRASSES & FERNS

Look for spittlebugs—tiny green insects hidden inside wads of white froth. They don't stay around long and aren't generally harmful, except on edible strawberries. If their numbers build up, rinse them off with a shot of water. Slugs reach their peak on the fresh foliage in April and May. Check hosta, iris, true lilies (*Lilium* spp.), and daylilies (*Hemerocallis* spp.).

Ants wander onto peony stems and buds. People sometimes say the ants make the peonies bloom, but actually they are just attracted to the sticky, sweet residue on the buds. Swish the flowers in a bucket of water to remove ants when cutting peonies for bouquets. They don't harm the peonies but they may alarm dinner guests.

ROSES

Rose thorn disease, a fungal infection that affects humans and animals, is uncommon but troublesome when it occurs. The disease (*Sporotrichosis*) is initiated by fungus present on rose thorns, hay, sphagnum moss, twigs, and soil. A thorny scratch may introduce the fungus below the skin. If the immune system is compromised in any way, the disease may occur more readily.

To prevent infection, wear protective gloves and long sleeves when pruning and handling roses, and use goggles when pruning if branches come toward your face. Open bags of soil or amendments carefully. Don't lean over and take a deep breath; always protect your lungs. Most gardeners will never see a case of this, but an ounce of prevention never hurts.

Blackspot and rust may show up on leaves. Manage with sanitation by removing affected leaves and pruning out canes that show inky blackspot lesions. Keep roses pruned with an open center for good air circulation. Keep leaves dry when watering.

SHRUBS

Twisted, puckered leaves indicate heavy aphid feeding. When damage levels are beyond the control of beneficial insects, apply insecticidal soap. Repeat every 7 to 10 days as new eggs hatch.

Voracious leaf-feeding caterpillars can appear almost overnight, camouflaged by their green color as they chew away. Leafrollers hide by curling the edges of leaves around them. Squish them on sight

Shrub roses produce blankets of blooms.

TO GROW ROSES WITHOUT PESTICIDES

In pursuit of perfection, gardeners may exert a large amount of effort and chemical products on their roses. Others may avoid roses altogether for their reputation of requiring lots of spraying. New plant trials at public gardens and partner sites in the American Rose Trials for Sustainability (A.R.T.S.®) have found that we can enjoy beautiful roses without all that fuss.

1. Choose roses adapted for your area and noted for disease resistance. Information is available at local Cooperative Extension offices and the A.R.T.S.® website. *Rosa rugosa* and many shrub roses are less bothered by leaf blights.

2. Don't be afraid to discard a rose that is persistently diseased. It's a great opportunity to introduce a strong variety in its place.

3. Plant roses where they will grow best: in sun, on moist soils with good organic and nutrient content, and not crowded by neighboring plants.

4. Provide a healthy but lean culture; sturdy plants are more resilient to pest attacks. Use organic mulch and fertilize modestly, especially if growth is good.

5. Water the soil, not foliage. Watering roses deeply over a broad area promotes deeper roots and more robust plants.

6. Keep the rose area clear of fallen leaves. Prune off heavily diseased leaves. Don't compost diseased rose leaves.

7. Learn how to correctly prune each rose according to its type and growth habit.

8. Perhaps most important, tolerate some imperfections and enjoy the flowers!

or leave them for birds and predator insects if damage isn't too severe.

Notched leaf edges on rhododendrons, evergreen azaleas, *Pieris*, and strawberry tree (*Arbutus unedo*) indicate adult root weevils are active. To reduce damage, keep lower limbs pruned up off the ground (adults come up from the ground to feed at night). Using a flashlight after dusk, drop handpicked weevils into soapy water. Or shake them onto a large sheet laid on the ground first. Commercial root weevil traps are also available. Contact your local Master Gardener clinic or Cooperative Extension Office for positive pest identification and control options if problems seem severe.

TREES

Avoid broadcast weed-and-feed lawn products that contain 2,4-D and other broadleaf herbicides. Trees are also broadleaved plants and can be harmed by repeated or over-applications of these products.

Flowering cherries (*Prunus* spp.) suffer many insect and disease problems, particularly west of the Cascades. Blossom brown rot blight enters blooms and causes twig dieback. Very tiny clumps of sawdust on the trunk and limbs indicate cherry bark tortrix borer is active. Borers are attracted to fresh wounds; avoid pruning until early September when mating season ends. Healthy trees are most resilient to both problems. Cherries grow best on sandy soil in open, sunny sites.

VINES & GROUNDCOVERS

Bloom failure on wisteria can occur when fertilizer and water have been generous and pruning has been modest. To encourage bloom, prune in early spring, cutting long, thin shoots back so three buds remain. Continue to prune out long, wild growth through the growing season. Withhold fertilizer, and allow the soil to dry out between watering.

Black sooty mold may appear on some groundcovers, thriving on secretions called honeydew dripping from aphids or scale-infested plants overhead. Sooty mold doesn't kill plants. Reduce sooty mold by managing the insect problem.

Ample light marks the character of this period in the growing season. The summer solstice, the longest day of the year, arrives around June 21. For plants, this is prime time for gathering energy and for flowering and reproduction. Growth continues, but at a slightly more moderate pace than in early spring. By summer's end, the blooms on many types of plants will have made their transition to fruit and seeds.

Every green leaf is hard at work in the process of photosynthesis—taking in the sun's energy with carbon dioxide and water to synthesize carbohydrates and release oxygen. The sugars and other compounds produced in the leaves provide the food for growth and development. Some of this energy is used immediately; some is stored in roots, stems, and other parts for the next growth cycle. Even on cloudy days, there is enough light for this process to continue.

Soaking rains are less likely to occur during summer months. It's time to keep an eye on soil moisture and to make sure new plants get enough water for early summer growth. A string of overcast days can be deceiving; rain might arrive, but never does. Or a brief shower may freshen the air but hardly dampen the surface of soil, leaving roots dry.

This is a lovely time to wander through the garden and enjoy the results of all the plantings and preparations you did last spring. Bring along a bucket and a couple of hand tools to handle some small but productive increments of care while you walk around. Pull weeds about to flower, probe the soil to check moisture, prune a branch overhanging a walkway, check ties on staked plants, and gather cuttings for an arrangement. Try this approach of doing a little bit of work more often instead of concentrating all your garden time into occasional longer sessions. You can catch some things before they expand into bigger issues. Even 15 minutes can make an amazing difference. And it's a nice way to enjoy the beauty of your garden and the seasonal cycles of growth and change.

PLAN

ANNUALS

Summer is here, but west of the Cascades, day and night temperatures can both be on the cool side. Choose warmer microclimate locations for tender annuals: tuck them against walls and in the sunniest spots within garden beds. East of the Cascades, provide morning sun with shelter from scorching dry afternoon heat.

BULBS

If you love arranging flowers, you'll enjoy the ornamental onions in bloom this month. Include some on your fall-planted bulb orders. The best ones for dried arrangements include *Allium* 'Purple Sensation'. Garden fireworks appear with both *Allium cristophii* and *A. schubertii*, with flowers in big globes nearly 12 inches across.

INDOOR PLANTS

Zones 4 to 6: Where inland summers stay hot, keep tropical plants such as schefflera and rubber trees shaded and cool on dry, hot days. Gauge your local conditions before settling plants outside.

Zones 7 to 9: It's difficult to keep plants such as angel's trumpet (*Brugmansia* spp.) and bird-of-paradise (*Strelitzia reginae*) warm enough for good bloom in cooler maritime areas. Most houseplants are generally tropical in origin and can move outdoors when nighttime temperatures remain above 50°F/10°C. Flowering plants, such as gardenias, princess flower (*Tibouchina urvilleana*), and flowering maple, will do well with morning sun in cool maritime areas but also need protection from the hottest afternoon temperatures.

LAWNS

Replacing the lawn where it isn't thriving in shade? Check nurseries for groundcovers sold under the Stepables™ name. If the area gets only occasional foot traffic, consider Irish or Scotch moss (*Sagina* spp.), barren strawberry (*Waldsteinia fragarioides*), or New Zealand brass buttons (*Leptinella squalida*).

■ *Blue star creeper makes a lush groundcover between stepping stones.*

Since all groundcovers need time to establish, you may want to replace lawn a few square feet at a time. Ferns provide additional interest and cover for shade. Add pavers or steppingstones for areas that get more foot traffic.

Is the lawn bouncy or spongy when walked on? This may be from thatch, which builds up at the base of grass blades. Thick layers of thatch, when they dry out in summer, repel water and can keep rain or irrigation from reaching turf roots. Next, check the lawn for soil compaction. Has your family worn patterns where they walk across the lawn? Will you need to add pavers on often-used paths? Grass roots get shallow and grass weakens on trodden, compacted ground. Core aeration helps get oxygen and water into the root zone, but it can't be done when lawns and soil are dry. Be sure to include it with fall lawn care tasks (see September).

ROSES

Feast your senses on rose bloom this month. Summer light shines over the garden and long evenings invite us to linger until dusk.

SHRUBS

Use shrubs to create colorful, drought-tolerant containers, alone or in combination with perennials. Buy shrubs in 6-inch or 1-gallon pots, with a plan to place them out in the garden in fall. Use large containers (5 to 10 gallons or more) for greater soil volume and water-holding capacity. Single specimens of dwarf conifers can be kept in large containers for a few years. Choose shrubs with striking foliage: *Hypericum* × *moserianum* 'Tricolor', *Weigela* 'Florida Variegata', *Spiraea japonica* Limemound®, smoke bush *Cotinus coggygria* 'Royal Purple', or the many selections of colorful barberries. Hardy fuchsia gracefully drape over container edges. Blooms to last the summer can also be found on pink elf hydrangea (*Hydrangea macrophylla* 'Pia') and *Caryopteris* × *clandonensis* 'Worcester Gold'.

TREES

Can you adjust planting areas to help trees and lawn coexist more effectively? Vigorous turf will stunt the growth of young trees. Lawns thin out under large, established trees. Mowers and string trimmers can seriously damage tree trunks. Roots

bulging through the soil surface get scraped and make mowing difficult. What can be done?

Maintain a generous ring of mulch beneath trees to eliminate turf competition and avoid mechanical damage from mowing. Place new trees in large beds and keep lawns to the open, sunny areas. With care to minimize soil disturbance, it is possible to create a planting bed beneath trees where turf has been shaded out. Start with a 2- to 4-inch layer of coarse, organic mulch over thinned out or dead grass. Don't bury skinned surface tree roots; keep them exposed to air to avoid decay problems. In fall, add new plants to the new bed.

VINES & GROUNDCOVERS

Many nurseries and garden centers have special sales this month. It can be a good time to stock up on extra groundcover plants to embellish thin plantings or to fill gaps as weeds are removed.

PLANT

ANNUALS

Tender plants can live outdoors this month, including annual flowers and warm-season vegetables.

Add culinary herbs to outdoor containers. Basil, the sumptuously flavored herb for Italian and Thai cooking, has a red-leaf form and dwarf 'Marseille' form in addition to the soft green standard type.

What to plant in the shade? For spots with three to four hours of sun, or filtered sun through taller trees and shrubs, there's a pick of bright colors with wax begonias (*Begonia* Semperflorens Cultorum Group). In lighter shade, try blue sapphire flower (*Browallia speciosa*), the colorful patterned foliage of coleus, and fragrant white *Nicotiana alata*.

BULBS

Dahlias and other summer bulbs happily go into the ground this month. If gladiolus, dahlias, or begonias show sprouts coming out before planting, handle them carefully. Plant out tuberous begonias, cannas, and caladium started indoors. Fancy-leaved caladiums with leaves in reds, pinks, whites, and striped green thrive in hot, east-side areas if given

HERE'S HOW

TO CREATE A PLANTING BED IN A LAWN

1 *Allow the grass to go dry. You can use a hose or heavy rope to lay out the shape, then cut the new edge in with a shovel. Use the lowest setting on your mower or a string trimmer to mow grass down to the nubs.*

2 *Put down a first layer of "sheet mulch" with several layers of newspaper, dampened to shape it tightly to the ground for added effectiveness.*

3 *Cover the area with about 6 to 8 inches of dampened mulch, such as wood chips or leaf mold. You can also put a layer of compost down first and top with coarse mulch for a total of 6 to 8 inches. This deep cover will smother roots and condition the soil for future planting. Add more mulch where any shoots poke through. The old turf will decompose in place, and worms and soil organisms will thrive.*

4 *By September, the bed will be ready for new plants. Push mulch aside to dig planting holes and place new plants.*

some afternoon shade. They do well in pots east of the Cascades. In cooler west-side areas, try caladiums in warm, glassed-in patios until leaves are larger.

If planting calla lilies now, soak the tuber for up to six hours in tepid water to give it a jump start.

INDOOR PLANTS

This is an easy time to multiply your houseplants. Succulents such as jade plant, aloe, and sedums root readily from broken-off leaves, and cuttings can be made of cactus. Allow the leaf or section to dry for 24 hours. Then tuck them about ¼-inch-deep into damp rooting medium, such as half-and-half perlite or pumice and coir fiber. Water and keep them away from full sun. (Don't cover these in plastic; the heavy-leaved cuttings can rot if left enclosed in moisture-laden plastic bags.) Check for new roots after two to three weeks.

LAWNS

Removing a lawn, if you choose to do so, can be done in summer. Try the easy, no-till approach shown on the opposite page.

PERENNIALS, GRASSES & FERNS

If you're new to growing herbaceous perennial flowers, observe how large they grow. Prepare to move crowded plants in early fall.

Peonies may be sold in bloom this month. Leave the plant in its nursery pot and sink it in a hole in the garden to hold for fall planting when the peony drops leaves and goes dormant. Do not disturb the roots in summer.

ROSES

Roses in nursery pots can be planted now. Add shade protection the first week after planting, especially in hotter areas. If newly planted roses droop even after watering, continue the shading.

SHRUBS

Don't transplant shrubs during active growth. Container plants installed now will need extra water and care. If you *must* plant, do it during the coolest conditions possible. Water containers

thoroughly the day before. Be prepared to provide temporary shading to reduce transplant stress. Don't forget to mulch.

Take softwood cuttings from shrubs. Look for strong shoots that are firm, but not yet woody.

TREES

This is not an ideal time for planting trees, especially where irrigation water is scarce. If you must plant now, do it on a cool day, and never in hot sun conditions. Soak rootballs beforehand and mulch after planting. Use a slow-release tree irrigation bag, and check daily for water needs.

VINES & GROUNDCOVERS

Zones 4 to 6: Early in the month, divide dense groundcovers to get more plants for other areas. Pachysandra, ajuga, vinca, sedum, and saxifrage are among those that may be divided now. Softwood cuttings can be taken of climbing hydrangea.

Zones 7 to 9: Herbaceous groundcovers can still be planted, particularly in areas that receive afternoon shade.

Softwood cuttings may be taken of variegated kiwi, clematis, cotoneaster, and climbing hydrangea.

CARE

ANNUALS

Protect annuals if temperatures drop below 50°F/10°C. These heat-lovers can be stunted if they get too cool.

Zones 4 to 6: At higher elevations, overnight frost is still a possibility. Protect young annuals and vegetable plants with a row cover (spun polyester garden cloth) or old sheets.

BULBS

Cut the tips on tall dahlias (over 4 to 6 feet) when they are about 14 inches high or when they have three pairs of true leaves. This will help them produce more blooms and sturdier stems. Loosely tie tall dahlias to stakes as they grow.

INDOOR PLANTS

Pay attention to houseplants taken outside for the summer. A sudden spike of 90°F/32°C in western areas along the coast can toast leaves exposed to sun. Thunderstorms, hail, and high winds can tear and damage leaves.

Zones 4 to 6: If garden conditions don't allow protection from extreme heat and drying winds, indoor plants are best kept inside.

LAWNS

During the warmest periods, raise mowing height about ½ inch. This can help keep roots strong and improve drought tolerance. Keep up regular mowing to remove only one-third of the blade height or lawns may suffer.

PERENNIALS, GRASSES & FERNS

Begin deadheading to remove spent flower heads. Many perennials bloom longer and stay more attractive if they don't go to seed. Removing the first spent flowers will result in new side shoots and blooms on campanulas, coreopsis, daylilies, lupine, lavender, sages, and many others.

■ Adjust the blade height on your mower to cut the lawn about ½-inch taller during summer.

■ *Many perennials continue to bloom after the spent flowers are trimmed off.*

Trim back spring bloomers that are finished. Plants such as columbine produce seeds freely and sprout up in corners and cracks. The seedlings aren't always the same color as their parent plants but may still turn out to be nice garden additions when they boom next summer.

Once established, herb gardens produce far more than any one gardener will need. Tidy up thyme and rosemary by selecting the longest shoots to give as small gifts. Rosemary varies in its productivity depending on zone. In zones 4 to 6, it needs indoor winter protection. Cultivars 'Madeline Hill' and a few others may survive to -10°F/-23°C if planted in protected spots. In zones 7 to 9, rosemary is mostly hardy. Larger cultivars can grow to 8-foot bushes and need regular pruning to keep them neat.

Prune off vigorous herb branches that grow over onto neighboring plants.

ROSES

Rose pruning this month takes on the form of simple "grooming." Pay attention to the overall form and habit as you do this work. For large bushes, such as ramblers, Alba roses, and old garden roses such as 'Cécile Brünner', which will bloom only once, do not remove withered blooms. As the flower petals drop, once-blooming roses set brilliant red seedheads (rose hips). Some shorter roses, including *Rosa rugosa*, have brilliant red to orange hips.

SHRUBS

Keep shrub beds weeded, especially around new plants. Minimize soil disturbance to avoid stirring weed seeds up to the surface. Dry soil makes weeds hard to pull. "Shave" them off at the soil surface with a shovel or hori-hori soil knife and cover the ground with mulch. Any weeds that grow back from the roots will be easier to extract from mulched soil.

Do not remove withered blooms from once-blooming roses in order to allow the colorful rose hips to develop.

Some shrubs start to sprout wild hairs, branches that shoot out of control. Prune these off vigorous shrubs that need more restraint than encouragement in summer.

Shape hedges so the base is wider than the top. Informal hedges can be shaped by removing individual long shoots with hand pruners.

Remove spent blooms on butterfly bush (*Buddleja davidii*) before they go to seed. *Buddleja* seedlings have been found to make their way into damp areas and creek sides, squeezing out native willows that butterflies require to rear their young; the plant is on regional noxious weed lists. Consider replacing shrubs that can't be kept deadheaded with sterile forms of *Buddleja*, such as 'Asian Moon', 'Blue Chip', or 'Purple Haze'. Chaste tree (*Vitex agnus-castus*) and the veronica forms of *Hebe* are nectar plants with floral spikes that are attractive to butterflies.

TREES

Create broad, soil-rimmed basins around young trees to aid water penetration over their root zone. Maintain generous areas of mulch around trees in turf.

Summer pruning can begin for many trees this month, including Japanese maples. Pruning should follow the tree's natural architecture, leaving it to look as though it were never touched by human hands. Use good, sharp tools. Remember to stand back frequently to look at the whole plant. Remove no more than one-quarter of the live branch area. Remove branches back to the point of origin at the main trunk or larger side branch. Prune at the branch collar, being careful not to cut flush to the trunk.

The first (and sometimes only) task is to remove dead branches. Next, work on any branches that are out of bounds with the rest of the tree or interfering with a walkway or building. On variegated or cut-leaf forms, remove any branches whose leaves don't match the rest. Branches of weeping or low-growing trees that drag on the

TO TURN AN OVERGROWN SHRUB INTO A SMALL TREE

Several kinds of shrubs, including rhododendron, redvein enkianthus, viburnum, camellia, and Japanese pieris, can be beautifully trained into small trees. This technique allows more light into garden beds and can be easier than trying to keep them trimmed low.

First, identify the lowest branches to keep. As a general rule, the canopy should take up about two-thirds of the total height. Remove the low branches back to the main trunk. Don't leave a stub; place the cuts at the branch collar. If the canopy is very dense, thin out a few long branches to allow filtered light to reach though the crown. This will enhance the appearance without leaving it looking like a lollipop. This training can be done in winter and summer for both evergreen and deciduous shrubs. Remember that the rule for summer pruning is to keep it light, pruning out less than 25 percent of live branches to reduce the potential for sunscald on remaining stems. Training a large shrub into a tree can add new life and beauty to old garden beds.

■ *A large shrub can be trained to resemble a small tree.*

ground should be lifted by thinning out the longest branches.

Small inner branches may be shaded out by outer branches. Lightly thin out some of the outer branches to allow filtered light to reach the inside. Don't remove all the inner branches, because they are important to overall tree health.

Disinfect tools between cuts within a tree and from tree to tree if there is evidence of diseases such as verticillium wilt or fire blight. Isopropyl alcohol in a spray bottle works well. Sanitizing pruning tools is not essential unless vascular diseases and stem cankers are present.

VINES & GROUNDCOVERS

Check supports and ties on vines, replenish mulch where it has gone thin, and prune back growth that is heading out of bounds.

Watch out for weeds camouflaged amid groundcovers this month and pluck them while they are small. Thin out the oldest stems on creeping rosemary to encourage new growth near the center and to prevent it from becoming too woody and bare.

WATER

Recently planted specimens can dry out quickly, while established plants are just fine. If the garden's verdant growth swallows small new plants, mark them with a bright ribbon tied to a stake to remind you where they are. When you water, be sure it has soaked in several inches and not just dampened the surface. It is equally important to allow the soil to dry out a bit between watering. Sometimes mulch will be dry on the surface, with good, moist conditions below. Dig in to check the soil when you water! Check containers daily. On extremely hot days, smaller containers and hanging planters may need water twice, morning and evening.

Keep extra washers on hand to fix leaky hose fittings. Adding quick-connect fittings will prevent lost washers and make changing hose connections easier.

If you have an automatic irrigation system, make sure the water is going where it's needed and is penetrating 6 to 8 inches deep.

Soaker hoses or emitter irrigation tubing woven through mixed planting beds with roses, perennials, bulbs, and annuals offer an excellent way to deliver water directly to the roots. This is also a great way to provide temporary targeted irrigation for establishment of new landscape plantings. Mulch can be placed over these systems for a better appearance and less evaporation. These slow-delivery systems need longer running times than sprinklers.

Zones 7 to 9: June may deceive gardeners west of the Cascades with gray skies but no soaking rains. Remember that plants continue to grow and use water on overcast days. When a light rain dampens the surface, it's a perfect time to irrigate and push moisture even deeper into the soil.

ANNUALS

Most annuals have low tolerance to drying out. Water thoroughly to drench the entire root zone.

BULBS

Summer-blooming bulbs require regular water. Spring-blooming bulbs are dormant in summer and do best when they are not irrigated.

INDOOR PLANTS

Whether indoors or out, all houseplants require more frequent watering in summer. Follow the routine of pouring excess water out of saucers after drenching the container.

LAWNS

Depending on what type of grass you have, if you decide to let the lawn go totally dormant, do not suddenly water enough in midsummer to revive it and then turn the water off again. This will weaken the lawn. In really dry years, it is all right to provide enough water to preserve roots without forcing green growth. Perennial ryegrass and fine fescue

lawns, the most common seeding mix in western areas, will need to have some moisture to keep the grass from severely thinning out by fall. If you do not provide an inch of water a week, at least give the lawn a deep watering once or twice a month.

Limit traffic on dry grass: footprints and scuffs add to stress on crowns and roots of grass.

PERENNIALS, GRASSES & FERNS

Some herbaceous perennials, such as tough Shasta daisies, recover well after leaf wilt. Others, especially the water lovers such as *Astilbe* and *Ligularia*, may collapse to the ground in an approximation of fainting. Continual water stress can kill some plants; consider relocating or replacing these.

ROSES

Deep soaking serves roses well. Avoid overhead watering (unless rain arrives!). Keeping leaves dry helps them resist disease.

SHRUBS

Many well-established shrubs can do fine with little to no summer irrigation, depending on the season and soil conditions. Watering shrubs less can also offer the benefit of slow-growing but healthy plants that require less pruning.

TREES

Keep new trees well watered their first three years. Irrigation bags (Treegator® and similar) are a great way to get extra water to new trees. Fill them about once per week, more often for first-year trees and in hot seasons.

Use caution when installing new irrigation near large trees: severe root damage results from trenching too close to trunks. Position lateral lines in a spoke-like fashion from beyond the drip line to minimize root impacts. Place heads so no water spray hits tree trunks. Adding frequent water to the root flare, where the trunk meets the roots, can lead to root rot and early death. Surface-installed emitter tubing offers a good alternative for providing irrigation to new plantings near long-established trees.

Slow-drip bags allow for steady watering that allows tree roots to absorb more water.

FERTILIZE

ANNUALS

Fertilize annuals in containers about every two weeks with a low-nitrogen liquid fertilizer, such as 5-1-1 fish emulsion or organic kelp. Annuals do not need as much phosphorus as once thought, and higher levels have been found to make plants leggy. High-phosphorus "bloom" fertilizers aren't necessary.

BULBS

Fertilize dahlias with a granular or liquid 5-10-10 product when plants are 8 to 12 inches high, watering it into the roots. Too much nitrogen results in weak stems and poor bloom.

INDOOR PLANTS

Fertilize as needed to support active blooms and new growth.

Cactus and succulents, which require relatively little fertilizing, can benefit from one-half strength fertilizer once a month in summer.

Timed-release fertilizers may be helpful for large indoor or patio garden plants with higher summer nutrient needs. Their outer coating dissolves with watering and minerals are released gradually over one to three months. Release rate depends on moisture and soil temperature, with about 70°F/21°C being most effective. Follow the package instructions.

LAWNS

Fertilize moderately to prevent lush overgrowth of grass. The more you fertilize, the more water and mowing your lawn will need. If you "grass-cycle," returning the clippings to the lawn will slowly add nutrients as they break down, often replacing the need for fertilizer at this time of year.

Zones 4 to 6: For inland gardens: if you did not fertilize at the end of May, fertilize now with a slow-release or organic source of nitrogen. However, if you do not plan to water your lawn this summer, do not apply fertilizer now.

PERENNIALS, GRASSES & FERNS

If fertilizer and mulch were applied in spring, most perennials won't need any fertilizer now. Delphinium benefits from a low-nitrogen fertilizer boost about now.

ROSES

Apply fertilizer four to six weeks after the last application. Water well before and after fertilizing. Do not use granular fertilizer on newly planted roses. If plants are growing well and setting buds, use a mild product, such as fish fertilizer.

SHRUBS & TREES

Annual fertilization is not required for established shrubs and trees. What if you see yellow leaves? Yellowing leaves can signal a number of different plant problems, including root rot, poor soil drainage, and some leaf diseases. Get an accurate diagnosis before adding fertilizer. If the plant suffers from root rot, fertilizer will not help and may worsen the problem.

VINES & GROUNDCOVERS

Hold back on fertilizing these plants during the warmest point in the growing season.

PROBLEM-SOLVE

ANNUALS

Basil is a favorite for slugs. Growing basil in containers can make managing slugs easier. Make a trap out of a plastic beverage bottle, cutting off the upper one-third of the bottle and inverting it like a funnel into the remaining half of the bottle. Add some beer or a yeast and sugar solution and set it on its side near your plants overnight. You can take the funnel section off to dump out the trapped, dead slugs and use the trap again.

BULBS

German iris (*Iris germanica*) may show signs of iris leaf spot. Brown oval splotches appear as summer progresses. Trim off affected leaves and keep them out of your compost. New leaf growth may also be affected. Leaf spot is more prevalent in warmer zones and coastal areas with high humidity. It can disfigure leaves. Good air circulation and sun exposure help subdue iris leaf spot.

Keep up on slug patrol, especially around newly growing dahlia shoots and lilies of all types.

Aphids multiply fast in warm weather.

INDOOR PLANTS

Gawky plants toppling in their pots or vines scrambling too far can be cut back this month and will fill in by fall. Make bushier plants of flowering maple (*Abutilon* cvs.), asparagus ferns (*Asparagus densiflorus* Sprengeri Group), begonias, grape ivy (*Cissus* spp.), *Dieffenbachia*, *Fatsia*, fuchsia, geraniums (*Pelargonium* spp.), philodendron, and *Tradescantia* by pinching them back.

LAWNS

Is your new lawn declining at the first dry days of summer? Many people have the unfortunate situation of finding themselves with a lawn that looks fine at first but declines rapidly after a few months. This is often traceable to poor soil preparation. Even the best quality sod can't cope with bad soil. Sod is sometimes unrolled over 2 inches of soil with hardpan beneath. If your lawn is persistently soggy, dies out in spots, or is hard to keep watered in summer, dig out a 1-foot-square section and check the soil quality under the roots. Plan to renovate the lawn in early September.

PERENNIALS, GRASSES & FERNS

Are your peonies failing to bloom but produce healthy leaves? They may be too young (less than three years in the ground) or planted too deep (more than two inches). If they are too deep, dig them up and replant them at the proper level in September or October.

HERE'S HOW

TO REUSE POTTING SOIL

Can you reuse potting soil? Yes, container potting soils can be used again. But if the plants growing in it had insect or disease infestations, toss that batch out (but not in your home compost).

Rejuvenating old potting soil isn't difficult. Dump it on a tarp, and shake out any old roots to remove them. Mix old soil with about one-quarter part gritty material, such as pumice or perlite, and about one-quarter part by volume of commercial bagged compost. This should give you a well-aerated, fertile mix. Homemade compost may not be sterile enough for use in potting mix.

ROSES

Deer seek out roses and many other plants in the rose family, such as apples. Keeping them out takes a sturdy 7- or 8-foot fence. Repellent can work, but should not be sprayed when sun is hot on the leaves.

Aphids multiply fast in warm weather. Birds and beneficial insects are good allies in keeping populations down. Aphids are more common on fresh new shoots and small leaves. Check under leaves when washing them off with water sprays.

SHRUBS

Rhododendron powdery mildew (*Erysiphe* spp.) often shows up with paler green patches on top of the leaf, with brownish or purplish splotches on the underside (but not the familiar white dust of the type that afflicts deciduous shrubs). Healthy plants are more resistant; grow rhododendrons on well-drained soil with organic mulch, good air circulation, periodic summer irrigation, and minimal fertilization. Some rhododendrons appear to be less susceptible, including *R. yakushimanum*, many of its small 'Yak' hybrids, and treelike *Rhododendron augustinii*. If you suspect this disease is on your rhododendrons, take a sample to a Master Gardener clinic or Cooperative Extension office for diagnosis and advice.

TREES

Often killing host trees, Dutch elm disease's first symptoms are the sudden wilting and browning of leaves along a single branch, called "flagging." Contact your local Cooperative Extension office or your community arborist or forester office as soon as you suspect this disease in your elm trees. Many areas of Oregon and Washington have active monitoring and control programs. Early control is important to limit its spread. This disease eliminated thousands of mature elm trees in the eastern United States.

Crabapples with apple scab and powdery mildew drop their leaves as weather warms. Rake up and destroy fallen leaves. Replace chronically affected trees with an alternate species or a disease-resistant crabapple for the best long-term solution.

Tent caterpillars, which appear on many trees and shrubs, are most troublesome on small trees. Knock nests off with a strong blast of water or clip them off if the tree has enough branches. Tent caterpillar cycles vary, and some years will have more infestations than others.

Trees with heavy aphid infestations may drip honeydew, leaving a sticky layer on anything that sits beneath them. This is most common on birch and tulip tree (*Liriodendron tulipifera*). Drought-stressed trees are more vulnerable. Providing mulch and adequate irrigation are helpful measures.

VINES & GROUNDCOVERS

Clematis wilt can take you by surprise, as beautiful, strong vines suddenly wilt and fail after blooming. This fungal disease, *Phoma clematidina*, invades stems near ground level, stopping the movement of water up the stems. Damp weather and active plant growth are ideal conditions for this fungus. The good news is that most vines will eventually replace the damaged stems with new growth, even in following years, so don't be too hasty to dig up roots on affected plants. Sanitation is important, so prune out infected stems at ground level and clear out the plant's dead leaves in the fall. The larger flowering cultivars are most vulnerable. To have clematis free of fungal problems, you can choose from several possibilities. *Clematis montana* (white, pink), *C. macropetala* (blue, early spring), *C. alpina*, and *C. viticella* are reported to be resistant, as are some of their cultivars, though they all bear smaller flowers.

July

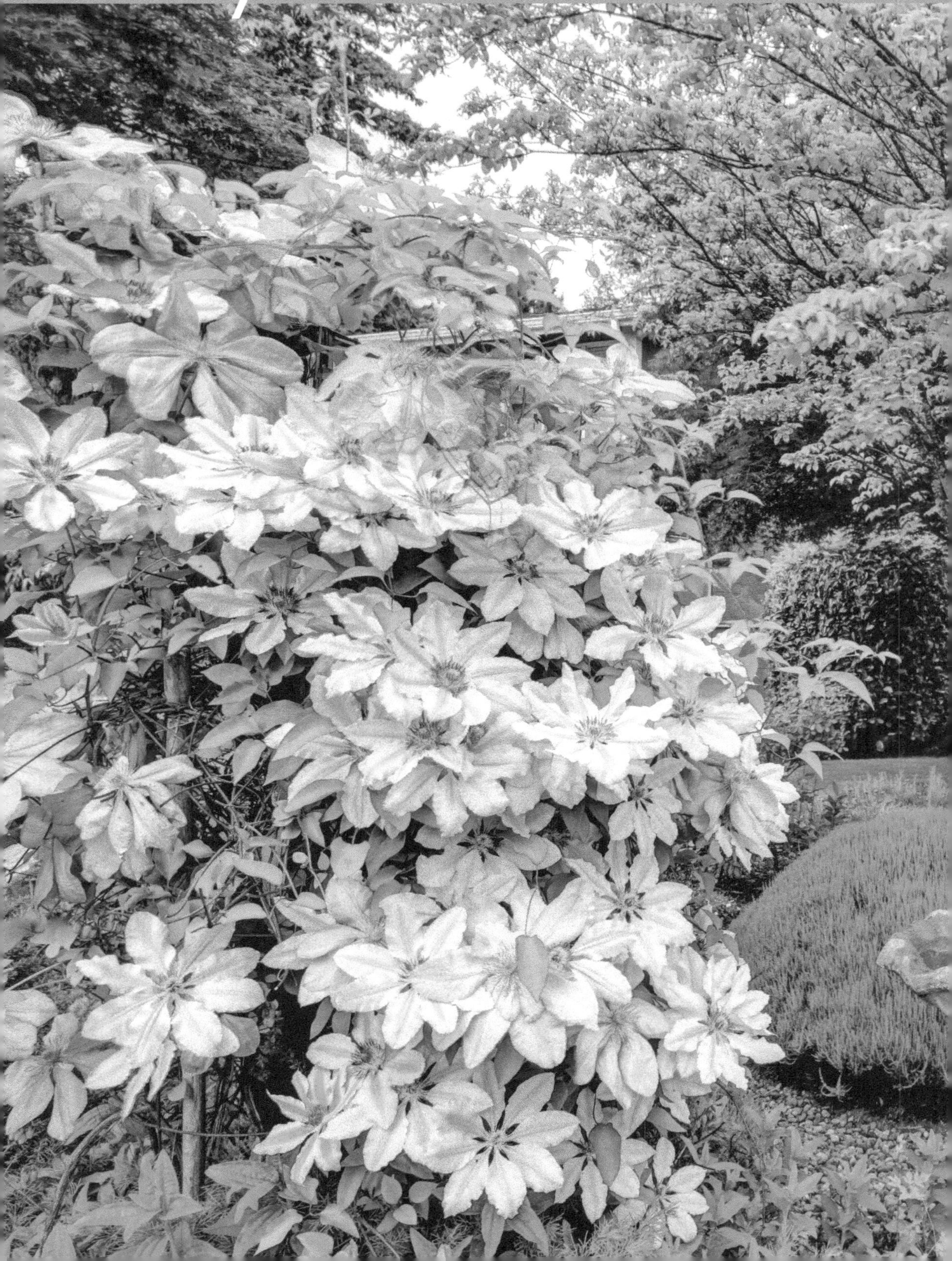

This is a time to delight in being outdoors. These are days of warmth and sunny skies, and all of those well-timed early season gardening tasks should pay off now, making this month's efforts for weeding and watering more manageable. Pause to revel in the beauty and bounty the garden has to offer. This is a time for picnics in the shade and leisurely strolls at local parks and gardens.

While the energy of spring goes toward adding leaves and size, summer is mostly about flowers, fruit, and seeds. We can gather cut flowers for arrangements and clip fresh mint for our iced tea. There may be berries to graze on and green beans to gather for dinner.

Summer's heat reminds us to keep the garden well watered. Heat waves put added stress on plants. Monitoring the garden and managing soil moisture takes priority over most other tasks. A string of warm, high-pressure days can quickly deplete soil moisture reserves. Seasonal containers and plantings added within the past year will be most vulnerable to heat stress.

With the concern for keeping things alive, it can be easy to irrigate more than plants really need. In the water-wise garden, the key is to track plant condition and soil moisture, and to provide just the amount of water needed for plants to stay healthy without adding extra growth. Soft, lush growth demands even more water to avoid wilting than do sturdy shoots of plants whose shoot growth has slowed and hardened off. Many drought-tolerant plants are so good at growing strong with any bit of extra moisture that they can trick us into watering them more often than actually necessary. Give priority to new plantings, seasonal containers, and food gardens. Water well-established plants and lawns less often and apply water slowly so it soaks in really deep.

Making the rounds to probe the ground and check soil moisture keeps us close to the lovely garden scenery and its details. Try to keep the garden pace more relaxed to enjoy the bright, long days of this season.

PLAN

This is truly the month to be outdoors and experience the unique atmosphere of your garden. Collect photos and notes for your garden log. Where do you spend most of your time outdoors? Review what changes would make these spaces more enjoyable or attractive, and begin planning to work on these in fall.

ANNUALS

Nurseries hold sales this month on summer annuals and hanging basket plants. Do you have containers to fill or an area to add a color accent? Some annuals are a bit more drought tolerant than average; look for verbena, zinnia, sweet alyssum, moss rose, calendula, and dusty miller.

BULBS

Many bulb suppliers offer discounts for early summer orders. Check these early catalogs for your wish-list plants. Bulbs will be shipped at the right time for fall planting. It may seem odd to think about daffodils now, but this is a great time to plan for fall season planting.

Photograph summer bulbs for a record of their performance.

INDOOR PLANTS

If you've been carrying along Christmas cactus, poinsettias, kalanchoe, and others that take special care for winter bloom, check out what you need to do now for flowers later. Christmas cactus is generally easiest to manage; poinsettias may do best as a summer houseplant to be discarded in fall. See September for details on fall needs for these winter-blooming plants.

Order Christmas amaryllis and paperwhite narcissus now from bulb catalogs.

■ *Mixed shrub beds are an attractive alternative for hard-to-mow, steep slopes.*

LAWNS

The landscape principle of "right plant, right place" fits right in with lawns. Some of the turf difficulties home gardeners encounter relate to planting grass in the wrong location with the hopeful optimism that a lawn will grow anyplace we want. Is the lawn getting enough sunlight? Turf should be placed in open, sunny locations; it is not well adapted for low light. Shade is not the only reason grass grows poorly under trees. The quality of light is reduced after wavelengths important for grass are filtered out by the tree canopy. Trying to prune trees for more light doesn't help in the long run.

Is the grass hard to mow? Lawn is not the best choice for steep slopes or for oddly shaped spots with obstacles such as trees, poles, or utility fixtures.

The best conditions for growing lawns are relative level, sunny locations with soil that is loose and well drained.

PERENNIALS, GRASSES & FERNS

The value of low-water-use plants can be very evident this month. Reliable and colorful selections include yarrow (*Achillea* spp.), various artemisias (*Artemisia* 'Powis Castle' holds up well), coreopsis (*Coreopsis verticillata* 'Moonbeam'), cottage and Cheddar pinks (*Dianthus plumarius* and *D. gratianopolitanus*), purple coneflower (*Echinacea purpurea*), and sun rose (*Helianthemum* spp.). During their first two summers, drought-tolerant plants need deep watering every 10 days or so until roots are well established.

Perhaps you have a pond or a spot that stays damp year round. For persistently moist spots, choose astilbe; filipendula, sometimes called Queen of the Prairie (*Filipendula rubra* 'Venusta'); *Ligularia dentata* 'Desdemona'; and carpet bugle (*Ajuga reptans* cvs.). European royal fern (*Osmunda regalis* var. *regalis*) has stunning foliage with contrasting upright fertile panicles. Add variegated grasses of *Carex* and *Acorus* to round out damp corners with contrasting color and texture.

ROSES

This is a prime time to visit public gardens to learn more about local rose culture and choices.

■ *Rose petals from organically grown roses can be collected for culinary uses.*

Edible roses? Roses add romance and sweetness to parties, from wedding showers to anniversaries. People don't generally nibble on bouquets, but you and your guests can eat rose petals as a cake garnish or have some rose hip jelly. Gather roses for garnishes from local organic growers where you know pesticides have not been used. Your own garden may also give excellent insecticide- and fungicide-free choices. Remember that many roses from conventional florists are generally treated with pesticides and cannot be eaten.

SHRUBS

Don't just rely on annuals and perennials for summer color; many of these herbaceous bloomers take a lot of water and attention. There is a hidden treasure of bloom, color, and texture on woody stems waiting to be gathered into our summer gardens. Well-placed shrubs with summer interest stick around for repeat performances in other seasons. With lower requirements for irrigation than many herbaceous plants, they make for more water-wise seasonal color.

Plan to include a few of these favorites: oakleaf hydrangea (*Hydrangea quercifolia*) bears large, creamy white blooms set against large, leathery leaves—with the added joy of orange autumn tints. Several forms of St. John's wort shrubs (*Hypericum*) produce sunshine-yellow blossoms by midsummer. Virginia sweetspire (*Itea virginica* 'Henry's Garnet') has fragrant white blooms and dynamic

■ *Oakleaf hydrangea is attractive in more than one season.*

with steppingstones? What are the sun and shade patterns this month? Are vines and arbors well placed, or are adjustments needed? Collect notes on changes that can be done now, such as installing pavers, and changes to complete in fall, such as transplanting.

PLANT

This month begins the quietest time for planting throughout much of the region, with the arrival of the year's warmest temperatures coupled with low rainfall and humidity. If you must plant now, choose the cooler evening hours, mulch well, be vigilant with water, and provide temporary shade from direct sun for a week or more to reduce water stress.

fall color for damp woodland gardens. Drought-tolerant tree anemone (*Carpenteria californica*) bears large, white flowers with bright yellow centers gaily set against evergreen foliage.

TREES

Trees provide a green backdrop in summer, and some even offer opportunities for color and fragrance. Look at existing gardens for exciting arboreal blooms. Some may be subtle, such as the small flower clusters dangling from pale green bracts on lindens (*Tilia* spp.). Robust catalpa trees boast oversized leaves and blooms. The fine features of *Stewartia* bring elegance to the woodland garden with its camellia-like blooms in midsummer. White lily-of-the-valley–style flowers appear in August on the petite sourwood (*Oxydendrum arboreum*), a tree with outstanding fall color. Golden rain tree (*Koelreuteria paniculata*) is a fine midsize tree for urban yards, with upright yellow flowers clusters followed by pinkish seedpods. It is drought tolerant and hardy to zone 5. Idaho locust (*Robinia* × *ambigua* 'Idahoensis') will grow in dry and poor soils, and it offers fragrant purple blossoms in June. Japanese tree lilac (*Syringa reticulata*) is a 30-foot-tall tree with cherry-like bark that bears fragrant pale blooms in June.

VINES & GROUNDCOVERS

Are there threadbare areas through the turf or groundcover areas that would function better

HERE'S HOW

TO PROTECT TREES DURING CONSTRUCTION

Misunderstandings about where and how tree roots grow has led to the untimely demise of many desired old specimens intended for preservation. Trenching and grade cuts too close to trees sever vital roots. Heavy equipment and grading work can cause soil compaction, which is fatal to root health. Even as little as 6 inches of fill soil can smother roots. The effects of construction damage may not be apparent until a few years later, at which time little can be done.

Healthy trees can tolerate some loss of roots; however, decline can occur in the following years if too much of the root area has been affected. Provide good care in the months or year prior to construction so trees are in good vigor and not drought stressed at the time of construction. Mulch the root area beneath the canopy with wood chips to protect the root zone and conserve moisture. Construction damage is far easier to prevent than to cure. Consult with an ISA Certified Arborist® to develop a plan for tree preservation and care before, during, and after construction events.

In zones 7 to 9, sow cosmos and zinnia in July for mid-September bloom.

ANNUALS

When purchasing sale-rack plants, choose healthy-looking plants that have white roots (not dark brown, matted, or mushy). Unlike some perennials, annuals that have been drought stressed may not rebound. Even when healthy, annuals that have been in nursery packs for weeks can become rootbound. Before planting, set them to soak in a deep tray of water until thoroughly dampened. Gently spread roots out when planting. If you see a thick, white mat at the bottom of the plant, peel it off before planting. Work in cool morning or evening, shade plants from the sun, and water frequently.

You may discover the stem of basil kept in a jar of water in your kitchen has sprouted roots. You can pot the rooted cutting in soil and grow it on for the rest of the summer.

Zones 7 to 9: Seeds planted now—such as cosmos and zinnias—will come into bloom in mid-September and last through October. Biennials and fall vegetables can be seeded the first half of the month. If you want a certain pansy for September, start seeds early this month. Pansies and violas will provide color throughout the winter if planted out in mid- to late September.

BULBS

July 15 is traditionally the latest time to plant gladiolus corms. Gladiolus planted this month bloom in late August or early September, when gardens are short of newly emerging flowers.

Check nursery sales this month for potted summer bulbs. Patio-sized dahlias, begonias, and even tender freesias refresh the garden in early July. If the weather is hot, plant in evening or early morning, and shade plants from bright sun for the first week.

INDOOR PLANTS

Take cuttings the easy way, in a jar of plain water. Plants that will obligingly root this way include the vigorous grape ivy (*Cissus* spp.), any philodendron, Swedish ivy (*Plectranthus verticillatus*), and zebrina (*Tradescantia zebrina*).

Make a cutting about 5 inches long, remove leaves that will be under water, and place the cutting container in light but not direct sun. Check and replace water weekly. Children can help with this,

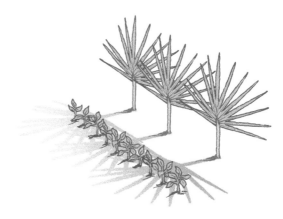

Stick some cut branches in the ground as temporary shade for new annuals.

and later in summer pot up and care for what could become their holiday gift plants.

LAWNS

Summer weather conditions prevent seeding lawns this month. It's possible (not optimal) to install sod, but be sure that the soil is well prepared and thoroughly watered before laying the sod. Expect to water every day or two for several weeks, or until fall rains return. Sod has been regularly watered and fertilized at the sod farm, and without good watering and installation, it can decline quickly.

PERENNIALS, GRASSES & FERNS

This is not an ideal time for planting. Maintain new plants in their containers.

ROSES

Nursery sales this month often have roses. Follow directions given in the June section when you plant. If conditions are really warm, you can maintain roses in their containers and plant them at a later time.

If you wish to propagate a favorite rose, such as creating new plants from a family heirloom, take cuttings in both June and July. You can also do this in September in zones 7 to 9. Best candidates are shrub roses, old roses, and climbers. Follow these steps:

1. Prepare a container of clean sand, or equal parts perlite and sand, and wet it.

2. Choose a strong new shoot with leaves that have five leaflets. If thorns break off with a snap, the shoot is ripe for propagating.

3. Keep the top two leaves with about 3 inches of stem below them.

4. Dip the cut end in rooting hormone.

5. Poke a hole in the sand, and gently press the cutting into place. You can put more than one cutting in a circle around the edge of the container.

6. Water, cover with a plastic bag, and keep the cuttings in a shady spot.

Rooting takes about eight weeks. Success isn't guaranteed, but it's great fun when a cutting takes root. Place rooted cuttings in their own containers to grow them for planting next spring.

SHRUBS

Avoid installing shrubs during periods of clear, hot weather in all but the shadiest garden spots. If you must plant now, keep plants cool and moist in the days before planting. Plant them late in the day so they have overnight to recover from the disturbance of being planted. Be prepared to set up shade tents. Or put off planting until September. To protect containers from heating up in direct sunlight, surround the sides with mulch to shade and cool them. Repot to a larger container if you see roots coming out the bottom.

Take softwood cuttings of barberry, flowering quince, hydrangea, heavenly bamboo, rhododendron, azalea, and many other deciduous and evergreen shrubs. Check for roots where low branches lay in contact with the soil. This is called layering, and the rooted section can be clipped free and dug out as a new plant. This can also be done intentionally by pinning a low branch to the soil and waiting patiently for it to root.

TREES

The peak dry heat periods of summer bring some of the harshest conditions for successfully planting trees. It is best to wait until shorter, cooler days return at the start of fall.

VINES & GROUNDCOVERS

Softwood cuttings of several vines and groundcovers, including variegated kiwi, five-leaf akebia, kinnikinnick, ceanothus, clematis, roses, and wisteria, can be done now.

CARE

ANNUALS

Keep up weeding: get them out while they are small. Stake tall sunflowers or cosmos that are vulnerable to being blown over, especially in zones 4 to 6.

BULBS

Stake taller true lilies very carefully, avoiding the bulb itself. If pierced, it will die. Bamboo stakes offer flexibility and strength. Some growers set them into the ground when planting the lilies. Shorter lilies do well with metal hoop stakes, such as those used with peonies. Staking protects from sudden summer wind and rainstorms.

■ *Bearded German iris should be divided when the rhizomes become overcrowded.*

Zones 4 to 6: Large, showy German iris (*Iris germanica*) can be dug four weeks after bloom and divided. Pry the entire clump of rhizomes gently out of the ground with a spading fork, shaking the soil from the rhizomes and roots. Discard any soft, damaged, or bad-smelling rhizomes, keeping only the most solid.

Separate rhizomes into smaller clumps, trimming back foliage if desired. Replant them in a triangle, setting three clumps about 9 inches apart. Plant rhizomes shallow, just barely covered with soil to allow sun to reach them. Water in well and keep watered while new roots form. New fans of leaves will develop after dividing. Complete this early in colder zones so that the iris will be solidly rooted when the ground freezes. Don't put old rhizomes or diseased leaves in your compost.

Keep dahlias and gladiolus trimmed, clipping off spent flowers. Gladiolus can't be easily deadheaded, since the stalk opens flowers from the bottom up to the top. Remove faded individual flowers. The entire stem can be removed when all bloom is over.

When blooms fade on true lilies, cut them back to the first leaves below the old flower. The leaves will continue to build bulb strength for next year's bloom.

■ *Grass that is cut too short is prone to scorching and drying out.*

HERE'S HOW

TO AIR-LAYER HOUSEPLANTS

Air layering is a fun way to renew elderly plants with trunks, such as *Dracaena*, rubber plants (*Ficus elastica*), or large, overwhelming climbers, such as big-leaved *Monstera deliciosa* and others. The process is slow and somewhat unsightly, but if done when the plant is outdoors in summer, the new section should be rooted by fall.

1. Choose a spot below the healthy leafy section where you want roots to form. Here, you will be peeling away a bit of bark to induce rooting. Score the bark with a knife, all the way around the trunk, in two spots about an inch apart, and remove the bark between the scorings to girdle the stem.

2. Put rooting hormone on the newly exposed surface.

3. Wrap about 2 cups worth of moist sphagnum moss around the stem to cover the wound and the stem area above and below it. Loosely bind the moss with twine. Then cover it completely with a plastic bag to completely enclose the moss. Tie the bag on firmly with twine or electrical tape (keep the tape off the trunk).

4. When roots are visible, cut the stem off below the new roots.

5. Pot up the new plant, watering carefully. Place a stick to support it in the pot.

The old plant will often resprout from the roots if the trunk is cut off down to about 6 inches.

INDOOR PLANTS

Prune out any damaged leaves. Prune branches back to a natural growing point, just as you would for any outdoor plant. Tie up any tall philodendron or other vining plants such as *Hoya carnosa*. They sometimes grow heavy enough to fall away from their supports and break.

LAWNS

Do not attempt to aerate a dormant lawn on dry soils. Schedule this task for early September or once the rain returns.

Lawns grow more slowly in summer, and mowing can be less frequent. If you haven't already done so, raise the cutting height by ½ inch and keep mowing regularly to remove no more than one-third of the blade height.

PERENNIALS, GRASSES & FERNS

Deadhead daylilies (*Hemerocallis*) to prolong their beauty. It's easy to snap off the dead flowers; each only lasts a day. They will be surrounded by several more waiting their turn to open. When an entire stalk is finished blooming, cut it to the ground, leaving the foliage.

A few summer bloomers, such as hardy geraniums and catnip (*Nepeta* 'Six Hills Giant'), will set flowers again if sheared now. Cut off all blooms and leave 4 to 6 inches of foliage. Water well after trimming.

Tall plants such as delphinium may need staking or retying.

For lavender sachet and potpourri, the scented oils preserve best if flowers are gathered just as the buds show color, before they open.

ROSES

Be sure the soil hasn't become compacted around your roses. Use a spade fork to gently pierce and slightly lift the soil without breaking any roots. Follow up with some mulch if the ground is getting bare. Continue grooming the repeat-blooming roses, and remember to leave the rose hips on once-bloomers for winter display and wildlife benefits.

■ *Stake tall flowers to protect them from blowing over.*

■ *To remove spent blossoms, cut rose stems back to a sturdy point at a leaf node.*

SHRUBS

Remove dead, damaged, or diseased stems. Prune the offending stems all the way to the ground or where they attach to a larger stem. Thin out wild stems that grow out of bounds or opposite the main direction of shoot growth. Mid-summer is an optimal time to prune shrubs you wish to keep smaller in size, as fewer new shoots will be stimulated now than after pruning in early spring. The rule for pruning in summer is to keep it light: remove no more than one-quarter of the total leaf area at this time of year.

Prune or shear hedges and topiary as needed to maintain their shape and size. Do not prune back to bare wood at this time of year. Hedges with large shiny leaves have a nicer appearance when shaped with loppers and hand pruners to selectively remove longer shoots. It avoids shredding the leaves and often results in longer intervals before shaping is needed again. It also prevents the accumulation of a wall of thick branch stubs that become too thick for cutting with hedge trimmers—a common problem with English laurel and other large shrubs.

TREES

Do not tie ropes or chains around tree trunks; they can cause serious damage. Check staking on young trees and remove it as soon as the support is no longer needed.

Inspect and photograph your trees. Walk all the way around to look at all sides. Look from the tiptop branches to the ground. Are there any dead branches or changes in leaf appearance? Compare with previous photos. Regular inspections can catch problems before they become severe. If you need help, call an ISA Certified Arborist® or contact your local Cooperative Extension office.

Remove any sucker growth emerging from the roots or below a graft union. Very small sprouts are easily removed by rubbing them off by hand. Use hand pruners on thicker sprouts; make a clean cut at the point of attachment, and don't leave a stub.

Low branches that hang down into walkways can be pruned back to the main trunk or larger side branch.

To reduce crown height and width, remove the longest branches back to the next largest branch within the crown. Trees pruned this way won't need pruning as often to maintain their size or form. Always prune moderately in summer, removing no more than one-quarter of the live branches at this time.

VINES & GROUNDCOVERS

Check for weeds that may be disguised amid groundcover plants, as many weeds are quickly going to seed this month. Herb Robert and cranesbill geranium will turn a pale red as summer heat peaks, poised to shoot its maturing seeds to cling to overhead foliage until fall rains wash them to the ground. Top-dress groundcovers with a ¼-inch layer of fine compost to maintain organic matter and appearance. Use a gentle water spray to wash down any bits of mulch sticking to leaves.

Fading blooms can be cut back on carpet bugle (*Ajuga reptans*) to encourage new leaves and keep plants tidy.

Check ties and supports to make sure rapidly growing vines aren't being girdled. Continue with selective thinning and shortening to manage summer vine growth. With its compact habit and modest growth rate, climbing hydrangea (*Hydrangea anomala* ssp. *petiolaris*) has fewer pruning needs than other vines. Provide light pruning to shape and thin as needed immediately after bloom.

WATER

This is typically the warmest month throughout the region. Water may roll off the surface of dry ground before soaking in, especially in groundcovers and lawns growing on slopes. Check the soil to be sure the water is going where you want it. If runoff is a problem, apply the water at a slower rate. One method is to run the water just to the point before it starts to run off. Wait a short while for the water to soak in, and then run the water again. Many automatic systems and timers have a repeat cycle option for this purpose. Really dry soil can be "hydrophobic"—water just beads up and rolls off. Try dampening the surface first with a wetting agent to reduce the surface tension and allow water to break through. Commercial garden products are available, or try a few drops of dish soap in a watering can for a similar effect.

Thunderstorms east of the mountains (and very occasionally on the west side) can damage gardens with wind or hail and fail to provide sufficient rainfall. Check the soil before skipping irrigation after one of those showers.

ANNUALS

Check for drought stress on annuals. Even those established since spring may need some temporary shading during extra hot days. Very lightweight spun polyester row covers make for easy cover.

Because sun hitting the sides of containers can affect the roots within, containers may need watering once or twice a day due to the extra heat. Dark black plastic containers can absorb so much heat that it kills roots within the soil. Keep this type container out of direct sun exposure.

BULBS

Spring-blooming bulbs such as daffodils and tulips have reached summer dormancy and don't need moisture. Indeed, they suffer if watered through summer. Water dahlias, cannas, gladiolus, and begonias with a soaker hose system to keep foliage

and flowers dry and reduce the development of powdery mildew and other fungal diseases.

INDOOR PLANTS

Sprinkling the leaves of houseplants may help remove dust from the leaves, but it's not a substitute for careful watering of the soil. Houseplants in inland dry areas need special attention to watering from now through August. They can desiccate quickly on a hot afternoon, so make sure they are shielded from harsh sun exposure. Leaf scorch can happen in these conditions, even if plants are watered well.

LAWNS

Water carefully. Do not over-irrigate. Probe the soil with a trowel to determine how much water has penetrated.

Be sure to keep new sod and newly seeded areas watered throughout the summer until roots are strongly established. Check the corners and seams of sod particularly, because these sections can pull apart if too dry.

If you haven't checked your soil type, do so now. Sandy soils need more frequent watering for shorter periods, because they do not hold water well. Clay soils absorb water slowly, so water should be applied more slowly.

■ *In hot weather, containers may need water twice per day.*

Loam　　　**Clay soil**　　　**Sandy soil**

Clay and silt

Standard soil

Sand and gravel

Knowing the soil type will guide you to the appropriate watering methods.

To get a quick idea of your soil type, dig out about a cup of soil from the lawn area. Put it in a quart jar, and fill the jar with water, adding ½ teaspoon of dish soap. Cap the jar and shake it thoroughly. Let it sit for about a week. Coarse sands and gravels will fall to the bottom; silt and clay particles will settle on top. A heavy clay soil may require longer settling out. The result is a general sense of the balance of sand and gravel to clay in your soil. Organic bits such as fallen leaves will float on top.

PERENNIALS, GRASSES & FERNS

Water perennials to the root depth once a week or often enough to keep them from moisture stress. Random sprinkling or waving the hose about above plants doesn't offer much benefit.

Even plants that are notoriously water-wise are likely to suffer, stress out, and even die when they are newly planted or exposed to severe conditions in the hottest months of summer and don't get enough water.

Daylilies, especially the repeat-bloomers such as *Hemerocallis* 'Stella de Oro', produce better flowers with regular water. Daylilies require less water when not in bloom, though occasional moisture will help keep foliage green.

ROSES

Water slowly and deeply once per week so that moisture goes down 8 to 12 inches. When using soaker hoses, bubblers, or drip irrigation, gently

dig and check how deeply water has gone into the soil.

SHRUBS

Shrubs in containers can dry out quickly. If water is racing through the container without soaking into the soil, adding a few drops of dish soap to a watering can full of water will improve absorption. You may need to keep pouring water through the container until the soil has soaked it up. A saucer to hold excess water is helpful when watering smaller containers that have gotten too dry.

TREES

Established trees that are not routinely irrigated may benefit from a deep soaking midsummer in very warm years. Apply water slowly to moisten the area beneath the canopy at least 8 inches deep. Watering now can prevent later summer drought stress and early leaf drop.

Always probe the soil before watering. Trees in waterlogged soil will also wilt, as the oxygen-deprived roots are unable to take in water. If you find waterlogged soil that smells bad, correct soil drainage and/or irrigation applications.

FERTILIZE

ANNUALS

Fertilize seasonal containers twice a month with a low-nitrogen application.

If annuals in flowerbeds grow strongly, have good leaf color, and normal bloom, fertilize only once toward the end of the month. Never fertilize dry roots. If fertile mulch has been used, additional fertilizer may not be needed.

BULBS

Most summer-blooming bulbs benefit from fertilization once per year after planting. Dahlias need a boost in midsummer. Apply a 7-percent nitrogen product to moist soil. Kelp- and fish-based fertilizers supply nutrients gradually and contain trace elements plants require.

If you're growing lilies, dahlias, or caladiums in pots with annuals such as impatiens or with perennials, fertilize them as a group with moderate-nitrogen fertilizer.

INDOOR PLANTS

If plants take off on a growth spurt that will make them larger than you want in the house, reduce fertilizer to once a month.

LAWNS

Do not fertilize established lawns in July or August.

PERENNIALS, GRASSES & FERNS

No routine fertilizer applications at this time of year.

ROSES

Mid-July is the last time to fertilize roses. You do not need to fertilize once-bloomers, since they will have finished their bloom cycle. But hybrid teas, bush roses, and floribundas need this application to support the new blooms.

Fertilize roses in containers twice a month.

SHRUBS

No general fertilization is needed at this part of the growing season.

TREES

The slowly decomposing organic matter from coarse mulches, such as composted wood chips, leaf mold, or coarse compost, replenishes soil nutrients and improves soil moisture-holding capacity.

VINES & GROUNDCOVERS

Are vines growing before your eyes and lacking bloom? This is a common symptom of excess nutrients. Back off fertilizing this season and next. Has the growth been stunted, with small, yellow leaves? Fertilizer may help, but make sure there isn't another problem causing this stress, such as excess shade or waterlogged soil.

PROBLEM-SOLVE

Wasp activity can be more noticeable now, and it's a nuisance to gardeners who get too close to their nests (see August). Keep a water source year-round to encourage birds and predator insects—your garden allies in subduing aphids and other insect pests—to stick around.

Monitor soft fruits, such as raspberries, blueberries, grapes, and strawberries, for the spotted wing fruit fly (*Drosophila suzukii*), a recently introduced pest that feeds on fresh and just-ripening fruit. Contact your local Master Gardener clinic for more information on how to detect and manage this pest.

ANNUALS

Remove annuals with a severe silky gray covering of powdery mildew. It is difficult to control once strongly established, especially if plants are in damp or shady locations. Aphids bother plants less this month. Plants resist aphid damage better after midsummer, when shoots are sturdier and less succulent.

BULBS

Aphids may build up on lush, well-watered dahlias. Birds and predator insects feed on aphids, but you may also use insecticidal soap to subdue heavy infestations. Slugs subside in dry weather. However, they may continue feeding on your lilies and hostas in moist garden beds. There'll be less damage as leaves toughen up in late summer.

LAWNS

Hand dig weeds if your lawn is small enough to make this feasible. Spot spray persistent perennial weeds. However, do not use any garden herbicides when temperatures are above 85°F/29°C. The selective chemicals that target broadleaf weeds but not grasses work on weeds that are actively growing. Read pesticide labels carefully before spot spraying. If the weeds and lawn have turned brown, dig by hand.

PERENNIALS, GRASSES & FERNS

If disfiguring powdery mildew appears in midsummer every year, look for resistant replacements. "Resistant" means varieties that show less damage or get less severe symptoms. Planting in sunlight with good air circulation helps with managing powdery mildew. Prune out isolated affected leaves, and regularly wash the plant with water to keep lighter infestations in check.

Early blooming perennials disappear as they go dormant. You'll discover foliage dying back on jack-in-the-pulpit (*Arisaema*), true poppies (*Papaver orientale*), and on native and cultivated bleeding heart (*Dicentra* spp.). This is the normal pattern of their growth cycle.

Perennials may bloom more sparsely when stressed by hot, dry weather.

ROSES

Blackspot is more troublesome in cool, humid conditions. Clip off affected leaves or whole stems. Consider replacing chronically infested roses with more resistant varieties.

Spheres that are smooth or mossy-looking may appear on stems. This is likely from a gall wasp, a beneficial insect that has laid its egg there. Often about the size of a quarter, the spheres are a growth

■ *Consider replacing perennials that have chronic problems with powdery mildew with a more mildew-resistant plant.*

reaction from the plant. They can be left alone. Trim off the hosting stem if you wish and lay the cut piece elsewhere in the garden where the larvae inside can grow and emerge. These wasps aren't particularly damaging to roses, and they eat aphids and other undesirables.

Calligraphy patterns or spots of yellow that appear on green leaves may indicate a viral infection loosely called rose mosaic. There are no controls. Rose mosaic is not fatal and isn't spread to adjacent plants. Sometimes affected roses may grow poorly enough to require removal.

SHRUBS

Leaf scorch symptoms may appear on drought-stressed plants as leaf tips and margins turn brown. This can be a signal that a shade-loving plant is getting too much sun. Excess fertilization can cause leaf scorch symptoms, even when the soil is moist. Always check soil conditions before watering these plants, as they may need additional care beyond watering. Plants most likely to scorch include rhododendrons, skimmia, and hydrangeas. Scorch damage will remain on the plant until affected leaves are shed and replaced. Make a note to provide mulch and additional watering next season for plants with repeated drought stress.

Regarding root rots and wilts: conifers such as arborvitae (*Thuja* spp.) suffering from phytophthora root diseases will suddenly turn brown. Curled leaves and single wilted branches may appear on rhododendrons and other shrubs infected with phytophthora root rot. Verticillium wilt, more common to maples, can also clog up the vascular system of hardy fuchsia, rose, spirea, lilac, smoke bush, sumac, and viburnum. These two soil-borne diseases can be spread on bits of soil clinging to tools and shoes. Root-rot diseases are more severe on waterlogged, poorly drained soils, and where organic content is severely lacking. Once the symptoms appear, the plants are not treatable. Contact your local Master Gardener clinic or Cooperative Extension office for diagnosis and management for nearby plants.

Watch for signs of spider mites on arborvitae growing in hot sunny exposures: dusty, off-color foliage with tiny mites and visible webbing. Yellow stippling on Skimmia plants in shade is caused by citrus red mite. Washing down infested foliage with water spray helps suppress spider mites.

TREES

Bronze birch borer may be first noticed with dead branches high in the canopy. Raised channels and D-shaped exit holes are visible on the trunks of affected trees. Maintain good tree vigor with mulch and summer water. Choose alternate shade trees where this pest is prevalent, because it is difficult to treat. River birch (*Betula nigra*) is less susceptible than the smooth, white bark birch species.

Port Orford cedar (*Chamaecyparis lawsoniana*), arborvitae (*Thuja* spp.), and evergreens suffering from phytophthora root disease will suddenly turn olive and then brown in summer when they can no longer take up enough water to survive. This disease moves in surface water and is more severe on waterlogged, poorly drained soils. Once these symptoms appear, the plants are not treatable.

Another type of phytophthora, called sudden oak death for the trees it was first noted to kill, infects a broad range of trees and shrubs. It is fatal to some. Less-affected plants display dead lesions on the leaves, and they can become an infection source to more vulnerable plants. Nursery growers have developed active programs to limit the spread of sudden oak death.

Verticillium wilt on Japanese maple may show up with the abrupt wilt and death of leaves on one or several branches, or even the whole tree. Some trees may survive with it for many years. This soil-borne disease can be spread on bits of soil clinging to tools and shoes. Disinfect tools after each pruning cut where this disease is suspected. Best care practices for trees with mild symptoms are to provide coarse, organic mulch such as wood chips or leaf mold and to water deeply every two or three weeks during summer months. Do not fertilize.

August

The warm, dry weeks of August take on a more leisurely pace than that of early summer. Late-blooming perennials, shrubs, and even some trees color the garden this month. Overall, growth slows down as the days become a bit shorter and soil conditions are drier. In the waning weeks of summer, the wear and tear of the growing season shows up in worn edges and slightly duller hues in the foliage. Summer dormancy appears in the shades of tan on nonirrigated lawns; some garden perennials take a similar lower profile during dry times.

Plant energy now is focused more on maturing fruit and storage than on new growth. The sugars and other compounds produced in the leaves during photosynthesis accumulate in roots and other plant parts, to be held in reserve for the launch of new growth next spring. To promote good plant health and winter hardiness, gardeners should follow this cue in how we care for our plants at this time of year. Too much water or fertilizer can disrupt a plant's ability to harden growth in preparation for dormancy and winter conditions.

Amid August blooms, maturing fruit and seeds add late-season texture and color to the garden. Dahlias begin their peak period of display this month and next. Roses, hydrangea, veronica, hardy fuchsia, and passion vine continue to produce new flowers. There is much to harvest in cut flowers, herbs, vegetables, and small fruits this month.

Managing moisture is a large concern in August. With the exception of annuals, vegetables, and fruits, most garden plants can tolerate moderate drought stress better now than in the early part of the growing season. If irrigation water has been restricted, special attention should be given to trees and shrubs with symptoms of drought stress: wilting or inner leaves that yellow and drop. These plants should receive priority for a slow, deep soaking. Unlike lawns and garden perennials, they are not so easily replaced if weakened or lost to drought. For gardens that have received ample weekly irrigation all summer, the schedule should be tapered back during the last half of the month.

PLAN

This is a good time to assess the most drought-resilient plantings in your garden and make plans to provide mulch and early season irrigation where it will help, and to replace plants that repeatedly struggle by this time of year. Some specimens might be transplanted to a shadier or damper location in fall. Review where irrigation schedules and system design were inadequate, and plan for improvements for next year. Remove failed plants now, and mulch bare ground in preparation for future planting.

If it's time for significant changes, you may want to enlist some assistance. Look for classes on plant selection and design offered at local public gardens, conservation districts, nurseries, or Master Gardener programs. If you are thinking about hiring professional help, look for services with credentials and memberships in landscape and nursery organizations. Some nurseries have a design and installation division, as do "design-build" landscape services. Landscape architects and landscape designers typically provide a plan to be installed by others. Many services specialize

■ *Start planning for fall changes to the garden with a diagram of the layout and key features.*

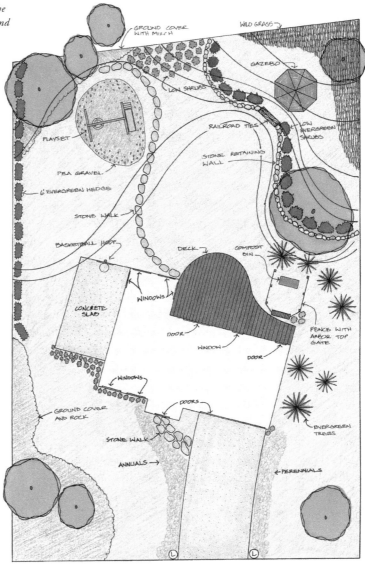

in specific landscape types, such as rain gardens, edible landscaping, habitat gardens, or drought-resilient designs. It's always helpful to interview more than one service and to ask for references in finding the right fit for your needs.

ANNUALS

Make note of which annuals did not do as well and why: were their color, shape, form, or perhaps location the problem? Visit display gardens and talk to professional gardeners to get ideas for late-season garden interest.

Check nurseries for seed sales. Scatter annual seed in late fall in zones 7 to 9, or in spring in zones 4 to 6.

BULBS

You can order spring-blooming bulbs from catalogs this month. While most companies take orders through October for zones 7 to 9, order now if you are in zones 4 to 6. Bulbs are shipped by planting dates for your hardiness zone. Consider some unusual summer bulbs, such as Peruvian lilies (*Alstroemeria*), foxtail lilies (*Eremurus* spp.), and wood sorrel (*Oxalis*), for next year.

INDOOR PLANTS

Repot houseplants that have outgrown their containers over summer. Dispose of unsatisfactory plants to make room for fresh choices or to give more space to your better plants. Nurseries may have sales on pots and potting soils this month.

LAWNS

After caring for the lawn all summer, your expectations for how much lawn you need may have changed. This is a good time of year to look at the eco-turf-style lawns planted with a blend of grass and broadleaf plants to get an idea of how they might work in your garden.

At one time, lawns were commonly cultivated in a blend with white clover. The clover fixes nitrogen and adds a darker green hue to the lawn. While we may have become convinced clover must be a weed, grass seed blends with dwarf micro-clover are again being sold alongside standard grass seed.

Grass and clover blends are making a comeback for their color and drought tolerance.

Carpeting groundcovers work well in place of turf around trees.

PERENNIALS, GRASSES & FERNS

August finds many gardens drought stressed and lacking in flowers. Take photos of cleverly designed, attractive gardens you see this month. Container plantings and late summer bloomers such as asters provide good sources for color and focal points. Ornamental warm season grasses such as *Miscanthus* and *Calamagrostis* shine with plumes of bloom not yet turned brown.

Make a list of important autumn tasks to prepare herbaceous perennial garden plants for winter and the next blooming season. Make notes of which plants to divide or move in September. Many perennials and grasses need to be divided every three or four years to stay vigorous and in scale with garden spaces.

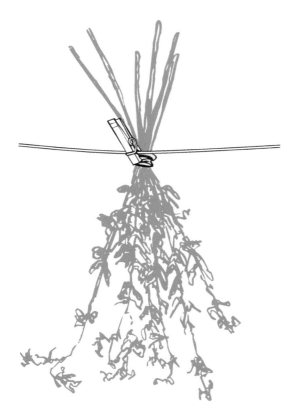

■ *Tie cut herbs and flowers in small bundles for drying.*

You can dry perennial flowers for bouquets: quaking grass (*Briza media*), globe thistle (*Echinops* spp.), statice (*Limonium* spp.), pincushion flower (*Scabiosa* spp.), strawflower (*Helichrysum bracteatum*), and yarrow (*Achillea* spp.) are among the flowers that preserve well if picked just as they show color. Select well-formed flowers, strip off all foliage, and bundle them for hanging upside down in a dark, dry place.

ROSES

Roses may bloom less this month, but many are getting ready for another round of bloom in September's cooler weather. Photograph and evaluate rose performance and display quality. Plan to remove and replace the poor performers. Giving up on a plant when it doesn't work makes space for one with better qualities.

Miniature roses combine smaller flowers with charming short stature. Well suited to containers, most hover between 18 inches and 3 feet, though some grow as tall as 4 feet. You can find the perfect shape of the hybrid tea rose or a fragrant floribunda bloom, but in a lovely, compact size.

Rose growers and breeders on the West Coast, especially Ralph Moore in California, produced some of the first miniature roses 50 years ago. Moore's 'Beauty Secret', a classic, warm rosy-red rose, received several American Rose Society awards of excellence. New miniatures appear yearly. They're among the easiest to grow, and you'll find them throughout the summer in nurseries.

SHRUBS

Green hues tire to dull khaki during these pre-autumn days. The best and worst of shrub performance is evident this month. Some plants experience a drought-induced dormancy in late summer. Repeated years of drought stress can weaken plants. Examine the soil. Provide a slow, deep watering to rehydrate roots. Cracked, dry soil conditions can be corrected with coarse organic mulches and early irrigation applications next season.

Go with the flow. Don't coax struggling plants into better shape. August is a good month to visit nurseries and look for better-adapted selections to plant in fall.

TREES

The term "shade tree" elicits thoughts of sultry summer days, soft breezes, and the cool cover of a green, rustling canopy overhead. Many of our favorite shade trees shift to lovely hues in fall before the leaves disappear for the winter. If you are longing for better shade by this time of summer, take a look at which kinds of trees in your area look good at this time of year. Planting deciduous shade trees on the southwest side of a house moderates the exposure to summer heat. Larger species, such as scarlet oak (*Quercus coccinea*) or European beech (*Fagus sylvatica*), might shade the whole side of a house, while those reaching 30 feet or less in height, such as paperbark maple (*Acer griseum*) or Amur maackia (*Maackia amurensis*), can serve as a cool natural umbrella over patios or entryways. Smaller-stature trees of 25 feet or less provide intimate shade for smaller garden spaces and are a must wherever power lines cross overhead. Amur maple (*Acer tataricum* subsp. *ginnala*) and American hornbeam (*Carpinus caroliniana*) are two hardy selections.

You can prepare the site now for fall tree planting. Clear away unwanted vegetation, turn the soil (if it's moist enough to dig), and cover a broad area with compost or mulch. After mulching, water thoroughly to support continued mulch decomposition and soil microbe activity. At planting time, rake mulch and compost away to expose the soil before digging the hole, then reuse it to mulch around the new tree.

VINES & GROUNDCOVERS

Survey shady corners where lawn has failed and plan to adjust the landscape for shade-adapted groundcovers. A carpet effect may be retained in damp shade with plants such as baby's tears (*Soleirolia soleirolii*) or Japanese spurge (*Pachysandra terminalis*). Include ferns for interest and function.

PLANT

This is one of the most difficult times of year to establish new plants. If you've picked up new nursery stock, keep the pots watered and store them in a cool, shady place until planting time. This is a good time to prepare the ground for early fall planting of woody plants, bulbs, ferns, grasses, perennials, and lawns. Remove dead or failing plants and weeds. Apply 4 to 6 inches of coarse mulch over the areas to be planted, and water thoroughly. By fall planting time, the soil will be easier to dig, weeds will be suppressed, and mulch will be in place for planting. Just rake mulch to the side to expose the soil to dig holes. Keep the mulch on the surface; don't mix it into the soil.

BULBS

Divide and replant German iris about every three years. Cut leaves back to 6 or 8 inches tall and reset the divisions in soil amended with fresh compost. Set the rhizomes just at soil level, not buried.

Zones 4 to 6: Iris need time to establish new roots before freezing weather. Divide and transplant

them by mid-August. Watch for new growth, and keep plants moist. Apply mulch to plantings in scorching, full sun. Special fall-blooming bulbs, such as *Colchicum speciosum* 'The Giant', 'Waterlily', or 'Album', deliver fresh energy to the fall garden. This is a fine garden plant that multiplies beautifully and is hardy to zone 4. (*Colchicum* is often referred to as autumn crocus, though it isn't really a crocus.) Plant them in sun to light shade where its foot-tall crop of spring leaves will be welcome. After several weeks, the leaves fade as the bulbs go dormant through the summer. Crocus-like blooms (but no leaves) emerge in early fall. It is very drought tolerant and naturalizes well in nonirrigated soil beneath large trees. A word of caution: this plant yields colchicine, a powerful, toxic drug present in all plant parts. It's not recommended for gardens with young children.

The fall-blooming *Crocus speciosus* shines clear blue and complements fallen yellow leaves from zones 4 through 9. Choose a spot with light shade or full sun and plant about 2 inches deep and 1 inch apart. Flowers pop up in late September, followed by leaves. Mulch them with 2 to 3 inches of compost.

INDOOR PLANTS

You can make new starts of plants such as philodendron, Swedish ivy, *Tradescantia*, spider plant, and strawberry begonia by layering their trailing stems and runners. Pick a long, healthy stem and pin it down firmly in a separate pot of soil with a piece of wire or old-fashioned hairpin. Keep it moist. Clip it loose from the parent plant in three to four weeks, after it has rooted. The "baby plants" that form at the ends of runners on spider plant and strawberry begonia can be started in a similar fashion or simply clipped off and planted in damp potting soil. Keep young starts well watered until roots fully establish.

LAWNS

Zones 4 to 6: August has poor conditions for any planting, especially in the inland high desert. If, however, you are able to water, seeding a lawn between August 15 and September 15 gives the best opportunity in the coldest areas to get it established before winter.

■ *Save dried seedpods of Siberian iris for dried floral arrangements.*

■ *Composting turns yard waste and even kitchen scraps into a valuable soil amendment.*

Zones 7 to 9: Overseed when temperatures cool down and morning dew returns for optimal germination with less applied water. This may be at the end of this month or not until September.

SHRUBS

Take more softwood cuttings this month, and check those you've started. Remove any that have mildewed or are shriveled. Remember to open plastic coverings periodically to vent moisture and bring fresh air to the cuttings.

TREES

This is the least advisable time for tree planting, but a good time to start shopping for fall planting season.

CARE

Look for weeds in flower or going to seed, and eliminate those first. Garden beds and lawns may be refreshed with a light topdressing of ¼-inch of damp compost. Give the areas you see and use most frequently higher priority for grooming. In less visible areas, do a little less grooming, and leave some patches of bare soil to maintain nesting and habitat sites for bumblebees and other native beneficial insects.

ANNUALS

Around August 1, loosely wrap expanding sunflower heads intended for harvest with cheesecloth to prevent squirrels and birds from nibbling seeds.

Continue to pinch off spent flowers. Cutting flowers for bouquets also helps keep plants such as zinnias, dahlias, and snapdragons blooming into September.

Weeds remain vigorous where irrigation has kept soil moist; keep scuffling the smallest ones and pulling the larger. Unchecked, they will be going to seed by August and spreading their nuisance offspring.

BULBS

Lily bulbs—Asiatic, Oriental, trumpets, and hybrids such as Orienpets—rely on the entire stem and foliage to generate growth for next season. When picking lilies for bouquets, guard bulb health by leaving at least two-thirds of the stem height intact. Check stakes on lilies and dahlias that may have become dislodged by wind. Deadhead spent blooms, a pleasant early morning task when the garden is still and cool.

Gladiolus will not produce additional flower stalks once finished. Remove spent stalks but keep the tall, green leaves.

Siberian iris produces intriguing stalks of seedpods that dry well and can add winter interest or be cut for dried arrangements.

INDOOR PLANTS

Yellowing leaves on lower parts of stems can be common toward summer's end. But yellowing leaves on new tip growth often signal root rot or other disease problems.

With vacations frequent in August, provisions for caring for container plants becomes a priority. The simplest and most obvious choice is finding a capable house and plant sitter.

Plants will manage for two to three days without care but need attention if you're away longer. Move plants away from bright windows for vacation mode. Nurseries sell capillary mat systems that water from the bottom; they're most easily used in a splash-proof area, such as a basement workshop. You may also find drip systems for indoor use. It's helpful to give these methods a trial period while you're still at home.

LAWNS

Mow as needed to maintain cutting only one-third of the grass blade height. Get lawnmower blades sharpened this month.

What conditions mean the lawn needs replacing? Taking out the lawn and replanting is a sufficiently big task that it's important to do it only when improving the lawn isn't possible with spot weeding, dethatching, aerating, and overseeding. Several years of neglect can result in a lawn outnumbered by weeds. Or construction damage during house remodeling or landscaping can kill

part of a lawn. Needing to replace a lawn because of diseases or insect damage is far less common. When preparing the seed or sod bed, make sure to remove roots of large perennial weeds such as dandelions. (See March for tips on installing a new lawn.) If garden irrigation is available, lawn replacement can be done starting in mid-August east of the Cascades to allow for good root establishment before winter. Mid-September is more ideal west of the Cascades.

If the presence of shade and competition from surface roots of trees is the source of poor performance, don't attempt to plant grass again. Stop watering. Cut any remaining grass close to the ground and apply up to 6 inches of mulch, such as wood chips or coarse compost, to prepare the area for fall planting with groundcover or a mix of ferns and woodland perennials. (See June for tips on "unplanting" a lawn, and September for tips on planting under large trees.)

PERENNIALS, GRASSES & FERNS

Lavender that's done blooming needs light shearing to remove flower stems. Though not as fragrant as last month, they still carry a fresh scent. Shear off about one-third of the outer foliage to shape and groom the plants. Do not cut back into older, woody branches.

Continue to deadhead coneflower, Shasta daisy, cosmos, and hardy geraniums. If you haven't sheared off flowers of garden mint (*Mentha* spp.) and catmint (*Nepeta faassenii*) cut them back now.

■ *Autumn crocus.*

■ *Deadhead spent flowers on perennials and garden herbs.*

The tattered foliage of plants such as daylilies (*Hemerocallis*) and lady's mantle (*Alchemilla mollis*) can be cut back now for a tidier appearance, or it can be allowed to remain. Some gardeners just remove the most unattractive leaves. As remaining old leaves decompose, they contribute to the life of the soil and its beneficial organisms. The old leaves will help provide some winter protection for marginally hardy perennials.

ROSES

Clean up any fallen leaves, especially those with disease problems. Do not add these to compost.

Deadhead flowers that finish this month, then let spent blooms mature into hips. Prune out any shoots (suckers) that emerge from below the graft. They usually have a different leaf shape; gardeners sometimes think, "My white rose turned red!" If not removed, sucker growth can overtake and weaken the top. For roses growing in their own roots, those new shoots are an asset, not a problem.

SHRUBS

Summer pruning can continue this month. Remove any branches that have reverted to solid green foliage on variegated or colored-leaved shrubs. If they are left, the whole plant may lose the fancy color or leaf shape. Prune lightly in summer: remove just a few problem stems and less than one-quarter of the total leaf area.

Watch for the occasional stem that drapes into walkways or grows out of bounds. If dead branches are numerous, pest problems or excess shade may be a culprit. Get the problem identified to deal with the source of the dieback.

TREES

Look closely at the largest trees on your property to monitor their general health and condition. Take pictures. If you notice unusual changes or problems, have them inspected by an ISA Certified Arborist® (see Resources).

Do not allow heavy vines to grow high up into trees where they can add weight and shade in the canopy. Always remove invasive species, such as English ivy, old man's beard, and kudzu. Heavier woody garden vines, such as *Wisteria* and *Actinidia*,

should be kept off trees. Also be sure to keep vines from blanketing lower trunks where they can hold in dampness and can conceal any developing problems at the root collar area.

Dead branches are easily spotted for removal in summer. Branches that hang down into walkways can be removed for overhead clearance. Prune these lower branches all the way back to the branch collar at the trunk for best effect. Keep pruning light.

VINES & GROUNDCOVERS

Tie up any loose vine stems. Prune groundcovers and vines as needed. Continue with monthly removal of long shoots on wisteria.

Softwood cuttings can be taken of kinnikinnick, sarcococca, ceanothus, jasmine, and grape.

WATER

Drought stress at the end of the season is typically less damaging than if it occurred in early summer. Some plants may simply go dormant earlier. Reduce the frequency of watering toward the end of the growing season to help plants harden off in preparation for fall and winter.

Soil that is not irrigated will be reaching its driest condition of the year and may become hydrophobic, a condition where water beads up and rolls off. Under these conditions, our usual watering techniques tend to be less effective than water delivered by gentle rains. If soil is dry, but the resident plants are coping, it may not be critical to water. To overcome hydrophobic conditions, apply water very slowly and in incremental stages. A wetting agent works wonders to break the surface tension—look for commercial products at garden centers or use several drops of mild dish soap in a large watering can for small areas.

If you have rain barrels, use the remaining water now, then drain and scrub out the barrels to remove algal deposits. Keep screening and rain barrel covers tight to prevent mosquitoes from laying eggs in them. Rain showers in late August may fill rain barrels again.

of the pot without reaching the roots within. If plants appear stressed, take them down once a week and immerse the containers to the rim in water—a wheelbarrow works well for this. Leave them for up to an hour. Check for water penetration to the center of the pot before hanging them back up.

INDOOR PLANTS

Some important reminders for watering indoor plants:

1. Apply water based on the requirements of the plant type—cactus and succulents get by with much less water than other houseplants.

2. What's the season? Plants need more water when in active growth and bloom.

3. Is the soil dry? Poke your finger in the soil about 1 inch down to find out.

4. Can excess water drain freely from the pot? Best practice is to water just to the point where some moisture emerges from the drainage hole. Keep a saucer or large old plate under each pot. Practice how much to apply so it will be caught in the saucer without it overflowing.

5. Don't let pots stand in excess water; constantly moist roots will rot. If plant pots sit in larger, decorative ceramic or plastic pots, make doubly sure water isn't accumulating in the bottom. Pots with attached deep saucers or self-watering pots can lead to excess wet conditions around roots and aren't the best options.

6. Water should be close to room temperature. Too cold or too hot can be hard on roots.

7. Type of water to use? Some indoor gardeners collect rainwater for their plants. Water straight from the tap is usually fine, except if the water is fluoridated or is alkaline or otherwise non-potable. Water with sodium fluoride added may lead to brown leaf tips on plants in the *Dracena* family (spider plant, dracaena, and lucky bamboo). Letting the water stand overnight will not reduce the sodium fluoride level or alkalinity, but using distilled water or rain water does solve this problem.

■ *Clean empty rain barrels and set them back up in anticipation of late summer showers.*

ANNUALS

These tender plants demand a continued supply of water. Check soaker hoses to be sure enough water is penetrating to the root depth. In hot, dry summers, distressed plants will reveal where the water system doesn't reach. Unfortunately, they often do that by dying. If annuals have turned brown, pull them out; they will not recover the way perennials might.

Containers and hanging baskets may need water twice a day in warmest weather. You may wish to move hanging baskets from hot, sunny spots to more shaded areas until weather moderates. Watch any July-planted starts for wilting during the day and provide some temporary shading (a bucket in the path of the sun or a wood shingle propped up) if they show stress.

BULBS

Keep summer-blooming bulbs watered. Give special attention to tuberous begonias in hanging baskets. Hang them where they'll receive gentle morning light and be protected from the hottest afternoon sun. In August, roots may completely fill the soil space and water may shoot down the sides

LAWNS

Fall rains help dormant grass revive but they can often be late in arriving. If you have not been watering weekly, be sure the lawn gets at least one deep watering this month to keep roots alive during the brown dormant period. Do not let turf go into extreme drought stress at the end of summer, which could cause roots to die. Watering in late afternoon or early evening helps more moisture reach roots without evaporative loss.

PERENNIALS, GRASSES & FERNS

Some fall-blooming plants, such as asters and chrysanthemums, won't develop good buds if they don't get enough water. Water any plants that were newly installed this year or have just been divided. In the herb garden, woody, gray-leaved herbs, such as lavender and rosemary, may need water only once every three weeks; soft-leaved herbs, such as mint, oregano, and catnip, need weekly watering. Most well-established ornamental grasses and ferns manage with less water. Brown leaves around their base are a sign of moisture stress.

ROSES

Keep blooming roses irrigated. Large mature roses that have finished their bloom and shrub roses such as *Rosa rugosa* may get by with one deep watering or none.

SHRUBS & TREES

Water woody plants less frequently toward the end of the growing season, but don't let them get too dry. Trees that have not received water all summer may show drought-stress symptoms: inner leaves yellow and drop as water supply becomes short, and early fall color may appear. Shrubs whose inner leaves turn yellow and drop are showing a similar drought-stress response. If drought gets severe, early fall color and total leaf drop can occur. A word of caution: these very same symptoms can show up when too much water drowns roots. Dig below the surface. If you find waterlogged soil that smells bad, soil drainage or irrigation applications probably need to be corrected.

FERTILIZE

Virtually no fertilization is called for this month, with the exception of a few specialized applications. Overall, plant growth needs to slow and harden in preparation for the end of the growing season and coming dormancy; extra fertilization may interfere with that process. Plants that are dry and stressed, including lawns, can be harmed by fertilizer application.

ANNUALS

Continue to fertilize blooming annuals in containers and hanging baskets every two weeks.

BULBS

Fertilize dahlias after watering. Too much nitrogen will retard or stop blooming. Use a half-strength of 5-percent nitrogen product only if plants show a need. Dahlias start their best bloom in August and continue until frost.

INDOOR PLANTS

Growth is slower now; scale back fertilization for most foliage plants. Fertilize cacti and succulents lightly from now through winter.

LAWNS

Don't fertilize during the height of summer. A very thin layer of fine, screened compost spread ¼-inch deep can be applied this month to refresh lawns and maintain organic matter.

Zones 7 to 9: West of the Cascades, soils trend toward the acidic side with a pH around 5. This is fine for most garden plants, and many lawn grasses can tolerate it as well. However, soil nutrients will be less available to grasses if the pH is too low. If you are planning to install a large new lawn in September, it is worth getting a soil test to check soil pH and get recommendations for potential lime additions. If needed, lime can be incorporated into the soil ahead of planting; it takes a while for lime to become effective. Do not apply lime and fertilizer at the same time. Soils east of the Cascades are naturally more alkaline and don't require lime.

■ *Refresh lawns with an evenly spread ¼-inch topdressing of screened compost.*

PERENNIALS, GRASSES & FERNS

Delphinium has high nutrient needs and may benefit from an application of a liquid 5-percent nitrogen fertilizer. Do not fertilize other perennials, grasses, or ferns.

ROSES

Fertilizer that was applied in mid- to late July will support September bloom. Do not fertilize this month.

SHRUBS, TREES, VINES & GROUNDCOVERS

No fertilization this month. Do maintain overall soil health and fertility with coarse compost or wood chip mulch, no more than 2 to 4 inches deep.

PROBLEM-SOLVE

Wasps and yellow jackets. Don't head for the wasp spray right away! These summer fliers can be a menace and hazard, but they are also one of the most beneficial insect predators. They differ from pollen-collecting bees that lazily buzz through the garden. Wasps are strong, fast flyers and are primarily meat eaters (aphid, whiteflies,

and caterpillars, besides the fare at your barbecue). They are more interested in their prey than people. One wasp can deliver repeated painful stings, unlike bees, which sting only once.

Do be careful gardening at this time of year. Before diving in to work on areas with thick growth, take a few minutes to study the area and look for flight activity. Wasps and yellow jackets are most active at the warmest, brightest periods of the day. If there is a nest, you will see a strong flight pattern to and from its location. The northern paper wasp and bald-faced hornet make a large, round, papery, hanging nest, while native yellow jackets and the German yellow jacket nest in the ground (watch where you step!). If you see a nest and

■ *Careful observation will tell you the difference between a wasp (left) and an ordinary bee (right). Both are beneficial in the garden, but wasps require a bit more wariness.*

can postpone the task until mid-winter, leave the colony to complete its summer life cycle and stay out of the area.

Commercial sprays advise to work after dark, but there may still be some "scouts" crawling over the nest. Proceed with great care, and consider calling professional help. In some situations, professionals use a vacuum to collect wasps from their nests for their medical use in allergy treatments.

Powdery mildew. The gray cover of powdery mildew may be thick on some shrubs, roses, and other garden plants by this time of year. Cool evenings and dry days increase the problem, as can excess nitrogen applications. For susceptible plants, the issue may be due to overcrowding and shaded conditions. For others, it's an end-of-season condition for which cleaning up and removing affected foliage is all that is needed.

Slugs. Slugs produce eggs most heavily in August and September. Almost perfectly round, the light tan eggs resemble small pearls of slow-release fertilizer granules. If you find a stack, under a log or some mulch, scoop up those bundles of 40 to 120 eggs and dispose of them anywhere but near the garden. Garden spiders and black ground beetles that roam that same territory include slug eggs in their diet and will do some of the work for you.

ANNUALS
Powdery mildew. This condition is often worse on annuals that have been overfertilized. Washing down leaves has been found to reduce or kill spores of most powdery mildew fungi, and frequent water sprays have been offered as one measure of control for annuals. Remove the most severely affected specimens.

BULBS
Thrips. These nearly invisible insects rasp gladiolus leaves and cause a stippled, even silvery appearance. They also deform the buds. Once symptoms appear, gladiolus can't be saved.

Viral problems. Lilies, dahlias, gladiolus, and other bulbs and herbaceous perennials suffer odd viral symptoms. Leaves may be streaked (lily streak virus) or mottled and marked with color.

Stunted growth is one of the most common and recognizable symptoms. A tall trumpet lily, destined to reach 6 feet, may stop at 1 foot if infected. Take a plant sample to a nursery or Master Gardener clinic for diagnosis. The only control is to remove the virus-infected plant from the garden. Since viruses do not survive outside of living tissue, you can plant new lilies and bulbs in the same locations next year.

Fungal botrytis. True lilies planted with poor air circulation may wither and appear covered in fine black powder. Clip off the diseased part and carefully slip it into a plastic bag to dispose of it and keep spores off the rest of the plant. Trim away encroaching vegetation to improve air circulation.

INDOOR PLANTS
Toxicity of houseplants can be a worry. Most houseplants may be only slightly toxic, producing limited symptoms when small quantities are eaten. Your local poison control center will have more specific information if you have a question about plants you grow. Common plants to avoid if potential plant chewing by household members or pets is a concern are: caladium, dieffenbachia, euphorbia (including poinsettias), schefflera, Jerusalem cherry (*Solanaceae* family), heart-leaf philodendron, and peace lily (*Spathiphyllum*).

While discomfort or symptoms from slight exposure to those plants may be minor, there are two common house and yard plants that could be fatal if ingested in small quantities and should be kept out of reach of animals and humans: castor bean (*Ricinus communis*) and oleander (*Nerium oleander*).

LAWNS
By the end of August, summer's difficulties show up as rampant weeds and considerate decline. Lawns can look pretty tired by this time of year. Whatever you plant, whether sod or seed, it will gradually evolve to consist of different grasses and texture than you started with. This change can still be green and attractive, but won't duplicate the groomed perfection of golf course turf.

Years of turf research at Oregon State University have given our region options for functional green lawns with modest water and fertilizer demands: innovative mixtures of grasses and broadleaf perennials, such as yarrow, strawberry clover, and English daisy. Sold as "Eco-Turf," "Fleur de Lawn," and other names, these blends resemble an all-grass lawn when mown. It's a different aesthetic for some, but also an opportunity to maintain lawn color and function through the summer with less maintenance.

For all lawn types, it pays to choose mixes best adapted to the location and the light conditions of your location. Kentucky bluegrass does not survive well west of the Cascades. Though it grows better as a pure lawn east of the Cascades, it requires lots of water and fertilizer. Blends with perennial rye and fescue are more drought-tolerant and adaptable to shade. West of the Cascades, cool-season grasses prevail: bentgrass, rye, and fine fescues. Dwarf micro-clover can be overseeded following fall dethatching or aeration to improve summer color and drought tolerance. Drought-tolerant lawn blends emphasize fescues, yarrow, and micro-clover. Local seed companies offer grass seed varieties and ecology blends well adapted for our region.

PERENNIALS, GRASSES & FERNS

Powdery mildew affects many perennials during periods of hot days and cooler nights, especially west of the Cascades. Since most will be winding down in their yearly growth cycle, treatment isn't necessary. Simply remove the old leaves from the garden.

Groom dead leaves from ornamental grasses that may have become drought stressed. Like lawn grasses, some may put on renewed growth next month.

SHRUBS

Camellias looking black and oily? Dark black, sooty mold on leaves signals an infestation of scale (camellia, holly, and maple scale) or aphids. The black mold grows on the sticky honeydew excreted by these sucking insects, and by itself it is not harmful. In dormant season, horticultural oil can be applied to smother aphid eggs and scale insects overwintering on the plants (see December). To improve appearance, heavy, sooty mold on evergreen foliage can be washed down with mild soapy water, though it's sometimes quite a scrub to get it off camellia leaves. Pruning out some of the affected branches can help improve air circulation on dense shrubs.

Leaves of tall Oregon grape (*Mahonia aquifolium*) commonly display the whitish patches of powdery mildew at this time of year. It is not usually extensive enough to cause serious damage, but can build up to problem levels in some locations. Mildew can be reduced by pruning earlier in the growing season to thin out crowded stems and improve air circulation. Remove fallen, infested leaves from around the plants.

Leaf edges of all species of Oregon grape may show leaf scorch, particularly after exposure to full sun, high heat, and dry soils. Old and damaged leaves will be shed and replaced over the next growing season. While *Mahonia* tolerate full sun, they prefer light shade.

TREES

Remove stakes from trees that were planted within the past year. Roots should be established into garden soil by now, and trees should stand on their own. Neglected old ties and stakes can cause serious trunk damage.

Wilt disease problems may continue to show up on deciduous and evergreen trees. (See "Problem-Solve" in July.)

Honeydew from aphids and scale feeding on birches, oak, maple, and other trees can result in black sooty mold on the plants below them. Insecticidal soap can be used for aphids and for the spider-like crawler stage of scale (you'll need a magnifier to see them). A dormant-season application of horticultural oil between December and March will help suppress these pests.

Branch dieback from borers and disease often shows up this month. Watch for symptoms of bronze birch borer, Dutch elm disease, Eastern filbert blight, and black locust borer. Drought-stressed trees are especially vulnerable.

Contact your local Master Gardener clinic or Cooperative Extension office for more information on suspected problems.

September

Change is in the air. A sweet dampness returns with cooler nights and morning dew—what a relief after the parched days of August. This is a productive time for gardening. Cool-season grasses and other plants put on a flush of new growth. Moisture is returning, and soil will still be warm enough to be pleasant to handle and to support root growth. Nurseries have good stock for fall planting season. Bulb orders arrive. Seasonal containers may be ready for a fall makeover. Enthusiasm for gardening is refreshed.

In warmer zones, weather can remain summer-like with warm temperatures and scant rainfall, but days are getting noticeably shorter. The autumn equinox (equal hours of daylight and dark) arrives around September 22. The changing light and cooler weather are seasonal signals for plants to shift into winter-season modes.

Old leaves, twigs, and seedpods drop to blanket the earth in a cover of natural mulch. Left in place, this plant debris will provide vital overwintering habitat for predatory insects and beneficial fungi. A wealth of nutrients and organic matter cycle back into the soil as plant debris decompose, nourishing root growth. While a common reaction may be to scour garden beds clean of fallen leaves and twigs, this practice goes against the cycle of the season. We do better to keep as much natural debris in place as possible and to compost the excess for later use.

Spider webs glistening with morning dew are an early marker the season is changing. Walking into one may be an unwelcome surprise, but we should really rejoice with their appearance. Spiders do some pretty serious work in pest control. They are more noticeable at this time of year when they are on the move in search of mates. Some species catch prey in finely crafted webs; others roam about in search of insects, other spiders, and even slug eggs to feast on. Despite many people's fears, spiders are largely harmless to humans. An estimated 25 different species of spiders are likely to be found in the average insecticide-free yard in our region.

SEPTEMBER

PLAN

This is a good time to think about rearranging shrubs for better performance. Notice the microclimate effects in your garden to help choose more favorable conditions for struggling plants. As the landscape changes over time, some plants may no longer grow as well as they once did. Sun-loving plants grow thin under decreasing light as young shade trees planted with them grow larger; full sun has evolved to partial shade. Likewise, the loss of a large tree or the removal of a tall wooden fence can suddenly expose plants growing comfortably in shade to more sun than they can handle. If such plants haven't recovered after the second growing season, they may need to be moved or removed. Also look at adjusting the spacing of plants that are too crowded or too far apart. Take new pictures of the areas you want to improve for reference while shopping for new plants.

ANNUALS

As summer annuals finish, consider fresh seasonal color with pansies, violas, and annual chrysanthemums. If you have perennial asters coming into bloom, or beautiful dark dahlia foliage, take flowers and leaves with you to shop for good colors to echo them.

■ *When shopping for fall annuals, consider color combinations that will complement plants, such as fall-blooming perennial aster, that you may have in your garden.*

BULBS

September is such a busy season for bulbs, it might as well be spring! Nurseries stock plenty of bulbs. Choose nice, plump bulbs free of any fungus for best blooms: the larger the bulb, the larger the bloom. If you are shopping on a hot day, keep the bulbs as cool as if they were a carton of eggs. Don't leave them in a hot car.

Tulips and daffodils can develop blue mold if left in warm, enclosed environments (such as plastic bags). Store them in brown paper or mesh bags in a cool, dry spot close to 60°F/15°C until planting time. Don't refrigerate or store them with fruit, which releases ethylene that can damage embryonic flowers.

INDOOR PLANTS

If you are moving, check with the Department of Agriculture to determine if live plants can be moved across the border. Moving companies seldom take plants. The best option is to winnow the collection to a few treasures that can be boxed up and carried via your own transportation. Water well and wrap the plants in brown paper for protection. You might also start cuttings of personal heritage plants months before departure, so you can take the small descendant with you.

PERENNIALS, GRASSES & FERNS

If a plant doesn't prove suitable to your garden or a given location after two or three years because of size or flower color, make a change now during fall garden cleanup. Find a new location in your garden, or share and trade with friends.

LAWNS

This is a good time to refresh, renew, or replace your lawn. Revitalize it where it adds visual value and function, and replace it with alternative plantings where it doesn't work. Consider renovating when unsightly weeds occupy more than 33 percent of the lawn, when thatch is over 2 inches deep, or when extensive areas show damage due to other problems. Opt for alternative landscape plantings in excessively shady or wet areas, in heavily trafficked areas, and on steep slopes.

HERE'S HOW

TO IDENTIFY GARDEN BULBS

Bulbs, corms, tubers, and rhizomes originate in many different parts of the world and thrive in different types of garden conditions. They are linked by an odd but practical reality: each are large, fleshy structures that can be dug up and moved around or stored without dying. We couldn't take a rooted plant such as a daisy out of the ground and expect it to survive sitting on a shelf for a while. But because bulbs have stored energy in their flesh, they can live out of the ground for several months while being stored or shipped.

Gardeners take a verbal shortcut by calling all of these plants "bulbs," but they each have different botanic form and names.

True bulbs. Tulips, lilies, hyacinths, daffodils, onion. True bulbs have distinct fleshy layers surrounding a central plant embryo. Small bulblets form along the outside of the base.

Corms. Crocosmia, crocus, gladiolus. Corms are firm and solid without layers. Pointed shoots sit at the top of the mature corm. They multiply quickly, with small corms (cormels) developing around the base of mature corms.

Tubers. Dahlia, sweet potato vine (*Ipomoea* spp.), cyclamen, tuberous begonias. Tubers are thickened sections of root tissue, with shoot buds (eyes) at one end. Cyclamen and tuberous begonias grow from round, somewhat flattened tuber structures that sit barely underground.

Rhizomes. Iris, cannas. Rhizomes are modified fleshy stems that lay flat along the ground. Rhizomes multiply into dense masses that can require periodic division.

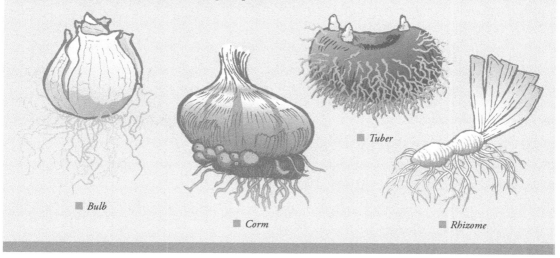

■ *Bulb*

■ *Corm*

■ *Tuber*

■ *Rhizome*

SHRUBS

Shrubs offer year-round structure and interest. Review locations for fall and winter interest. Oakleaf hydrangea offers stunning colors at the foot of an evergreen backdrop. Beautyberry (*Callicarpa bodinieri* var. *giraldii* 'Profusion') has brilliant purple berries and golden-to-purple fall color. Stunning fall color is found among deciduous viburnum. Choose shrubs with colorful berries for visual affect and to add wildlife value. Also consider placement of shrubs for winter interest in the locations you pass daily or are most visible from inside views.

TREES

In arid zones, it is wise to choose the most drought-adapted tree species for long-term display and benefits. Look to the predominant native and garden trees that thrive in your area as indicators for choosing species with similar adaptations. Some highly ornamental, drought-tolerant species hardy to zone 5 include evergreen Chinese juniper (*Juniperus chinensis*) and limber pine (*Pinus flexilis*); summer-blooming Idaho locust (*Robinia × ambigua* 'Idahoensis') and Japanese pagoda tree (*Styphnolobium japonicum*); specimen shade trees European hornbeam (*Carpinus betulus*) and silver linden (*Tilia tomentosa*); early blooming Cornelian cherry dogwood (*Cornus mas*) for smaller garden spaces; and Persian parrotia (*Parrotia persica*) and sourwood (*Oxydendrum arboreum*), with brilliant fall color. Many of these flowering trees are also attractive to bees and other pollinators.

Good soil management to improve moisture-holding capacity is equally important. Even a drought-tolerant species will struggle on heavily compacted soil. Plan to thoroughly prepare problem soils weeks before planting. Turn compacted soils and add modest amounts of organic matter to surface layers as needed. (See the Introduction for more soil-preparation information.) At a minimum, maintaining coarse, organic mulches over droughty soils will improve the moisture-holding capacity.

VINES & GROUNDCOVERS

The Pacific Northwest hosts many native groundcover plants that make for excellent companion plantings under trees and shrubs. Many of these have been exported as garden plants for other regions of the world. Browse the native plant sections in local nurseries for native ferns, kinnikinnick (*Arctostaphylos uva-ursi*), woodland and coast strawberry (*Fragaria vesca, F. chiloensis*), low Oregon grape (*Mahonia repens, M. nervosa*), false lily-of-the-valley (*Maianthemum dilatatum*), fringe cup (*Tellima grandiflora*), prostrate juniper (*Juniperus communis* var. *montana*), and others.

■ *Persian parrotia is a drought-tolerant tree.* Parrotia 'Vanessa' and 'Ruby Vase' have a narrower form.

PLANT

Roots add new growth while soil remains warm and moist, which is one reason why fall is a good time for planting trees, shrubs, cover-crop seed, and bulbs.

Plant cover crops to protect soil over winter in a temporarily vacant flower or vegetable bed, future lawn or landscape areas, or bare ground around a home under construction. Sown in September, a cover crop will protect the soil, enrich the ground, and crowd out weeds. Sometimes called "green manure," these plants can be turned into the soil just before they go to seed. Let the ground rest for several weeks to allow for decomposition before replanting.

Crops in the legume family, such as crimson clover, vetch, and field peas, fix nitrogen in the soil. They can all be planted from mid-August through mid-October (through mid-September in zones 4 to 6).

ANNUALS

Fall- and winter-blooming annuals go into the ground or seasonal containers this month. Chrysanthemums will billow into nurseries with many different colors. Plan to install them this month for best performance. Pansies come in dozens of attractive colors, from white through pinks, true blues, even almost black. They last well through the winter in zones 7 to 9. In zones 5 to 6, they offer color in early fall, but are killed by heavy frost.

BULBS

If you marked tulips or daffodils to be dug up and replanted, you can do that now and plant them along with any new bulbs.

Zones 4 to 6: Plant spring bulbs this month— snowdrops, crocus, daffodils, tulips, hyacinths, allium, and lilies. They need time to initiate root growth before the ground freezes. As bulb expert Brent Heath observes, "Once roots are initiated, the bulb's cellular walls join in, becoming more elastic and resistant to freezing." It's wise to plant early in the month.

INDOOR PLANTS

No one container material is necessarily better than another; drainage is the single most vital need. If you've chosen a container without drainage holes, consider drilling about three holes in the bottom. Or set a smaller pot with drainage holes inside the larger decorative container. Also look for attractive saucers to set under them. Old dinner plates with nice patterns recycle well for this purpose.

Plastic containers come in many forms and colors; some are a close mimic to clay pots. Their advantages are lightness of weight, variety, and lower cost. Soil in plastic pots may not dry out as quickly as in terracotta clay.

Wood containers may be natural or painted. Its rustic appearance is more ideal to a porch or balcony, but remember that wood gets heavy when wet. Wood is slightly porous to air and water and eventually suffers slow disintegration.

Foam and composite containers, made of new, lightweight materials, some including recycled content, offer endless forms, textures, and colors. Some mimic ceramic, stone, concrete, and even wood. Because they are molded, these containers can copy just about anything the maker chooses. They excel in being lightweight and in holding water well. Most are sold without the drain holes punched through, but be sure to do that before use.

Pottery, including beautiful stoneware and clay pots, can add strong accents to décor. High-fired stoneware is nearly indestructible unless dropped; clay and terracotta pots may be either quite soft and breakable or more durable. Air and moisture move through soft clay pots, and they may need watering more often than plastic or foam. Many people love the classic look of terracotta pots. White deposits from salts in fertilizer may accumulate on their sides, but can be wiped off. Clay pots should be scrubbed clean of deposits when plants are repotted. After a time, clay pots develop a natural patina.

LAWNS

Using either seed or sod, follow these dates for planting:

- Zones 4 to 6: Plant new lawns between August 15 and September 15. Weather may turn to sudden freezes after September 15, halting growth of new grass.

HERE'S HOW

TO PLANT BULBS

Depth: Two to three times the height of the bulb, measured top to bottom.

Soil: Well-drained soil is vital. Amend sandy or gravelly soil with compost. If you have heavy clay, bulbs may do better in pots or raised beds. Optimal soil temperatures for planting bulbs are no warmer than 60°F/15°C. For best effect, most bulbs should be planted in clumps.

Fertilizer: The plump, fleshy bulb tissues contain energy stores for next season's growth. Bulbs don't require fertilizer at planting. Plan to fertilize in spring when blooms fade and leaves are still green (see May).

Mulch: After planting, cover with lightweight, coarse mulch. Fully composted leaves or other coarse compost are good choices, as well as 2 to 3 inches of pine needles (pine straw). These materials also serve as a slow-release nutrient source.

Water: Water new plantings in well if soaking rains are not imminent.

Containers: In zones 4 to 6, use large plastic containers for spring bulbs; a nursery pot about 15 inches deep and 12 inches across is a good size for 8 to 10 daffodils or medium tulips. Plant early and sink the container into soil to protect it from freezing while roots form. Mulch the container. For zones 7 to 9, use containers 3 gallons or larger for enough soil volume to protect roots during cold spells.

- Zones 7 to 9: Plant between September 1 and October 15. Cooler, darker weather after mid-October inhibits germination and development.

If you aerate or dethatch now, overseed with lawn mixture developed for your region, type of use, and sun exposure. Perennial ryegrass is a good choice for areas that will get traffic, such as play areas. Be sure to water newly seeded areas regularly if fall rains stay away. (See March for details on planting new lawns.)

PERENNIALS, GRASSES & FERNS

Install new plants between now and early October in colder zones, about four weeks before hard freezes; through mid-November is a good target for zones 7 to 9. Soil conditions may remain dry this month. After digging the planting hole, presoak it before planting by filling it with water and allowing it to drain. This presoaking assures the plants will have damp soil around their roots after planting: it can be difficult to get water to soak through the planting hole if just watering from above. Set stakes to mark less visible plant crowns to avoid disturbing them during other garden activities.

Many garden perennials and ornamental grasses establish and naturalize well without the need for regular dividing. Keep an eye out for crowded clumps, diminished bloom, or for plants that have gotten too broad for their space. On average, you shouldn't need to divide a perennial or ornamental grass more than every three or four years. Ferns that have grown into massive clumps with multiple crowns can be dug up and separated for replanting. Spring division works for all zones in our region, but some plants are better done in fall.

Herbaceous garden peonies—the kind with leaves that die down in winter—do best planted and divided in September and October. Garden peonies are long lived and can be left undisturbed for decades. Divide only if you need the space or want extra plants. Wait for a cool fall day when the ground is damp and the foliage has begun to die

down. Use a garden fork to carefully lift the roots from the soil. You'll have a tangle of heavy, thick, fleshy roots slightly smaller than the diameter of a garden hose. Wash dirt from the roots, then use the serrated side of a hori-hori soil knife to cut the clump into sections with three to five "eyes"— the spots where the foliage arose. Protect peony divisions from the sun.

Peonies grow best in rich, humus soil. Amend the planting area with compost, if needed. Plant the roots with the eyes 1 to 2 inches below ground, no deeper: they will not bloom well if planted too deep. Space them about 1 foot apart. Mulch around the plants but only lightly over the top. Do not fertilize at this time. Division may retard bloom, so don't be concerned if the peony doesn't bloom the first season.

Tree peonies (*Paeonia suffruticosa*) have woody stems and are shrubs, with a different growth habit from their herbaceous perennial kin. They can also be planted in fall.

ROSES

Zones 4 to 6: Sink roses in nursery pots into the ground and cover with a light, fluffy mulch, such as pine needles. Keep mulch away from the trunk.

Zones 7 to 9: Rose cuttings may be started this month, following directions listed under July.

SHRUBS

Install plants from nursery containers now. If transplanting, wait for deciduous plants to lose their leaves first. Evergreens may be transplanted starting now through late winter. Be sure the ground has been well watered before planting.

Softwood cuttings can still be made on several shrubs: strawberry tree, aucuba, camellia, holly, and yew.

TREES

Fall planting allows time for new roots to grow before top growth begins next spring. These plants have lower irrigation requirements as they become established during their first summer.

■ *Fall is a great time to plant trees.*

Drought-tolerant species benefit from fall planting and will still need summer water their first two or three years in the ground. Remember to water deeply and mulch at planting.

CARE

In the most northern parts of the Pacific Northwest, diminishing light can be a frustration; some adventurous gardeners have resorted to head lamps (like those used for camping) to extend the gardening day.

The seedheads from many annuals, perennials, and ornamental grasses that gardeners often whisk away as they tidy up the garden may actually have more function left in them. Consider keeping more of them in place. In addition to being a great food source for many birds, the seedheads of globe

thistle, Pacific coast iris, and others add interesting texture and pattern through the dormant season.

Refresh mulch to cover any patches of bare soil in garden beds.

ANNUALS
Select the tender geraniums, fuchsia, and begonias you wish preserve over winter. They can stay outside until October, but trim off any damaged or very long stems now. Allow the final blooms of zinnias and other annuals to go to seed for future plants and wildlife value.

Zones 7 to 9: Continue to harvest flowers from cutting gardens and to deadhead annuals still in active bloom. You'll notice renewed bloom on plants cut back in July. Sweet alyssum often puts on a flush of new growth about the same time lawns perk up. Trim back any dried stem ends to allow for the fresh flush of leaves and bloom.

BULBS
Keep dahlias picked as they continue to bloom. They will offer cut flowers until knocked back by frost.

■ *Many perennials and ornamental grasses can provide seeds or winter protection for birds.*

HERE'S HOW

TO PLANT GROUNDCOVERS & COMPANION PLANTS UNDER LARGE TREES

The shady, root-laden area under large trees tends to become a barren zone as lawn grasses and other plants fail to thrive under the shade and root competition. Attempts to encourage better growth by pruning the trees and adding more water are rarely effective solutions in the long run, and may even harm tree health.

The good news is that there are several types of groundcovers and companion plants well adapted to grow with trees. Think about the kinds of plants that would naturally grow in woodland environments. Drought-tolerant sword fern (*Polystichum munitum*), wood rush (*Luzula* spp.), low Oregon grape (*Mahonia nervosa*), Oregon wood sorrel (*Oxalis oregana*), and inside-out flower (*Vancouveria hexandra*) are rugged selections that can be grown in combination beneath large conifers or deciduous trees. Complement them with naturalizing bulbs, such as snowdrops, daffodils, scilla, and grape hyacinth. For a carpeting effect, plant low-profile, spreading groundcovers, such as *Euonymus fortunei* 'Kewensis', Japanese spurge, or barren strawberry (*Waldsteinia fragarioides*). Selections of *Geranium sanguineum*, creeping comfrey (*Symphytum grandiflorum*), and *Epimedium* offer good foliage cover and flowers.

Stay away from garden plants that require annual digging and cultivation, or that require high fertility and moisture. Don't add or remove soil under trees, as grade changes can harm roots. Consult with an ISA Certified Arborist® beforehand if grade changes are planned near large trees.

PLANTING TIPS:

- Take advantage of fall-season planting benefits when adding new plants near large trees.

- Keep digging and planting activities to a minimum to avoid disturbing large and small roots. Don't try to turn or rototill soil under trees. Don't dig trenches or add new underground irrigation lines close to trees. Use no-till soil preparation methods before planting.

- Cover the area to be planted with coarse mulch, such as shredded leaves, leaf mold, or wood chips. Do not bury the trunk or buttress area. Use plants from 6-inch to 1-gallon containers to minimize digging and disturbance where there are dense tree roots.

- Do not try to plant right next to tree trunks; it's bad for the trees and the new plants. Stay a few feet away—the larger the tree, the farther out. Use spreading groundcovers that will fill in on their own. Position larger-growing plants near the outer edge of the canopy for better light and fewer tree root conflicts.

Soaker hose or emitter tubing provide the most efficient ways to get water to new plants without overwatering the trees. Don't allow irrigation spray to repeatedly wet tree bark: it's an invitation to basal trunk rot.

TO SAVE SEEDS

You can easily save seeds from many types of annuals and biennials. Some can be left to self-sow in the garden. Sweet alyssum, forget-me-not, and parsley are good candidates. Collect brown seed heads from hollyhock, zinnias, marigolds, cleome, nigella, and others. Make labels to keep with the seeds. Shake or pull out seeds and spread them on a paper towel to dry for about 10 days. You can also tie short stems together and hang them upside down in a paper lunch bag to dry, and then use the bag to store seeds that have been shaken free of their pods. Keep seeds in a cool, dry spot (heat and humidity are the enemies of stored seed). Seed in envelopes store better in closed jars or in plastic kitchen containers with tight lids. You might slip in a small amount of powdered milk in a twist of paper or a small packet of silica to help manage humidity.

Seeds from hybrid plants such as Zinnia Profusion series or *Coleus* 'Merlot' will produce different-looking plants. A hybrid plant has two different parent plants that contribute characteristics to the offspring: that same combination of parent plants has to be repeated to get the same plant again. Plant breeders select the best-desired characteristics for beauty, pest resistance, or fruit production when making these crosses. When flowers are open-pollinated in the garden, new parentage combinations occur, and as a result you may get perfectly lovely, but different, flowers.

Standard plants, such as species cosmos, columbine, or California poppy, will produce consistent seed year after year, and they often self-sow in the garden, where they will germinate for the next growing season.

Amaryllis foliage begins to yellow slightly toward fall. Bring them indoors this month. Store them in a dark, dry spot at room temperature, laying the pot on its side. Stop watering and allow the foliage to brown. Leave it for 10 to 12 weeks without water or attention before bringing it back out for forcing in December.

INDOOR PLANTS

Bring houseplants back inside before night temperatures drop below 50°F/10°C. For zones 4 to 6, this could be the first week of September. Tender plants can come back inside toward the end of the month in zones 7 to 9.

Prune back any plants that have gotten too tall. As for all ornamental plants, selective removal of entire stems will maintain the natural form and overly dense growth at branch tips. Plants pruned in September seldom add much growth over winter.

Mid-September is the time to start forcing poinsettias for December or January color. It's a challenge some gardeners find inviting. Poinsettias require 14 hours of complete darkness per night and bright light for 10 hours; they will need a designated space where they can get these conditions without any interruption to either light cycle. Nurseries manage this by setting timers and using dark cloth that slides over plant benches.

LAWNS

Lawns bothered by red thread, slow drainage, and thin growth are good candidates for core aerating. You can hire a service or rent a machine to do this. Coring is most effective on damp soil, so be sure to water a few times before aerating, or choose a time when a few good rains have moistened the ground. Aerating allows air and water to move more easily through aerated soil and creates stronger grass roots. Remember to overseed this month after dethatching or core aerating.

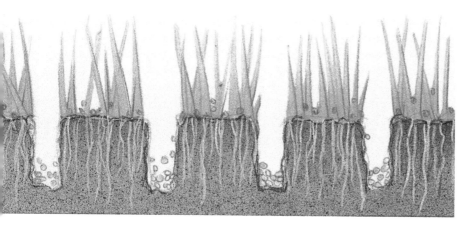

■ *During September, you can do all the lawn care chores that were possible during April and May. This is an ideal month for proactive lawn care, such as core aeration.*

PERENNIALS, GRASSES & FERNS

Many perennials and ornamental grasses can provide seeds or winter protection for birds. Dahlias, and all the composite flowers including daisies, cosmos, coneflowers, yarrow, and asters, are just a few to consider.

Remove seedheads from any grasses known to be at all invasive, such as Mexican feather grass (*Stipa tenuissima*).

In the coldest zones, dead leaves provide winter protection; keep them in place and supplement with additional mulch. In warmer zones, many gardeners prefer to cut dead foliage away for a neater appearance, but it is not essential. Mulch should be added to help protect plant crowns over winter. In all zones, dispose of diseased foliage.

Zones 4 to 6: Daylilies begin to go dormant. Trim foliage back, and cover with mulch for winter.

ROSES

Check rose cuttings: those taken eight weeks ago should have roots by now. A gentle tug will let you know if the cuttings have rooted. In zones 5 to 6, prepare a sheltered spot to store rooted cuttings over winter. A cold frame or cool greenhouse where plants won't freeze is ideal. Or sink the pot into the ground in a protected site and cover with pine needles or other loose mulch when the rose leaves

drop. Next spring, bring them back out gradually, and keep the cuttings in their pots until the roots are strongly developed.

Zones 7 to 9: Stop pruning spent blooms on roses to help promote dormancy.

SHRUBS

Pruning efforts should be minimal this time of year. Prune only to take care of the occasional errant branch that blocks a walkway or window. Wait until later, January or February, to begin dormant pruning.

It is not necessary to prune all shrubs at planting time, but do remove any branches that are weak, dead, or broken.

Zones 4 to 6: Get containerized shrubs ready to bring under winter protection before the first frost.

TREES

Remove staking from young trees as soon as they can support themselves.

Cut heavy vines out of trees.

Avoid pruning large limbs from deciduous trees just before they go dormant. Do remove dead or broken limbs as needed.

Do a final pruning of long whips from wisteria.

VINES & GROUNDCOVERS

Do a final pruning of long whips from wisteria. Prune other vines lightly this month. Excessive or messy shoots can be partially clipped back to keep them in bounds and from blowing about during winter.

Zones 4 to 6: Prepare tender potted vines for overwintering. Water about half as often to encourage hardening off and dormancy. Remove dead leaves. Tie stems together for easier handling and storage.

WATER

Fall rains may not arrive until late in the month. Though irrigation should be tapered off at this time of year, do water enough to avoid severe drought stress. Continue to water containers, as they are not likely to get enough moisture from early rains.

BULBS

Keep new plantings of spring-blooming bulbs watered, because they cannot root in dry soil. If roots begin growth and then dry out, bulbs can be damaged or killed. Maintain water for dahlia and gladiolus still in bloom.

INDOOR PLANTS

Reduce watering frequency as plant growth slows this month. Water when soil starts to get dry, not just by the day of the week.

LAWNS

All lawns may need some water during September if weather stays warm and dry. Keep new sod and newly seeded lawns irrigated if rain is insufficient. Reduce the frequency for lawns that have been irrigated all summer. Brown, dormant lawns may need just enough water to keep root crowns alive.

ROSES, PERENNIALS, GRASSES, FERNS, SHRUBS, VINES & GROUNDCOVERS

Non-irrigated areas are usually their driest at this point in the growing season, and it will take some time for seasonal rains to fully wet the ground again. Established evergreen and deciduous shrubs, as well as perennials, will benefit from a good soaking if they have been drought stressed. Plants that are well hydrated going into winter will be more resilient against cold damage.

Newly installed plants should be checked at least once a week for watering until rainfall is sufficient to keep the ground moist.

TREES

Water recently planted trees. Check the original rootball soil, as it may dry out more quickly than the surrounding native soil. Water any trees that have become extremely dry so their roots are recharged with moisture before winter dormancy. Established trees that received some irrigation over summer should not need supplemental water unless conditions remain very warm and dry.

FERTILIZE

As the growing season winds down, so should applications of fertilizer for most garden plants. Landscape plants kept in lush growth late in the season miss the opportunity to harden off and produce protective compounds to carry them into dormancy.

ANNUALS

For containers and hanging baskets still in active bloom, you can provide one application early in the month. Don't apply for plantings that will be removed soon.

BULBS

Top-dress established bulb plantings with compost and/or coarse organic mulch to maintain soil structure and fertility.

INDOOR PLANTS

Fertilize once this month.

LAWNS

Grass goes through a growth spurt with the cooler, damper weather. Fertilization will boost blade and root density before winter and promote good vigor for next season. Dense lawns are less open to dense weeds or moss. Choose products with at least half of the available nitrogen in slow-release form. Nitrogen is the most important element, so choose formulations with lower or no phosphorus. Drop spreaders are most efficient at delivering an even application directly where it's needed: make two passes in opposite directions for an even application. Avoid fertilizing right before heavy rain, and don't be tempted to apply more than recommended. It is likely to leach away without being absorbed by roots, contributing to runoff pollution.

■ *Drop spreaders avoid "overspray" problems. Only apply fertilizer to moist ground or it will burn the lawn.*

Phosphate-free fertilizers are a good choice for fall lawn care.

A light application in early September is usually sufficient: one pound of actual nitrogen per 1,000 square feet. If you've been grass-cycling (mulch mowing) and the lawn is dense, it's probably getting adequate nitrogen and this application could be skipped or done at half the rate. Another method for providing a slow-release source of nutrients is to top-dress the lawn with a ¼-inch layer of finely screened compost or manure–compost blend. This will also help maintain soil organic matter.

SHRUBS & TREES

No standard fertilization is recommended at this time of year. Trees and shrubs may already get some "spillover" from nearby lawn fertilization.

Fall applications of compost and/or organic mulch are a good way to maintain soil organic matter and the slow release of nutrients. This is consistent with the natural nutrient cycle in forests, as falling autumn leaves "mulch" the forest floor.

VINES & GROUNDCOVERS

Similar to fall treatment for lawns, herbaceous groundcovers that spread by underground stems will benefit from a light application of nitrogen fertilizer the first half of this month (no more than 1 pound of actual nitrogen per 1,000 square feet), particularly if their growth has become thin.

PROBLEM-SOLVE

Zones 4 to 6: Flathead cedar borers attack drought-stressed arborvitae, juniper, and cedar trees and shrubs. It often goes unnoticed until plants have died back or gone completely brown.

Slugs will be busy reproducing at this time of year. Look for the small piles of pearly eggs (smaller than BB shot) in stacks of 40 to 120. Look under mulch, woodpile edges, and woody refuse lying on the ground. You may come upon them while weeding. Scoop them up and destroy them by dropping them in soapy water (but not in your compost pile, where they will hatch and multiply!). Continue to set slug traps near vulnerable plantings. Remember that garden spiders and black soldier beetles that take cover under mulch and leaves include slugs and slug eggs in their diet.

ANNUALS

Remove and discard annuals disfigured by powdery mildew. You'll notice it most on zinnias.

BULBS

Discard any dahlias that show virus symptoms: stunted plants, leaf mottling, odd coloration, and mosaic or ring patterns on leaves (see August).

INDOOR PLANTS

Survey plants carefully before bringing them indoors. Slugs, aphids, and earwigs may hitchhike inside. Thoroughly wash leaves and trim out any damaged by insects or diseases. Some gardeners briefly soak the plant in a bucket of water up to the soil line (for less than an hour), and then let it drain.

LAWNS

Concerned about crane fly? Crane flies get a lot of attention this time of year, in part because the adults emerge in late August and early September, resembling large clumsy mosquitoes. If you see adult crane flies, it doesn't automatically mean there will be lawn damage in spring. Other animals eat them. Both adult and larvae crane flies are essential food for birds, fish, and other insects. September is not the right time to treat for crane flies, and even before treatment, you should check for damage. (See October for information on how to monitor for crane fly.)

SHRUBS

By the summer's end, the effects of powdery mildew may be evident on many garden shrubs. Deciduous azaleas, some native *Mahonia*, privet, and lilacs are particularly susceptible to powdery mildew. Make sure that plants have good air circulation. Avoid shearing shrubs that have been prone to powdery mildew in the past, and do some remedial thinning in the dormant season. Remove mildew-coated fallen leaves to reduce spore sources for next year. If powdery mildew remains a looming battle each year, consider transplanting or replacing the affected plants with less-prone selections.

Parasitic nematodes can be applied to moist soil around any rhododendron, azaleas, and *Pieris* that have significant amounts of leaf notching from root weevils. It also helps to keep lower limbs pruned up off the ground, so the weevils don't have an easy route from the ground to the branches. If only lower limbs have seen damage, pruning may provide adequate control.

TREES

Extremely heavy rains that soak deciduous trees still in leaf sometimes add enough weight to severely bend or even break weaker branches. Gently shake bending branches on young trees to release the weight load. Have larger trees with broken limbs inspected and pruned by an ISA Certified Arborist®.

Fall webworm nests stand out now in some trees, though the worms have been feeding for quite a while. The occasional nest is not too problematic for healthy trees, and at this late point in the season, there is no point to control. This is a native critter, most prevalent on willow, poplar, and alder. Caterpillars begin feeding in early summer, but they seldom do as much damage as do tent caterpillars, which appear much earlier in the season.

VINES & GROUNDCOVERS

Zones 7 to 9: Once touted as a great all-purpose vine and groundcover for the coastal northwest, English ivy is now on noxious weed lists in British Columbia, Washington, Oregon, and California. It can be a nuisance in cultivated gardens and is a threat to native forest land. It requires frequent pruning to keep it in bounds, because unchecked vines smother garden plants. Accumulated growth in trees can add weight and wind sail, contributing to failures in storms. It is a poor soil stabilizer: slopes have fallen away beneath the cover of ivy after very heavy rainstorms. If these reasons aren't enough to dissuade its use, large expanses of ivy have also proven to be ideal havens for rats.

This is a good time of year manage English ivy. Keep the edges of existing garden ivy trimmed and contained. Slow seed dispersal by cutting off flower heads that form in fall to avoid a new crop of spring seeds. Remove ivy groundcover wherever possible.

October

October might be dubbed "leaf appreciation month." As foliage changes color, it can be as if each tree and shrub steps into a spotlight, taking a curtain call before shedding its leaves. Newly fallen leaves carpet the earth with a final display of color. And all those fallen leaves call out to another level of appreciation, for they offer a rich bounty for garden mulch and compost.

The best fall color years will have lots of sunny days combined with crisp, cool nights. The appearance of such striking color where there was once solid green is truly amazing. Yellow and orange carotene pigments only become visible after chlorophyll breaks down. Red and purple anthocyanin pigments are produced in leaves of some trees and shrubs during early fall (and in some types of conifers with red or purple winter hues). If these pigment names sound familiar, they are one and the same with the antioxidants found in the colorful and healthful fruits and vegetables we are advised to eat. These same antioxidants also act as protective compounds in plant life.

While weather is a factor, gardening practices can also influence fall color quality. If too much nitrogen and moisture are available through the end of the summer, dormancy will be delayed and colors will be less brilliant. On the other hand, stressed plants may shed their leaves early. In terms of plant health and good fall color, allow plants a period of *mild* stress with less water toward the end of summer. It will help them harden off and promote the development of the colorful, protective pigments.

With the return of fall rains, soil fungi—the masters of decomposition—move into action on the leafy debris and other organic material lying on the soil. Beneficial mycorrhizal fungi thrive in moist ground where decomposing leaves and other organic matter are present. These fungi bolster root function, improving moisture and nutrient uptake, and, in some cases, offering a protective coating against disease fungi. All this is lost if gardens beds are routinely blown and raked completely bare of all fallen leaves.

PLAN

Fall brings a new variety of interest and color. Take photos with broad views of your garden to take with you to shop for new plants to add some zest to your garden palette. Visit local gardens to see plant combinations with stunning color.

BULBS

Take a last walk through your garden before shopping local bulb sales and wrap up bulb plantings by the end of the month.

INDOOR PLANTS

Houseplants give us a way to stay connected to gardening over indoor winter months. They add interest to interior spaces, and the process of caring for them can be relaxing. Peace lily (*Spathiphyllum*), Chinese evergreen (*Aglaonema*), and snake plant (*Sansevieria*) are among the easiest to grow under lower light conditions. Find some books on indoor plants to learn more about what can be can be grown in different interior settings.

■ *Low-light houseplants with variegated leaves help brighten the indoors over winter.*

SHRUBS

While trees may dominate our thoughts for fall color, don't overlook the many shrubs whose blazing colors complement and complete this seasonal tapestry. Visit nurseries to see shrubs in peak color, and bring some home to plant for instant gratification. *Aronia* × *prunifolia* 'Autumn Magic' has red to purple hues, beautyberry (*Callicarpa bodinieri* var. *giraldii* 'Profusion') produces almost iridescent violets, and compact burning bush *Euonymus alatus* 'Fire Ball' delivers intense red. *Fothergilla* has a warm golden color, beautiful next to the deep wine-colored foliage of oakleaf hydrangea (*Hydrangea quercifolia*). *Viburnum* species turn to lovely shades of yellow, orange, and red, with all three colors appearing together in the cultivar *Viburnum dentatum* 'Ralph Senior'.

TREES

Deciduous trees stand out boldly as they turn color. The timing will vary by zone and elevation, with trees at higher elevations and in cooler areas coloring first. Bright sunny days followed by rapidly cooling night temperatures cause greater amounts of sugars to remain in the leaves, which combine with leaf pigments to produce greater colors. Fall seasons with cloudy, rainy days and moderate temperatures have more subdued colors (typical for areas west of the Cascades). Some trees produce consistently brilliant colors. Ginkgo (*Ginkgo biloba*) is clear yellow in fall. Japanese maples produce a range of reds, oranges, and yellows. Japanese stewartia (*Stewartia pseudocamellia*) brings warm reds and purple. Katsura (*Cercidiphyllum japonicum*) has apricot to orange fall color and emits a sweet cinnamon scent as leaves fall. With a continuum of yellow to orange to scarlet, Persian parrotia (*Parrotia persica*) creates a color show within one specimen. Scarlet oak (*Quercus coccinea*) is true to its name, and equally deep scarlet reds appear on sourwood (*Oxydendrum arboreum*).

Zones 4 to 6: If you are considering getting a living Christmas tree this year, now is the time to determine the planting site and cover it with a thick layer (8 inches or more) of wood chips or with straw bales to insulate the soil from freezing. (See "Plan" in December.) You may even find good selections at local nurseries to purchase now.

PLANT

ANNUALS
Zones 4 to 6: Gather seedheads to save for next season as you clean up fading annuals.

Zones 7 to 9: Bring some annual seeds along when you are out planting bulbs. Forget-me-not, calendula, Shirley poppies, California poppies, larkspur, sweet pea, and sweet alyssum can be scattered now for early spring bloom (don't layer deep mulch over seeds). Edible and colorful varieties of chard and kale may go in as seed or from potted starts.

BULBS
Start paperwhite narcissus indoors for December bloom. Allow about six weeks from planting to bloom.

Zones 4 to 6: Finish planting bulbs well before the ground freezes. Mulch helps keep the soil warmer longer, an aid to planting and root growth.

Zones 7 to 9: Get the earliest blooming bulbs and corms in first. The typical sequence is snowdrops, snow crocus, large Dutch crocus, small daffodils, larger daffodils, small tulips, hyacinths, large tulips, and allium. In colder zones, they can go in about the same time. Plant some in pots to use later in spring containers.

Plant winter-blooming *Cyclamen coum* and *C. hederifolium* corms now.

Tubers of *Anemone blanda* and *A. coronaria* come looking like little buffalo chips. They will plump up and grow faster if soaked overnight in tepid water before planting. They produce brilliant flowers in spring.

INDOOR PLANTS
Select small attractive pots to plant up cuttings or plantlets rooted in late summer to offer for holiday gifts. They'll look better if they've had six to eight weeks in their new pots.

LAWNS
Zones 4 to 6: In eastern inland areas, October is too late for seeding and sod.

HERE'S HOW

TO PLANT CROCUS IN A LAWN

Crocus bulbs add an early-season "meadow" effect to lawns. Brightly colored Dutch crocus (*Crocus vernus*) work best. Scatter about 10 bulbs per square foot randomly across the lawn and plant them where they lie. Use a circular bulb planter to cut out a planting hole, and drop the crocus bulb in, about 3 inches deep. Crumble the soil from the plug to backfill the hole and replace the plug of grass to grade level with the rest of the lawn.

Another method is to roll back a square of turf, plant the bulbs, then lay the sod back down and gently tamp with the back of a garden rake. Crocus can work especially well with eco-turf lawns. The first mowing should come after blooms are done and bulb foliage has had some time to mature. Crocus survives best in sandy, well-drained soil. They may diminish over time on clay soils, making it necessary to replant them every few years.

Zones 7 to 9: Plant until October 15 in warmer western areas. Good grass types include perennial rye and fine fescue blends. Late fall plantings may be colonized by winter weeds, and the later you sow, the more grass seed you will need to use to ensure coverage.

PERENNIALS, GRASSES & FERNS
Zones 4 to 6: Finish planting about one month before hard freezes to give plants time to establish new roots. Apply coarse mulch while soil is still warm to help retain heat for a longer time.

Zones 7 to 9: Replant containers for winter display with small evergreens, evergreen grasses and perennials, ferns, kale, and pansies. Allow about 3 inches of soil around the edge of the pot as insulation for roots. Potted perennials that are too crowded and rootbound are more susceptible to winter freezes. Repot them if needed.

■ *Replant containers for fall and winter display.*

and perennial groundcovers can be planted now for a jump start on next season. Remember to mulch and water them in if conditions are dry.

CARE

Compost or shred raked leaves to recycle them back into your garden: they are one of the best materials for soil amendment and mulch you can get. Some gardeners use their lawnmower to shred leaves, placing a layer across the lawn and then running over them a time or two before collecting them. Damp, deciduous leaves packed into plastic bags with a couple air vents poked in them and aged for six months to a year will decompose into a beautiful material called "leaf mold." It's not really moldy, but rather deliciously dark brown and crumbly. Turn the bags over occasionally to speed up the composting process. You can also compost shredded and raked leaves in a stack or wire cage. The piles must stay damp to decompose well over winter.

Zones 4 to 6: Winterize birdbaths, pottery, and garden art to avoid cracks and chips from freezing. Clean and store them under cover in a garage or upside down under an overhang where they won't collect water. For items too big to move, drain and cover securely to keep moisture out.

ROSES

Zones 7 to 9: Planting and transplanting roses is appropriate now. You can remove leaves if they haven't dropped yet.

SHRUBS & TREES

Fall is a great time for planting shrubs and trees, although in zones 4 to 6, less hardy species will fare better if planted in spring. In all zones, magnolias tend to establish better when planted in early spring. You may need to water if rainfall has been light. Place a generous mulch ring around each new plant. Be sure to keep mulch a few inches away from the trunks and stems.

VINES & GROUNDCOVERS

Plant, divide, and conquer! Groundcovers with spreading root systems can be divided now. Woody

■ *Use a soil knife (or hori-hori) to divide and replant smaller perennials.*

A combination yard blower/vac/mulcher is one way to pick up and shred leaves for use as mulch.

ANNUALS

Chop up dead annuals for faster composting, but keep diseased or insect-infested material out of home compost. Clean out hanging baskets and store them empty. Mulch exposed ground in annual beds over winter.

Begonias, geraniums, and fuchsias may be wintered over indoors. Keep geraniums and begonias as houseplants if you have sufficient light and space. Water them sparingly over winter. Geraniums can also be stored dormant: pot five plants to a 10-inch pot; trim back both roots and foliage to prepare them. Rootballs should be about 4 inches in diameter, and foliage area about 6 inches in diameter. Label them and water in. Store them at 40° to 45°F/4° to 7°C. Water lightly each month and check for shriveling.

Tender basket fuchsias can take light frost. In zones 7 to 9, they may survive winter if cut back to 6 inches and buried in the ground or set under a porch and mulched. In colder zones, store them indoors in a cool location where they won't freeze. They won't need much light but will die if their roots dry out.

BULBS

After the first light frost, dig and store summer bulbs. Grape hyacinth (*Muscari*) and Dutch iris send up leaves in late September and early October. Mulch with 2 to 3 inches of coarse compost in zones 4 to 6.

Dahlias: Trim off dead foliage and use a spade fork to gently lift tubers from the soil. Wash the soil off and spread them out to dry for three to four days in a sunny spot, protected from frost. Keep them labeled so you can tell them apart next season. Divide dry tubers, making sure each has the central stalk in place. Store the tubers in barely damp sawdust or coir fiber.

Gladiolus: Dig and store in zones 4 to 6. They are hardy in zones 7 to 9 and may be left in the ground. If left in the garden, trim off dead foliage and cover with 3 to 4 inches of mulch. They produce dozens of small new corms, and grow better if divided every couple years.

Dig and store dahlias over winter.

■ *When leaves start to die back, use a spade fork to gently lift frost-tender bulbs from the ground.*

■ *Cut stems down to 1 inch and shake soil from the roots. Allow them to dry out for a few days.*

Lilies: Divide overcrowded true lilies when they turn thoroughly brown. Dig carefully, as it's easy to pierce bulbs with a shovel. Replant with the largest bulbs.

Most tropical plants decline when temperatures drop below 40° to 50°F/4° to 10°C. Dig and store tuberous begonias, cannas, callas, and caladium. Follow the directions for dahlias, except for the dividing. Shake soil off and let them dry for a few days before storing in boxes of dry sawdust or coir fiber. Store at about 65°F/18°C. Caladium may also be grown as a houseplant.

INDOOR PLANTS

Tender blooming plants, such tuberous begonias, that come inside for winter will grow better under light systems. Geranium 'Stella' series, scented geraniums, florist's cyclamen, and African violets bloom better with auxiliary light during winter.

Light stands are commercially available and might make a thoughtful present for a houseplant collector.

■ *Label and store bulbs in dry sawdust or coir fiber.*

Many are attractive enough for living room use. Or you can build one yourself. Simple construction of an A-frame with a shelf makes care easy.

Standard fluorescent bulbs work well: use a shop-type fixture with one cool-white and one warm-white 40-inch bulb to provide full spectrum light. Light bulbs specifically designated for growing plants aren't essential.

LAWNS

To get the lawn ready for winter in all zones:

1. Continue mowing as long as grass keeps growing. Mowing height can be lowered by ½ inch if it was raised during summer.

2. Keep leaves off the lawn. If leaf cover is not too heavy, mulch-mow them to the size of confetti. Studies have found that mulching

■ *Keep thick leaf fall raked up; if leaf cover is thin, it can be mulch-mowed into the lawn.*

HERE'S HOW

TO PROMOTE FLOWERS ON CHRISTMAS CACTUS

Christmas cactus (*Schlumbergera* spp.) may need another nickname, since many of them bloom throughout winter. These live for decades if well cared for and often become living family heirlooms. They bloom reliably with just a little fall care. Flower buds are prompted by a combination of drought, cool temperatures, and short day length.

1. Place the plant where it will get cool temperatures at night, down to 40°F/5°C.

2. Keep them in medium light during the day and then about 13 hours of continuous darkness. In zones 7 to 9, they will often set bud when kept outside on a covered, unlit porch or other protective cover, which offers both cooling and shorter daylight.

3. Do not fertilize.

4. Once buds appear, water more often. Allow the soil to dry out partially before watering.

5. Set the plant in a location with good light where you can enjoy the bloom. Clip off segments that have bloomed once the flowers fade.

Allow soil to get dry this month. Water infrequently, enough to prevent wilting.

leaves into the lawn improves overall lawn health and suppresses weed problems such as *Poa annua* (annual bluegrass).

3. The lawn should be well mown and free of large wet leaves going into winter. A final edging completes the package with a neat appearance and head start for next spring.

4. East of the mountains, water the lawn deeply before hard freezes to reduce winter injury from desiccation.

5. Stay off lawns during winter when they are frozen and when ground is saturated.

PERENNIALS, GRASSES & FERNS

Rake heavy, fallen leaves from garden beds where smaller plants may get smothered. Retain some leaves to protect bare soil, or where they may lend protective cover to plants such as daylilies.

ROSES

Rake up and discard fallen rose leaves. Don't put diseased leaves in home compost.

Zones 4 to 6: After the first freeze, protect grafted roses from winter damage. Cover the ground and graft union with a foot of pine needles or similar lightweight mulch. In very cold areas, some gardeners wrap the tops of the bushes with burlap, making the outline of a lollipop.

Zones 7 to 9: Roses can be reluctant to go dormant, staying in leaf and bud into fall. Toward the end of the month, you can remove the remaining foliage. Strange as it sounds, it's a way to clear away any diseased leaves and also nudges the plant into dormancy. This can be helpful for special specimens of hybrid tea and English roses. Roses will survive if you don't remove the leaves, and the task is impractical for large scrambling climbers or huge shrubs.

SHRUBS

If falling leaves from deciduous trees pile up on top of shrubs, they can quickly smother the life out of them, especially evergreen shrubs. Rake them away, but don't be too tidy about removing all leaves. Allow smaller leaves to join the mulch

on the ground beneath. Clear away any leaves that have accumulated directly against the stems near the ground.

Zones 7 to 9: Prepare shrubs in containers for winter as first frost dates approach. Be prepared to move more tender species under cover if deep freezes are forecast. Have some old blankets or bubble wrap ready to provide quick insulation for pots that won't be moved under cover. With cooler weather, less watering is needed, though rainfall rarely wets containers very well.

General shrub pruning work should be done later in the dormant season, not in fall.

TREES

Fallen leaves can feel like a big nuisance when they flood the yard, but they are great mulch waiting to happen. Allow smaller-sized leaves to remain on the ground if possible, without letting them

■ *Allow smaller-sized leaves to remain on the ground if possible, without letting them accumulate against stems or over low plants.*

accumulate against stems or over low plants. A combination yard blower/vac/mulcher is one way to pick up and shred leaves for use as mulch. A hopper-style leaf shredder is another good tool for reducing fallen leaves to use as mulch or to compost into leaf mold.

With the exception of removing dead limbs, this is not the best time for pruning deciduous trees. Wait until later in the dormant season for routine pruning. Conifers may be pruned now.

VINES & GROUNDCOVERS

Keep thick layers of leaves raked up where they accumulate on top of groundcovers, lest they smother out the plants. Shredded leaves are great mulch to tuck under groundcover plants.

WATER

By this time, fall rains should start doing their work, and gardeners can turn their attention to other tasks. Make sure evergreens that have been dry over summer are well watered now. Plants that go into winter cold suffering from drought stress are more likely to be damaged by freezing.

Start putting your irrigation equipment away for the winter. Drain and coil garden hoses. Collect sprinklers, nozzles, and watering cans for dry storage.

Zones 4 to 6: Winterize and drain automatic irrigation systems and protect exposed hose spigots. Drain and store rain barrels so they remain empty through the freezing season.

Zones 7 to 9: Begin winterization toward the end of the month when hoses and irrigation are no longer needed.

INDOOR PLANTS

Plants need less water now. Make sure to allow soil to dry part way between watering.

LAWNS

Keep any newly seeded, emerging lawns watered if rains are scarce. Established lawns won't need irrigation.

PERENNIALS, SHRUBS, TREES, VINES & GROUNDCOVERS

Make sure new plants and any plants that were severely drought stressed over summer are well watered by rain or irrigation by the end of the month.

FERTILIZE

Discontinue fertilization as heavy rains return to the region. Organic mulches will slowly add nutrients to the soil as they decompose over winter, reducing the need for fertilizers.

INDOOR PLANTS

Use a half-strength mix for foliage plants once this month, if needed. Do not fertilize succulent plants, such as jade plant and cactus-type plants.

Flowering plants grown under lights require fertilizer once a month to support active growth and bloom.

LAWNS

Zones 7 to 9: West of the Cascades, irrigated lawns may benefit from a last fertilization early this month. Use a low- or no-phosphate fertilizer at 1 pound of actual nitrogen per 1,000 square feet.

PROBLEM-SOLVE

Spider webs can be seen glistening with early morning dew at this time of year. Their beautiful patterns stretched across shrub beds indicate that effective natural pest control is on duty. Spiders actively hunt and feed on insects throughout the growing season. Some work from webs, while many roam in search of prey. Spiders thrive with the protection of dense plant growth (such as shrubs and groundcover plants), leaf litter, and some moisture. Maintain some plant debris on the ground throughout the year to provide adequate habitat, and resist the urge to stomp them when they catch you by surprise.

BULBS

Protect crocus and tulips from squirrels by placing a square of hardware cloth over the ground. If you are in deer territory, snowdrops and daffodils won't be bothered, but tulips and lilies are likely to be grazed on. If you don't have a deer fence, grow vulnerable bulbs in containers that can be moved to safer locations.

INDOOR PLANTS

Fungus gnats that followed plants in from outside will multiply on plants that are overwatered, but will not survive dry soil.

Low humidity in heated homes will be a particular difficulty in colder zones 4 to 6. Grouping plants together helps raise the humidity for all of them, but misting does not offer lasting benefit. Setting plants on pebble-filled trays can lead to problems from waterlogged soil at the bottom of the pots. Devices used for raising house humidity for the entire family will also benefit houseplants. Plastic enclosures are an option for plants on light stands. While winter life comes with lower light and dry air, most plants will recover in spring without special measures.

LAWNS

In late summer, lawns can look pitiful even without any help from crane flies. Often, it's a result of compaction, lack of nutrients, thatch buildup, or even lack of water. Crane fly damage seldom shows up before spring, because winter's cold temperatures and bird predation tend to reduce the populations. Treating for them in fall makes no sense.

You can check for crane-fly larvae now; look for bare or dying spots in the lawn with holes. In late winter or early spring, the larvae may even be out of the ground on the top of the soil or sod. Birds may be feeding in flocks. If you see these signs in late winter, dig up a square foot of lawn and count the larvae. Healthy lawns can tolerate about 40 or fewer crane flies with no other treatment. Scaling back on irrigation so the soil is drier toward the end of the summer is also a helpful measure to suppress crane fly damage.

ROSES

Funny looking balls on rose stems? You may notice these oddities on bare stems after leaves drop. They are likely the work of gall wasps, beneficial garden predators. Adults emerge in spring, around May. Galls tend to be more numerous on plants that are drought stressed. Galls wasps are not harmful to healthy roses, or to humans (see July).

SHRUBS & TREES

Too much water or fertilizer late in the growing season will delay dormancy and cold hardiness, as well as lessen fall color. If your trees are staying lush longer than others of their kind, reduce irrigation and eliminate fertilization next season.

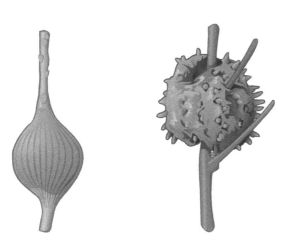

■ *Stem gall on roses indicates the presence of beneficial predators.*

■ *Install protective collars around the base of young trees where winter rodent damage can be a problem.*

HERE'S HOW

10 TIPS FOR HEALTHY TREES

1. **Be kind to the roots.** Cultivation, trenching, and raising or lowering the grade can seriously damage roots. Planning a remodel or construction near established trees? Call in an ISA Certified Arborist® well before you break ground to help determine if and how the tree can be preserved.

2. **Protect the bark.** Avoid wounding or breaking the bark with nails or equipment. Don't tie ropes or chains around trees that can chafe bark or girdle the trunk. Bark wounds can invite the start of decay. Painting wounds doesn't help; prevention is the best cure.

3. **Avoid turf versus tree conflicts.** Place a broad ring of coarse organic mulch around trees. This prevents damage from mowers and string trimmers and reduces root competition for nutrients and moisture. Don't use "weed and feed" turf fertilizers near trees; they contain broad-leaf weedkillers that can be absorbed by tree roots.

4. **Mulch.** Coarse, multitextured mulch provides many benefits to root growth and tree health. Apply mulch where the ground is bare, and in place of turf around the base of trunks. Don't let mulch contact the bark; keep a few inch width of bare soil next to the trunk.

5. **Prune to natural form and don't top your trees.** Good pruning preserves the natural branching habit. Get instruction or hire a professional. Topping can permanently disfigure and weaken smaller trees and create future hazards in large trees.

6. **Plant with care.** Planting a tree correctly will ensure its future health and performance in the landscape. Use the right tree in the right place, don't plant it too deep, and water during the first three years of establishment.

7. **Don't overstake.** Overstaking can impair trunk strength on young trees, and forgotten ties that embed in the bark cause more damage than not staking at all. Stakes should be removed from young trees within the first year of planting.

8. **Water.** Give your trees an occasional slow, deep soaking if the soil gets extremely dry, especially later in summer. Don't overwater and don't allow irrigation spray to soak tree trunks.

9. **Remove invasive and heavy vines.** Ivy, old man's beard, wisteria, or kudzu can be heavy enough to make trees more vulnerable to wind damage.

10. **Know when to call a professional.** Call in an ISA Certified Arborist® before construction work near valued trees, for risk assessment and other problem diagnosis. And any work off the ground is best done by someone trained and equipped to work safely in trees.

Install protective collars around the base of young trees where rodents may chew through the bark over winter, often under the cover of snow or mulch that is too close to the bark.

VINES & GROUNDCOVERS

The effects of compacted and infertile soil often show up as bare areas. Such barren areas can be improved at this time of year with organic mulch. Break up hard surfaces with a spade fork or hard rake before mulching. Don't work or tromp on wet soil, lest you cause more compaction. With the moisture from autumn rains and the action of soil insects and microbes encouraged by the organic materials, compacted and infertile soils will show improvements by next spring.

November

Daylight hours wane, and the sun sits lower in the sky; the quality of light in November is subdued. A fleeting period of brighter days may arrive when the last autumn leaves fall to reveal new vistas and more sky. While October's days are marked by falling leaves, November days are marked by precipitation. At the start of our winter rain season, November is often the wettest month of the year.

In the coldest areas, the garden will be settling into full dormancy. In warmer zones, full dormancy may not set in for several weeks. West of the Cascades, there's still a bit of good gardening to do: a last run at clearing leaves, a few bulbs left to plant, perhaps even another mowing for the lawn. Garden activity slows or shifts to rest mode for the duration of winter weather conditions.

In all areas, the cycle of this season is about the return of rain and snow. This is a good time of year to observe how winter precipitation interacts with your garden. Does it soak in well, stand in temporary pools, or run off? The moisture absorbed by the soil over winter will be an important part of the moisture supply for trees and garden plants during the next growing season. Bare soil is prone to erosion and compaction from rain impact, making it less able to absorb water. A simple cover of coarse mulch, shredded leaves, straw, or even burlap will increase infiltration. Mixed plantings of evergreen and deciduous trees, shrubs, and groundcover plants intercept and capture a good amount of precipitation; large expanses of lawn or barren ground, not so much.

Managing runoff in winter and conserving water in summer are large concerns for this region. Many municipalities and water districts have programs promoting rain gardens and swales designed to slow, capture, and filter rainwater runoff (see Resources).

Soggy soil is easily damaged from cultivation or being trod on. Let the ground rest for now. November is a time to take a step back and appreciate the return of good rain.

PLAN

Look through photos taken over the seasons this past year, and enjoy the images of your garden at its best moments. Review what has provided the best function and enjoyment with minimal care. Make plans to repeat those successes in other areas of the garden.

Cultivating a natural garden ecology that takes lessons from natural systems can increase garden success and beauty. When plants are combined and placed according to their natural qualities, you won't be fighting nature to achieve good growth.

Study, photograph, and map out how water moves and collects in different parts of the garden. This information will be valuable to developing appropriate changes for next year, particularly if you are considering installing a rain garden.

BULBS

Allow enough time if you want to force bulbs indoors. Most spring-blooming bulbs and corms need about 10 to 16 weeks of temperatures below 45°F/13°C before bringing them indoors. In zones 4 to 6, look for "pre-cooled" bulbs to pot

■ *Map how water collects and moves through the yard in winter.*

up in early November and keep in cool storage for about three weeks, until they have set buds, before bringing them indoors. Some of the best tulips for forcing include 'Single Early', 'Christmas Marvel', 'Beauty Queen', and any of the 'Emperor' forms.

Forced daffodils, tulips, and paperwhite narcissus will do better in cooler house locations, such as an enclosed porch, with temperatures between 45° to 55°F/7° to 13°C. If kept in higher temperatures, bloom life is shortened. In zones 7 to 9, they can be placed on front porches for decoration. Bring them indoors if temperatures drop below 38°F/3°C.

INDOOR PLANTS

If you have ever stood under a tree when stressed, you know the presence of plants provides benefits that transcend the aesthetic. Being around plants helps reduce physical and mental stress, accounting for their presence in hospital gardens and therapeutic programs.

When we walk into even a small conservatory area, we can recognize a freshness to the air. Even a few plants gracing indoor spaces can change the physical and psychological atmosphere.

Stores stock holiday plants this month. Look for Christmas cactus with large blooms and buds. Pick poinsettias late this month, with firm color on the bracts, closed center flower buds, and bright green leaves. Be sure to wrap them securely to keep them out of drafts and chilly air on the trip home. Warm the car, and keep transportation time to a minimum. Plants should be kept out of reach of pets and children, as the milky sap can cause vomiting or diarrhea if ingested.

LAWNS

Anyone who's lived in cold winter climates knows that the normal winter color for grass is doormat brown. But west of the Cascades, mild winters allow the lawns to maintain some shade of green. Gardeners expect no less, hoping that the lawn will set off winter shrubs and conifers with magazine-photo emerald color. Not surprisingly, lawns that look best through winter have had good care during the other three seasons.

PERENNIALS, GRASSES & FERNS

Consider how long your perennials stay in bloom (two to three weeks may be the average) when choosing new plants. Also look for nice foliage effects, as found on epimedium, huchera, hosta, or variegated Japanese forest grass. Add variety to extend overall bloom period and to improve habitat for butterflies and beneficial insects. Allow seedheads to mature on perennials such as Echinacea and on ornamental grasses to provide forage for overwintering birds (who may also glean overwintering insects from your garden).

ROSES

Zones 4 to 6: Keep notes on roses that survive winter cold and have performed well in your area. Replace stressed or dead roses in the spring with some hardy performers, such as Canadian Explorer Series and Griffith Buck roses.

SHRUBS

Look at which shrubs contribute nicely to the winter scene. Both deciduous and evergreen shrubs provide continuity and structure through the seasons.

West of the Cascades, broadleaf evergreens thrive and are plentiful in gardens. Many bear colorful blooms at some point in the year: rhododendrons, camellias, glossy abelia, silk-tassel (*Garrya* spp.), and *Pieris*. The flowers of some are discreet (*Sarcococca* and boxwoods), while others show off colorful berries, such as heavenly bamboo and skimmia. All provide rich texture and color year round.

East of the Cascades, the winter landscape is highlighted by needle-leaf evergreens, such as pines, juniper, and arborvitae, as well as deciduous shrubs with colorful stems or berries. The deciduous winterberry holly *Ilex verticillata* 'Winter Red', beautyberry *Callicarpa dichotoma* 'Early Amethyst', and *Aronia melanocarpa* 'Morton' (Iroquois Beauty™) all offer strongly colored winter berries and thrive in zones 5 to 6. All prefer damp soils and sun.

TREES

As the quality of light shifts and the clutter of foliage recedes, the architecture of large trees comes into focus. The unique structure and beauty of each tree's trunk and limbs are revealed anew. The fine texture and colors of conifer foliage complement the leaf color and bare stems of their deciduous neighbors. Trees preside like silent sentinels over the garden in winter, their forms punctuated with the beauty of a light snow or thick frost. They create a sense of place, of permanence through the seasons.

Trees with interesting foliage, bark, and branching patterns stand out at this time of year. The almost iridescent pale bark of the Himalayan birch (*Betula utilis* var. *jacquemontii*) is brilliant against an evergreen backdrop. Paperbark maple (*Acer griseum*) has delicate, peeling, cinnamon-color bark. In larger spaces, the wide, spreading limbs of *Ginkgo biloba* stand out with deeply furrowed, light gray bark. Weeping trees offer a dramatic focal point in winter silhouette.

This is a good time to assess spaces lacking in trees for potential well-placed additions. In zones 7 to 9, trees may still be planted. Plan for early spring planting in colder areas.

VINES & GROUNDCOVERS

Trees are often considered a great ready-made support for garden vines, but be thoughtful about which vines you choose. Some vines can be complementary companions: a climbing hydrangea on a tall expanse of bare trunk on a Douglas fir, or the surprise of blooms on a shade tree where petite clematis has woven through the crown. At other times, vines can spell doom (or a maintenance nightmare) when heavy growth consumes the host tree. English ivy (*Hedera*) and old man's beard (*Clematis vitalba*) are on the noxious weed lists: they cause damage as they grow to heavy, dense proportions. Vigorous garden vines can also be too much for trees to handle: wisteria, kiwi, honeysuckle, and grape are some that should be kept out of trees. Less rampant growers, such as hybrid clematis and some of the climbing roses, may be more easily kept in balance when grown on a sturdy tree. Just like those grown on built arbors, annual pruning of vines to a low framework is essential to keep them in scale.

■ *Ornamental kale brightens the early winter garden.*

PLANT

Zones 4 to 6: Wrap up planting early in the month, well before hard frost and freezing weather set in.

Zones 7 to 9: Planting of trees, shrubs, vines, some perennials, and sod may be done during periods of moderate weather, when temperatures are above freezing and soil is not soggy.

ANNUALS
Zones 7 to 9: There's still time to add another ornamental kale or pansy. Hybrids of ornamental kale come in astonishing color combinations of purple, greens, and white. They perform best in sunny locations.

BULBS
Paperwhite narcissus (*Narcissus tazetta* hybrids) are an easy, enjoyable bulb to force for the holidays. Unlike other types of daffodil, this one doesn't require a chill period and blooms four to five weeks after planting at normal household temperatures. You may see these grown in gravel, but bulbs do better in potting soil. A 6-inch pot holds about five bulbs. Tuck them in with about one-third of the bulb exposed. Keep them in a cool place for about 10 days until rooted. As shoots start to expand, bring them into bright light. Plant them around November 15 for bloom at Christmas and New Year's. For extended display, store extra bulbs in a dark, cool place and pot a few up every two weeks until January or February.

Zones 7 to 9: Weather permitting, continue to plant hardy bulbs and corms.

INDOOR PLANTS
Repot amaryllis saved from last year. Shake off the old soil and plant in a compost-amended potting mix. Water and keep it in a warm, bright area. About the time amaryllis appear in stores for holidays, the saved bulb should be beginning its growth. Fertilize lightly then. Flowers should open in about four to six weeks.

LAWNS
Zone 7 to 9: It's too dark now for good seed germination. Sod can go in nearly any time as long as the ground isn't frozen or saturated and can be well prepared.

PERENNIALS, GRASSES, FERNS, ROSES, SHRUBS & TREES
Zones 4 to 6: Complete planting work early in the month before freezing weather sets in.

Zones 7 to 9: Continue planting and transplanting as long as weather permits and conditions are neither too wet nor freezing.

CARE

Zones 7 to 9: Make another sweep to clean up any heavy, wet leaves lying on lawns and plants in garden beds. Compost autumn leaves in discrete piles or mix into general garden compost.

■ *A self-contained indoor terrarium garden is a perfect way to continue gardening when you can no longer garden outdoors.*

TO CREATE A TERRARIUM

Terrariums—glass cases that hold small plants—give rooms a touch of the Victorian age, when fern cases adorned every proper parlor. Aquariums with glass lids cut to rest on top, open round vases, or large canister jars will all work fine. The ideal terrarium balances water needs, requires no fertilizer, and thrives in warm spaces with moderate light. Avoid direct sun or total shade. The best plants to use are small ferns and foliage plants with small leaves, such as *Fittonia* or *Peperomia*. Variegated leaves add interest.

1. Clean the container thoroughly.

2. Place about 1 inch of charcoal on the bottom; unlike all other container plantings, this is necessary for the closed environment.

3. Add about 3 inches of moistened, clean potting soil (without fertilizer).

4. Water plants before installing. Allow to drain.

5. Arrange plants in the soil. Decorative stones or other ornaments may be included.

6. Leave the top off for a few days, and then cap it. Moisture on the sides is common in the morning but it shouldn't get soggy.

A terrarium without a lid will provide humidity and shelter for plants but takes more watering. Planted terrariums are also available at many garden centers and florists.

Put garden tools away for the winter, cleaned and sharpened. Sand and treat wooden handles with linseed oil or similar wood oil to prevent wood from drying and cracking. Clean and oil lawnmowers and other power tools; empty gas tanks.

ANNUALS

Plan to shelter large outdoor containers against freezing. Some may be moved into a garden shed or garage. Smaller containers may be partially buried and surrounded by mulch or leaves.

Zones 7 to 9: Winter freezes typical to these zones seldom harm containers larger than 15 inches in diameter. Put containers up on "feet" to promote better drainage and avoid potential freeze damage. Use small wood blocks or specially designed pot feet to raise containers about ½ inch off the ground. Be prepared to cover containers and plants with burlap or light blankets should a deep cold blast set in. Smaller containers should be moved into shelter in case of hard freezes.

Cut bloomed-out chrysanthemums back to about 6 to 8 inches. Some may survive as perennials.

BULBS

Mulch all newly planted bulbs with shredded leaves or coarse compost about 3 to 4 inches deep for winter protection.

Zones 4 to 6: Summer bulbs should all be pulled and put in winter storage by now (see October). Pots should be moved into protective storage, or sink the whole pot in the ground over winter.

Zones 7 to 9: Bring tuberous begonias in before the hardest frosts. Shake the soil loose and lay plants on dry newspaper until the foliage withers. Store the tubers in dry sawdust or sand. Divide stored dahlias, keeping a stem with each tuber. Sections without a stem will not grow next season. Place them in sawdust or coir fiber and dampen with a light spraying of water. Store at room temperature.

INDOOR PLANTS

See sidebar on page 185.

LAWNS

Worried about mushrooms? Mushrooms are fruiting bodies attached to an underground network of fungus mycelium. During dry weather, the underground web of fungal life goes unnoticed, but with the onset of fall rains, the spore-producing structures appear. The fungal mycelium perform the essential job of decomposing dead plant debris and cycling nutrients and organic matter back into the soil. Many of the fungi we

TO MAKE LEAF MOLD

In natural settings, fallen leaves play a vital role in landscape ecology. They protect the soil and provide essential habitat for beneficial insects and fungi. As leaves decompose, nutrients and organic matter are cycled back into the soil, fostering a good environment for healthy roots.

It pays to learn how to manage autumn leaves for the health and benefit of your garden. Large, wet leaves that pile up on garden plants can smother the life out of them. Clear those leaves away, but move them to a place where they will protect exposed soil or compost them for leaf mold.

■ *Set up a leaf-only compost pile.*

A leaf-only compost pile aged for about a year can be used as coarse, organic mulch. It will still contain visible bits of leaves and twigs. Aged longer, it will break down into dark humus that is suitable as a soil amendment or for blending into potting soil.

Leaves and twigs are rich in nutrients, tannins, and other compounds that are released when they decompose. They contain valuable concentrations of calcium, magnesium, and trace minerals. These are all important components to productive soil.

You can compost all types of fallen tree leaves. Pine needles are slow to break down, but they can be mixed and chopped up with large broadleaf leaves before composting. Where possible, keep some as mulch beneath the trees they fell from. If you have a walnut tree, those leaves should be kept separate and used under the tree they came from: walnut trees contain allelopathic compounds that are poisonous to many herbaceous plants. They should never be used in or near vegetable gardens.

Super-simple leaf compost. Stockpile damp leaves and allow them to break down over time. Store them in a bin, such as a portable compost cylinder, or make a bin with hog wire fencing. Set these piles where they can be kept covered and moist during the summer, such as on the north side of a building or in a shady corner. Piles that are turned every couple months will break down more quickly.

Bagged leaf compost. Fill large plastic garbage bags with damp leaves and poke a few holes in the bag. Turn the bags over a time or two over winter. Composted leaves are often ready to use as mulch the next spring and early summer.

Shred large and leathery leaves for faster processing. This can be done by spreading them out in an even, shallow layer over the lawn and going over them a few times with a rotary lawnmower. Some garden blowers have a shredding function. Dedicated garden shredders are valuable for gardens with larger quantities of leaves to handle.

Finished leaf mold will have a coarse, crumbly texture and uniform dark color. It should have a sweet, earthy smell. It should not smell sour, which can happen if it gets waterlogged. If that happens, set it aside to dry out, and then compost normally before using it in the garden.

TO MEASURE INDOOR LIGHT LEVELS

The strange old term "foot candles" is still used to describe light intensity. The term indicates how much light falls a foot away from a burning candle.

Outdoor light far exceeds the brightness of any space inside of a window. A simple way to get a general idea of available light requires only a piece of white paper. Do this now to measure light in the dark season and do it again in March and June. Note how indoor light can change as the position of the sun moves each month.

1. Place the white paper where you want to set your plant.

2. Hold your hand about 12 inches above the paper during the brightest part of the day. Now look at the shadow your open hand casts on the paper:

   • A clear shadow with crisp detail signifies high light.

   • A fuzzy shadow but distinguishable as a hand is medium light.

   • A blurry shadow with no recognizable outline is low light.

   • No shadow at all indicates that the area is too dark for most plants.

The high brightness areas in spring, summer, and fall can be medium to low in winter. Light patterns will also vary during the day: east-facing areas with bright light at noon may darken toward afternoon. Becoming accustomed to how light moves and changes is a central skill of indoor and outdoor gardening.

see in fall are beneficial types with important roles in root health and function. So, don't worry: mushrooms are rarely a problem for lawns. If they bother you, knocking them over and raking them up is the best tactic.

Zones 7 to 9: Keep leaves and twigs raked. In mild years, mow as needed if grass gets long (don't wait until spring). Sharpen those mower blades! And stay off a frozen lawn: footsteps can damage grass blades.

PERENNIALS, GRASSES & FERNS

Zones 4 to 6: Lightweight winter mulch (such as pine needles) should go down now where perennials lack protection from walls or fences, and around transplanted or divided perennials. Aim to finish this task by mid-November.

Zones 7 to 9: Do a rotation of weeding to remove the small rosettes of fall-germinated weeds or undesired excess perennial seedlings. Some of those excess perennial seedlings and new ferns that often

■ *Use a cold frame to protect potted plants over winter.*

pop up along the bottom of fences or under larger plants may be potted up and tucked into a nursery bed over winter—either in a cold frame or bedded into mulch—and saved for spring planting.

Cut off dead stalks from euphorbia. Trim back and dispose of any diseased foliage and keep it out of the compost bin. Problems such as peony botrytis can persist through the winter on infected foliage. Retain some old flower stalks that have gone to seed for overwintering birds. Do not cut back hardy

■ *Remove fall-germinating weeds and cover exposed soil with mulch.*

fuchsia, red hot poker, hardy cyclamen, or bishop's hat at this time of year. Leave ornamental grasses alone, unless they are too tall or have been knocked about in the weather. Large leaves of bear's breeches (*Acanthus mollis*) may stay attractive through winter.

ROSES

Postpone pruning until spring. Rose hips should be left in place for winter display and for the birds.

Zones 7 to 9: If leaves and shoot growth persist on hybrid tea and winter-tender roses, it may help to remove their leaves to prompt them to go dormant. Cover roots and the graft unions of tender roses with 2 to 3 inches of lightweight mulch.

SHRUBS

Install winter protection for tender plants as needed in all zones. Move tender container plants under cover and water them thoroughly. In areas with heavy snowfall, wrap vulnerable evergreens with burlap or twine to protect against snow load damage. Set up protective cover or fencing where deer browsing increases in fall and winter.

No major pruning is needed at this early part of the dormant season. You can attend to dead or damaged limbs. Clip stems with attractive fruits or seedpods to enjoy indoors. Look beyond the usual

for interesting textures in bud, bark, and fruits. Always make the pruning cut back to ground level or at the point of attachment on a larger stem—don't leave branch stubs on your shrubs!

TREES

Clear away any mulch or leaf debris that may be piled up against the lower trunk. This debris can hold harmful moisture against the bark, and in colder areas it provides protective cover for rodents that chew on the bark.

Install an 8-inch-tall ring of wire mesh around the base of young trees vulnerable to rodents chewing on them over winter.

Zones 4 to 6: East of the Cascades, protect the trunks of young trees planted within the past three years from winter sunscald. Start at the bottom so that the layers overlap like shingles, which will help shed water. You will remove the tree wrap in early spring, just before new growth begins. Once the outer bark of the main trunk has thickened, this winter protection should no longer be needed.

VINES & GROUNDCOVERS

Zones 7 to 9: Bring in tender containerized vines. Clean up dead leaves and tie stems together for easier handling. Check hardy vines for secure

■ *Rose hips left on bushes will offer food for birds, as well as an interesting winter display for you.*

attachment to their supports. Trim back any excessively long stems that might catch in the wind.

With routine pruning and grooming provided earlier in the year, robust woody vines can lend a beautiful form to the garden in their dormant state. Accentuate the pattern of a wisteria, grape, or hardy kiwi by adding a string of lights to the arbor.

Make a final pass at cleaning up accumulated leaves from prostrate groundcovers.

WATER

This is typically the wettest month of the year. Irrigation systems should be drained and winterized by now. Drain and store hoses under cover to protect from freezing. Tie them in large coils or coil them inside a large trash can.

Zones 4 to 6: When conditions are above freezing and natural moisture is lacking, give newly planted garden material a deep, occasional soaking to prevent not-yet-established rootballs from drying out. Make sure all evergreen plants have moist soil before freezing temperatures set in: they will continue to lose moisture when exposed to sun and wind. Check plants in dry shadows near building eaves and overhangs.

ANNUALS
Zones 7 to 9: Containers of winter annuals on a covered porch may need watering.

INDOOR PLANTS
All houseplants need less water in winter. Allow the top of the soil to dry down to about 1 or 2 inches. Plants such as philodendron or Swedish ivy will need close observation, because they can suffer when too dry.

LAWNS
Make sure your irrigation system and equipment have been winterized.

PERENNIALS, GRASSES, FERNS, SHRUBS & TREES
Zones 4 to 6: Monitor new plants when there is no snow and temperatures are above freezing. Water

as needed to soak down to the root depth for any plants that have become dry.

Zones 7 to 9: Check on water needs of any plants under the cover of cold frames or other protection.

VINES & GROUNDCOVERS
Zones 4 to 6: If the ground is dry early in the month, thoroughly water groundcover plantings before the ground freezes to reduce the incidence of cold injury. This is especially helpful for evergreen plants, which can continue to lose moisture when exposed to sun and wind, and for plants in dry shadows under eaves and overhangs.

FERTILIZE

Hold off on broadcasting fertilizers, as heavy rains can result in rapid leaching of nutrients. Organic mulches may still be applied on drier days (to avoid tromping over soggy ground).

BULBS
Forced bulbs do not require fertilizing.

INDOOR PLANTS
No fertilizing will be needed this month unless you are growing flowering plants under lights. Blooming gift plants have been fertilized at the nursery and do not require anything extra.

LAWNS
Zones 7 to 9: For highly maintained lawns, a winter application may be made between November 15 and December 7. Choose a slow-release form of nitrogen fertilizer with no phosphate, such as a 7-0-2 NPK, and apply at 1 pound or less of actual nitrogen per 1,000 square feet. Don't apply when heavy rains are forecast. Lower-maintenance lawns and those that have been mulch-mowed won't require fertilizer at this time.

Gypsum has been promoted as a soil conditioner that can magically improve soil structure. Wouldn't that be great? Gypsum is calcium sulfate, and it is sometimes recommended to add calcium to an alkaline soil, since it doesn't increase the pH as lime does. Gypsum can produce rather miraculous results, but only for those rare cases of soils with an excess sodium problem. This problem is rare in the Pacific Northwest and never occurs on the moist, west side of the Cascades.

PROBLEM-SOLVE

Some gardeners are meticulous about cleaning leaves out of garden beds in an effort to subdue slug and root weevil populations. The downside is that it will also suppress the valuable populations of predatory beetles that feed on those pests. Clear out around sensitive plants, but keep some leaves and mulch nearby. Slug traps and baits set out during rainy periods this month will help suppress the population.

Nestle pieces of cut limbs and small logs into mulched beds; the rotting wood provides valuable habitat for beneficial insects and fungi.

INDOOR PLANTS

The lower light in winter means a lull in growth for indoor plants. Be meticulous about removing yellowed or fallen leaves, and keep the soil surface cleared of plant debris. Keep watch for early appearance of potential insect problems when grooming your houseplants.

If you see tiny black flies around your houseplants, they could be fungus gnats. They are often a sign of overwatering or of standing water in plant saucers. Allow the soil to dry out well before watering. You can also use sticky traps.

LAWNS

In spite of what industry advertising might suggest, fall is not the time to treat for crane fly. Regional Extension specialists advise that the best line of defense is to allow birds and other natural controls to do their work on reducing the population over winter (see October).

PERENNIALS, GRASSES & FERNS

Zones 4 to 6: Check small plants for frost heaving, which can leave tender roots exposed to air. Tuck them back in and cover the soil around them with mulch to reduce repeated occurrence.

SHRUBS

Browsing damage from deer can occur between late fall and early spring. As winter food sources diminish and deer get very hungry, applied repellents often lose effectiveness. It can take a lot of work to keep up on protection measures, and it still may not be possible to protect all your favorite plants from deer damage.

There are several shrubs that deer avoid that you can incorporate into your garden. Make note of which parts of your existing landscape remain unscathed, and use this list to build a garden less inviting to deer appetites. Locate vulnerable plants far from observed deer trails. Feeding patterns will vary with seasonal conditions, alternate food sources, and taste preferences of the local population. Expect to protect young, newly planted shrubs until they reach larger, less-tender dimensions. Here is a partial list of shrubs to start with:

- Barberries (*Berberis* spp.)
- Boxwood (*Buxus* spp.)
- Cotoneaster (*Cotoneaster* spp.)
- Forsythia (*Forsythia* spp.)
- Heath (*Erica* spp.) and heather (*Calluna* spp.)
- Leucothoe (*Leucothoe* spp.)
- Lilac (*Syringa*)
- Mexican orange (*Choisya ternata*)
- Mountain laurel (*Kalmia latifolia*)
- Pieris (*Pieris japonica*)
- Potentilla (*Potentilla fruticosa*)
- Red vein enkianthus (*Enkianthus campanulatus*)
- Rhododendron (*Rhododendron* spp.)
- Rosemary (*Rosmarinus*)
- Sagebrush (*Artemisia tridentata*)
- Silk-tassel bush (*Garrya* spp.)
- Smoke bush (*Cotinus coggygria*)
- Spirea (*Spiraea* spp.)

Native plant species commonly foraged by deer include new growth on Douglas fir, western red cedar, mock orange, snowberry, wild rose, deer bush (*Ceanothus* spp.), salal, and sagebrush.

TREES

While it's impossible to predict what kinds of storm events may arise, taking some time to look at your trees, large and small, will help to prepare for whatever kind of weather arrives. Most healthy trees withstand the impacts of winter, and many of the common causes of tree failures in storms can be prevented if noted in time. Some are as simple as pruning large dead limbs before they are blown off. Larger trees with structural defects have greater potential to become hazardous than smaller trees.

Here are some common signs of potential problems in both evergreens and deciduous trees that merit attention. Evaluating tree condition, and the seriousness of any defects, is best done by an ISA Certified Arborist® (see Resources). Look for the following:

- Large dead limbs or hanging branches: have them pruned now, before they are knocked out in the wind. Dead trees should not be left standing (though they may be cut into a habitat snag in some locations).

- Large conks or mushrooms on the trunk, especially near the base.

- Large open cavities, cracks, or loose bark on trunks and large limbs.

- A new lean spotted on a previously upright tree can mean it's become unstable. Look for any signs of humps or cracks in the soil at the base the tree.

- Co-dominant or multiple trunks of near equal size with a layer of bark pressed between them.

- Recent construction activity near the roots. Grade changes, trenching, or other construction activities can seriously damage supporting roots and leave the tree unstable to strong winds.

- Heavy growth of English ivy and other woody vines in the crown can add weight beyond the tree's normal capacity, making it more vulnerable to limb breakage and increasing wind sail.

- Previously topped trees are more prone to storm damage, especially when several new leaders have grown from the cut top.

- Trees near power lines. Contact your local utility if you have any concerns about trees near lines.

Always check on your trees after any serious storm activity to look for any damage or changes. Regular tree care can help reduce tree problems and prolong tree life.

VINES & GROUNDCOVERS

Zones 4 to 6: Be sure that groundcovers and vines planted the previous year are mulched to protect roots from freezing and fluctuating temperatures over the winter. Cover plants for winter protection where extremely cold temperatures persist and snow cover is sparse. Evergreen boughs and burlap can be used. Be sure the materials are secured tightly to the ground.

Zones 7 to 9: Temperatures may remain frost free or rapidly plunge from mild to below freezing in a sudden cold snap. Have materials ready to provide hasty cover for vulnerable plants, such as new transplants or those whose growth has not yet hardened off. Old lightweight blankets, sheets, tarps, or burlap are good quick cover. Be sure to remove them as soon as temperatures return to above freezing.

The dormant season is a good time of year to look closely at any vines growing on trees. If you find trees being overcome by invasive or planted vines, trim or remove the vines. Remove as much of the old vines as possible, especially heavy woody trunks, as seen on English ivy and wisteria. For larger trees, this job is best done with the help of an ISA Certified Arborist® who can safely climb and work in the trees. Uproot as much of undesired vines as you can from all the way around the trunk, and follow up to keep a 3-foot-wide zone around the base of the tree free of any new vine shoots.

If it is a garden vine that has gotten out of hand, cut it back to short stems and begin an annual schedule of pruning to keep it in scale with the tree. Look up and keep an eye out for any vines that may have quietly slipped away from a support structure into nearby trees.

December

This is the quietest of months for activity in the garden. Much of garden flora and fauna will be dormant, hibernating, or mostly inactive. The sun hangs toward the horizon as we approach the shortest day of the year at the winter solstice around December 21. In gardening and the natural world, this is a time to take rest and shelter.

Compared to summer, the winter landscape is simple and subtle in its aesthetic qualities. Bare stems present interesting color and textures against snowy or evergreen backdrops. Winter berries and dried seedheads are key features of garden scenery with their color, texture, and the birds they attract. Dried seedheads of asters, grasses, globe thistle, bachelor buttons, and native and garden perennials are a winter food source for overwintering small birds. Black-capped chickadees and bushtits will be busy gleaning seeds and berries as well as overwintering insects and their eggs from bark and stems. Bushtits move from plant to plant in large, lively groups, hanging sideways and upside down to graze on insect protein. Small birds find shelter in evergreen and deciduous shrubs in beds or hedgerows, and they appreciate the shelter of that small pile of brush left over from fall. We can appreciate the insect suppression provided by overwintering birds.

Winter brings us brightly colored stems and seedpods that make for interesting features in cut arrangements and wreaths. Pine cones, variegated leaves of broadleaf evergreens, stems with bright berries, and strands of grape vine are wonderful additions for indoor and outdoor decorations. A closer examination of the garden in winter may reveal many other interesting opportunities for collecting cut material. Festive strings of cranberries and popcorn on evergreen plants are an old standard seasonal decoration that can be enjoyed by humans and overwintering birds.

With the shorter, darker days at this time of year, it is fitting there is less to attend to in the garden this month. Take in the subtle qualities of light and color in the garden. This month offers a respite from the usual pace of gardening tasks.

PLAN

As winter weather delivers rain and snow, continue to observe how water moves or lingers on your property, and use this information to plan for improvements. This is not the time to dig or disturb soil. Instead, take lots of pictures. The photos will be a valuable reference for work during the dry season. Gather information on local resources and requirements that may apply to your property if you are considering adding a rain garden or bio-swale. Professional assistance is often required for work on areas with slopes greater than 10 percent or with other environmentally sensitive conditions.

BULBS

Plant paperwhite narcissus and amaryllis for extended indoor winter display.

INDOOR PLANTS

Choosing indoor plants for winter holiday decoration, such as tabletop Christmas trees or other living evergreens, requires thought. Many will thrive only briefly indoors. Dwarf Alberta spruce (*Picea glauca* var. *albertiana*) can be purchased pre-decorated or plain. This perfectly shaped miniature Christmas tree needs cool temperatures when indoors. Not reliable as a houseplant, it will need to be placed back into cool conditions after the holiday season. In zones 4 to 6, store it with other containers under winter protection. In zones 7 to 9, acclimate them to store them outdoors or to plant directly into large seasonal containers. Norfolk Island pine (*Araucaria heterophylla*) is a well-adapted, permanent houseplant that can serves as a Christmas tree every year. Native to Norfolk Island in the South Pacific, they're in the same family as the odd-looking

■ *Old seedheads on grasses and perennials are winter forage for birds.*

monkey puzzle tree grown outdoors in zones 7 to 9. Norfolk Island pine do best with daytime temperatures of 68°F/20°C and night temperatures a bit cooler. Keep them near a bright window and turn them one-quarter turn per week to keep them symmetrical. If a light system is available, they benefit from 16 hours of artificial light. Water sparingly with rainwater or distilled water. In winter, allow the soil to get dry before watering.

ROSES

Roses need good drainage. Check drainage patterns in areas you're considering for roses to help select optimal locations.

SHRUBS

Shrubs with winter interest can brighten gloomy days and add beautiful details against a backdrop of snow: junipers with waxy green cones, arching stems of cotoneaster lined with neat red berries, tight spiraled stems strung with golden catkins on Harry Lauder's walking stick (*Corylus avellana* 'Contorta').

Zones 7 to 9: Visit garden centers for gardening gifts in the form of shrubs with winter interest or fine tools for the gardener, in anticipation of the coming growing season. Gardening books with ample color photographs offer inspiration for the coming growing season.

TREES

The prospect of saving your Christmas tree as a plant for your garden can be very enticing. Practical as it sounds at first glance, it takes serious consideration and special care to make this a successful project. The first step is to make sure you have enough space in your garden for a tall conifer; it will need an open, sunny exposure and well-drained soil.

Nurseries and Christmas tree growers stock special selections of living trees, including true firs (*Abies* spp.), Douglas fir (*Pseudotsuga menziesii*), and pines (*Pinus* spp.). Double check the nursery tags and mature sizes for the listed species or cultivar. Trees are sold in large containers, or balled and burlapped. Balled-and-burlapped trees will be protected from damage and be easier to handle if placed in a large pot. Rootballs can be very

heavy; smaller-sized trees will be easier to handle. The next vital step is to have a cool storage area, such as an unheated garage, to acclimate the tree between outdoors and in. It will need to be kept there for a few days again before taking it back outdoors. The high temperatures and low humidity inside homes are stressful to trees, and they shouldn't be kept inside more than one week. Set the thermostat as cool as possible and place the tree away from fireplaces and heat vents. Keep the rootball moist but not sopping wet. Coat the needles with an anti-dessicant such as Wilt-Pruf to help hold moisture in. Use "cool" lights and modest decorations.

Plant your tree as soon as possible. This is more easily done in zones 7 to 9 than in colder areas, where there is a greater difference between indoor and outdoor temperatures, and where the soils are likely to be very cold or frozen. In colder zones, you'll need to select the site early and mulch it heavily with straw or woodchips to keep the soil from freezing.

VINES & GROUNDCOVERS

The areas closest to the entrances to your home get noticed more than anywhere else in the garden at this time of year. Does the view please you as you come and go? Or are these planting areas barren or dull at this point in the season? Add colorful, bold-textured plants to the areas you see the most. Groundcover such as low Oregon grape (*Mahonia repens* and *M. nervosa*), varieties of prostrate *Cotoneaster* with colorful red berries, and Russian arbor-vitae (*Microbiota decussata*) are among the choices for striking winter color.

PLANT

Zones 7 to 9: Continue planting and transplanting evergreen and deciduous trees, shrubs, and groundcovers when weather permits.

LAWNS

Zones 7 to 9: This is not an optimal time of year, but if necessary, sod can be installed when temperatures are above freezing and ground isn't water saturated. Seeding lawns will not be successful.

CARE

Winter winds may stir things up and leave gardens looking a bit messy. While it's desirable to tidy up areas of high use and visibility, having some plant debris in the garden over winter is not all bad. A garden stripped too bare of all organic detritus is likely to lose beneficial organisms. Large, leathery leaves provide the protective cover, dampness, and dark needed by nature's decomposers—fungi, millipedes, worms, ground beetles, and other organisms that help maintain a healthy garden ecology.

BULBS

Amaryllis need warm temperatures; keep them out of drafts and in locations that remain above 65°F/18°C. Blooms on paperwhite narcissus and other daffodils will last longer when kept in a cooler room overnight (or on a sheltered porch in zones 7 to 9 when temperatures remain above 35°F/2°C).

Zones 7 to 9: Outdoors, watch for emerging spring bulbs toward the end of the month in mild years. Pull away protective mulch or evergreen branches when their new leaves show through. You may see inch-high leaves of crocus, snowdrop, muscari, and early daffodils. They will survive cold temperatures—even some snow—without damage.

INDOOR PLANTS

When you acquire gift plants, remove any foil or plastic wrappers; view a decorative cover as purely temporary. But if you do wish to keep the colorful wrap, poke about 10 holes in the wrapper bottom to allow drainage. If wrapping plants to present as gifts, make a care tag that identifies the plant and describes its needs. Lamination adds to their useful life. You can create a nice presentation for a gift plant by tying this tag on with yarn, raffia, or ribbon.

Poinsettias keep best if stored in cooler temperatures at night, around 55°F/13°C. Throughout winter, be meticulous about removing yellowed or fallen leaves.

LAWNS

Zones 4 to 6: East of the Cascades, lawns are fully dormant over winter. Even if it looks totally brown and dead, turf remains ready to grow again with warm spring temperatures. However, extreme moisture loss from wind and exposure can result in dead turf. Windy sections of the inland regions and the Columbia Gorge can present such conditions. Tops of hills and other areas with high wind exposure are most affected, since bitter cold alone does not kill dormant turf. Turf that goes into winter healthy and well hydrated will be more resilient to winter desiccation.

Zones 7 to 9: West of the Cascades, lawns may continue to grow when temperatures are moderate and never really develop cold tolerance. A sudden Arctic freeze can damage grass blades, causing the tips to turn brown. A prolonged freeze may cause more damage, especially if a frozen lawn gets foot traffic.

Keep lawns mowed if they are actively growing. In very mild years, mowing once or twice this month may be needed.

PERENNIALS, GRASSES & FERNS

Don't worry if you didn't groom fading perennials at the end of the season. Finches, chickadees, and bushtits will visit to glean seeds from fennel, globe thistle, bachelor buttons, asters, and ornamental grasses.

Zones 7 to 9: A few mild days may entice gardeners outside to do some grooming and trimming of tattered plant ends. It can be satisfying to start some of these tasks now, though it is not critical to do them yet. Allow foliage and stems to remain on hardy fuchsias and chrysanthemums.

ROSES

Zones 7 to 9: Are your roses still bearing buds and leaves? A rose on Christmas Day may charm you, though the flowers are likely to be damaged by wind and rain. Heavy frost will prompt dormancy, but it may not set in when temperatures stay moderate. If it's practical, it can be helpful to

Always prune back to a point of attachment when collecting branches for cut decoration.

of garden shrubs. Different forms of holly, *Sarcococca*, and conifers are good choices. Use your imagination as you save trimmed stems for winter arrangements, looking for interesting colors and textures found in deciduous stems with remnant berries or seed pods. Long, whippy stems might be coiled as a base for a wreath. When you cut for decorating, follow standard pruning practices by cutting back to natural points of attachment—don't tip branch ends or leave stubs.

Zones 4 to 6: Apply a layer of mulch after the ground freezes to prevent frost heaving, especially for smaller plants that went in last fall. Snow cover that remains at 2 or more inches will also provide good insulation.

TREES
Check trees after wind- or snowstorms for broken or damaged limbs, or other storm damage.

Save some of your dormant-season pruning tasks to provide interesting branches for holiday decorations. Always use selective cuts to remove branches so the pruning looks natural and inconspicuous. Branches from evergreens, such as western red cedar and arborvitae (*Thuja* spp.), pines, Douglas fir, and English holly can be blended for attractive wreaths and arrangements. Brightly colored deciduous stems provide interesting contrast against evergreen foliage.

VINES & GROUNDCOVERS
Zones 4 to 6: Save evergreen boughs to provide winter protection for tender vines and groundcovers.

Zones 7 to 9: It is still a good time to clean up any leaves that have become matted over groundcovers and even to add some mulch to spots of bare soil.

WATER

OUTDOOR PLANTS
Check containers in winter storage and water if the soil is dry.

remove the foliage from hybrid tea, floribunda, grandiflora, and English roses to encourage dormancy. Allow old flower heads to remain.

SHRUBS
Heavy snow can bend and break shrub branches. Use a small broom to lightly shake them free of snow. Leave them alone during icy conditions, which can cause branches to snap. Inverted baskets and light blankets can provide a quick cover to protect tender shrubs when a cold front descends.

When temperatures are above freezing, you can gather holiday greens by doing some light thinning

Zones 7 to 9: Be sure outdoor containers drain freely and have not become waterlogged.

INDOOR PLANTS

Holiday gift plants will need regular watering and good drainage. Florist's cyclamen with butterfly-like white or red flowers, Jerusalem cherry (*Solanum pseudocapsicum*), kalanchoe (*Kalanchoe blossfeldiana*), and even holly can appear along with the poinsettias and Christmas cactus. Most of these bloom three to four weeks before fading. *Kalanchoe*, with its brilliant red or yellow flowers, grows well as a permanent houseplant. This succulent plant should be watered more sparingly than the other holiday plants. Be sure soil is dry at least 2 inches down before watering. Keep it in the brightest possible light. Kaffir lily (*Clivia miniata*) blooms during late winter with showy, fragrant flowers. Do not water for six to eight weeks in winter: stop around the first of December and resume when buds appear, usually in February.

FERTILIZE

None to worry about this month.

PROBLEM-SOLVE

BULBS

If voles or squirrels have been bothering bulbs, lay hardware cloth over the plantings and cover it with mulch.

INDOOR PLANTS

Cooler nighttime temperatures will benefit most houseplants.

LAWNS

Zones 7 to 9: The fungal disease called fusarium patch may show up as water-soaked spots up to 6 inches across, often with masses of white or pinkish mold. It is sometimes called "snow mold" because it appears in lawns as snow melts east of the mountains. Good air circulation, moderate fertilization, and drier conditions can help manage and prevent this problem. Get an accurate diagnosis from your local Master Gardener or Cooperative Extension Service if you think your lawn is affected.

PERENNIALS, GRASSES & FERNS

Zones 7 to 9: Review the soil conditions in perennial beds over winter: far more perennials die from drowning in waterlogged soil than are lost to cold. If water stays in puddles in part of the garden, it's worth the trouble of digging out the affected plants and moving them to a better-drained location.

SHRUBS

Rodents may chew bark and cause damage, especially where there is thick snow cover. To deter them, don't allow mulch to be piled up close around the trunks of shrubs. Install a ring of 8-inch-tall wire mesh around the base of shrubs that are vulnerable to winter rodent chewing.

TREES

Zones 7 to 9: Apply dormant oil in mid-December to spruce trees (*Picea* spp.) that had heavy needle damage from spruce aphid last season. This aphid feeds over winter and disappears by the time the older damaged needles fall off the next spring. Trees in shade (and even the shady side of a tree) are more heavily affected. Thorough coverage by the dormant oil is essential, and larger trees may need to be done by a spray service. Colorado spruce (*Picea abies*) is one of the most susceptible species. To avoid the annual burden of spraying, consider replacing spruce trees growing in too much shade with better-adapted plants, such as Serbian spruce (*Picea omorika*), which is resistant. Spruce aphid is not a problem east of the Cascades, where these trees are better adapted to the climate.

VINES & GROUNDCOVERS

Vines and groundcovers less favored by deer include clematis, cotoneaster, creeping rosemary, dwarf bamboo (*Pleioblastus pygmaeus* and *P. variegatus*), heath (*Erica* spp.), kinnikinnick, honeysuckle, native strawberry, wisteria, and native wood sorrel (*Oxalis oregana*).

Zones 4 to 6: When colder weather sets in and food sources diminish, deer browsing intensifies. Protect vulnerable vines with wire fencing. Evergreen boughs can protect newly planted groundcovers from both freeze and browse damage.

Zones 7 to 9: Keep materials such as lightweight blankets or burlap sheeting ready to provide hasty cover for vulnerable plants in case of extended periods of below-freezing temperatures.

Cut dead stems from dormant perennials after there is no value left to their seedheads.

Resources

MASTER GARDENER WEB SITES

Master Gardener programs provide gardening information and local plant diagnostic clinics for the public. Find local gardening information and how to become a Master Gardener through these websites:

- Master Gardener Association of British Columbia: www.mgabc.org/resources

- Oregon State University Master Gardeners: www.extension.oregonstate.edu/mg

- University of California Master Gardeners: www.mg.ucanr.edu

- Washington State University Master Gardeners: www.mastergardener.wsu.edu

WEEDS AND INVASIVE SPECIES

- British Columbia Ministry of Agriculture— Weed Management: www.agf.gov.bc.ca/cropprot/weeds.htm

- Washington State Noxious Weed Control Board: www.nwcb.wa.gov

- Oregon Department of Agriculture: www.oregon.gov/ODA/programs/Weeds/Pages/AboutWeeds.aspx

- California Department of Food and Agriculture, Encycloweedia: www.cdfa.ca.gov/plant/ipc

COOPERATIVE EXTENSION

Washington State University

- Gardening in Washington State: www.gardening.wsu.edu

- WSU Hortsense IPM information: www.hortsense.wsu.edu

Oregon State University

- Gardening in Oregon State: www.extension.oregonstate.edu/gardening

- OSU Pest Management: www.extension.oregonstate.edu/mg/resources-pest

University of California

- Gardening in California: www.ucanr.edu/Gardening

- UC IPM: www.ipm.ucdavis.edu

British Columbia Ministry of Agriculture

- Pest Management: www.agf.gov.bc.ca/cropprot/index.htm

TREE CARE

- International Society of Arboriculture (ISA): www.treesaregood.com

- Pacific Northwest ISA: www.pnwisa.org

- Western Chapter ISA: www.wcisa.net

THE GARDEN PROFESSORS BLOG

Blog posts, articles, podcasts, and discussions on the science of gardening and other topics from professors in Washington, North Carolina, Michigan, and Virginia: gardenprofessors.com

RAIN GARDENS AND BIOSWALES

- British Columbia Capital Regional District Green Infrastructure: www.crd.bc.ca/education/low-impact-development

- 12,000 Rain Gardens in Puget Sound: www.12000raingardens.org

- Oregon Sea Grant—The Oregon Rain Garden Guide: seagrant.oregonstate.edu/sgpubs

- Coastal California Rain Gardens ANR Publication 8531: www.anrcatalog.ucanr.edu

REGIONAL HORTICULTURE LIBRARIES

These libraries provide local lending and reference services, as well as online information on local gardens, garden tours, and plant sales.

- Yosef Wosk Library and Resource Centre at VanDusen Botanical Garden, Vancouver, B.C.: www.vandusengarden.org/learn/library

- Elisabeth C. Miller Horticulture Library at the University of Washington Botanic Gardens, Seattle, Wash.: www.millerlibrary.org

- Helen Crocker Russell Library of Horticulture at San Francisco Botanical Garden at Strybing Arboretum, San Francisco, Calif.: www.sfbotanicalgarden.org/library

PUBLIC GARDENS

Find information on gardens you can visit from a regional horticulture library: www.ilovegardens.com

GARDEN CLUBS AND PLANT SOCIETIES

Joining a garden group is a great way to learn more and meet others with shared plant interests. Contact your local Master Gardener clinic or regional horticultural library for listing of plant organizations near you.

NATIVE PLANT SOCIETIES

- Native Plant Society of British Columbia: www.npsbc.ca

- Washington Native Plant Society: www.wnps.org

- Native Plant Society of Oregon: www.npsoregon.org

- California Native Plant Society: www.cnps.org

Bibliography

Brenzel, Kathleen Norris, ed. *The New Sunset Western Garden Book*, 9th edition. Menlo Park: Sunset Publishing Corp., 2012.

Brickell, Christopher and David Joyce. *The American Horticultural Society Pruning and Training*, revised edition. New York: DK Publishing, Inc., 2011.

Chalker-Scott, Linda. *Sustainable Gardening: the Oregon-Washington Master Gardener Handbook*. OSU Extension Catalog EM 8742, 2008.

Detweiler, Amy Jo and Stephen Fitzgerald. *Fire-Resistant Plants for Home Landscapes*. PNW Extension Publication PNW 590, 2006.

Dunn, Terri and Ciscoe Morris. *Jackson & Perkins selecting, growing, and combining outstanding perennials: Northwestern Edition*. Minneapolis, MN: Cool Springs Press, 2003.

Grissell, Eric. *Insects and Gardens*. Portland: Timber Press, 2001.

James, David G. *Beneficial Insects, Spiders, and Other Mini-Creatures in Your Garden: Who They Are and How to Get Them to Stay*. Washington State University Extension Publication EM067E, 2014.

Kourik, Robert. *Roots Demystified*. Occidental: Metamorphic Press, 2008.

Krukeberg, Arthur R. *Gardening with Native Plants in the Pacific Northwest*, 2nd edition. Seattle: University of Washington Press, 1996.

Kukeilski, Peter. *Roses Without Chemicals: 150 Disease-Free Varieties That Will Change the Way You Grow Roses*. Portland: Timber Press, 2015.

Lancaster, Roy and Matthew Briggs. *What Houseplant Where*. New York: DK Publishing, 1998.

Link, Russell. *Landscaping for Wildlife in the Pacific Northwest*. Seattle, WA: University of Washington Press, 1999.

Logan, William Bryant. *Dirt, the Ecstatic Skin of the Earth*. New York: Riverhead Books, 1995.

Murphy, Elizabeth. *Building Soil, A Down-to-Earth Approach*. Minneapolis, MN: Cool Springs Press, 2015.

Olkowski, William, Sheila Daar, Helga Olkowski, and Steven Ash. *The Gardener's Guide to Common-Sense Pest Control*. Newtown: The Taunton Press, 2013.

Predny, Mary. "Gardening and Your Health: Protecting Your Knees and Back." Publication 426-065, Virginia Cooperative Extension (2015).

Reichard, Sarah H. *The Concientious Gardener*. Berkely, CA: University of California Press, 2011.

Tallamy, Douglas W. *Bringing Nature Home*. Portland: Timber Press, 2009.

The Xerces Society, Deborah Burns, ed. *Attracting Native Pollinators: Protecting North America's Bees and Butterflies*. North Adams, MA: Storey Publishing, 2011.

Index

Photo Credits

Tom Eltzroth: 54, 108, 182 (top)

Katie Elzer-Peters: 16 (bottom), 18, 34, 55 (all), 58 (top), 72 (both), 81, 79 (top), 81, 86, 90 (both), 92 (both), 93 (all), 96, 97 (top), 98 (top), 102 (top), 104, 112 (bottom), 125 (top), 127 (bottom), 129 (bottom), 131, 139 (bottom), 143 (right), 156 (all), 158 (bottom), 168, 197

Bill Kersey: 22 (bottom), 25 (all), 29 (left), 40, 41, 45, 58 (bottom), 66, 80, 97 (bottom), 98 (bottom), 99 (both), 101, 112 (top), 114, 125 (bottom), 127 (top), 128 (all), 129 (top), 132, 140, 153 (all), 170 (bottom), 176 (left), 184 (bottom)

Crystal Liepa: 43 (bottom), 60

Shutterstock: 10, 23, 24, 26, 28, 29 (right), 32, 35, 38, 52, 58 (top), 65, 68, 70, 73, 79 (bottom), 87, 88, 102 (bottom), 106, 113, 117, 120, 122, 123, 124, 134, 136, 139 (top), 142 (left), 143 (left), 147 (bottom, both), 150, 152, 154, 158 (top), 159, 162, 166, 171 (bottom), 173 (bottom), 174, 178, 182 (bottom), 185, 186 (both), 190, 192, 195

Richard Smaus: cover, 6

Lynn Steiner: 47, 48, 76

Bryan Trandem: 116

Jessie Walker: 57

Barbara Wise: 170 (top)

Meet Christina Pfeiffer and Mary Robson

Christina Pfeiffer is a Seattle-area horticulture consultant and educator with over 35 years of experience in landscape horticulture. Sustainable and efficient landscape techniques are a special area of interest and expertise. She is a regular speaker at professional seminars, natural yard care programs, Master Gardener training, garden clubs, and at the Northwest Flower & Garden Show. She is a pruning instructor at Edmonds Community College, and has also taught courses in arboriculture and landscape management at South Seattle College and the University of Washington. She is a part-time consulting associate with Urban Forestry Services Inc., and a member of the Magnuson Community Garden. Christina is a contributing writer and member of the Washington Park Arboretum Bulletin editorial board. In her earlier career, she led landscape management efforts for the Holden Arboretum and at the Washington Park Arboretum. She holds degrees in horticulture from Michigan State University and the University of Washington, and is an ISA Certified Arborist®. Tending her home garden provides an ongoing source of pleasure, observation, and learning.

Mary Robson, consultant for this book, is a retired Horticulture Extension agent for Washington State University. She also wrote a garden column for the *Seattle Times* from 1988 through 2007, particularly enjoying readers' questions and comments. She speaks to garden groups of all types, knowing that an effective speech means finding the focus for issues. Since moving to the Olympic Peninsula, she has appreciated the edge of where gardening knowledge meets natural history. Her interests now include native wildflowers, mosses, lichens, and birds.

■ *Mary (left) and Christina (right).*